ANALYSIS OF CACHE PERFORMANCE FOR OPERATING SYSTEMS AND MULTIPROGRAMMING

THE KLUWER INTERNATIONAL SERIES IN ENGINEERING AND COMPUTER SCIENCE

PARALLEL PROCESSING AND FIFTH GENERATION COMPUTING

Consulting Editor
Doug DeGroot

Other books in the series:

PARALLEL EXECUTION OF LOGIC PROGRAMS,
John S. Conery ISBN 0-89838-194-0

PARALLEL COMPUTATION AND COMPUTERS FOR ARTIFICIAL INTELLIGENCE
Janusz S. Kowalik ISBN 0-89838-227-0

MEMORY STORAGE PATTERNS IN PARALLEL PROCESSING
Mary E. Mace ISBN 0-89838-239-4

SUPERCOMPUTER ARCHITECTURE
Paul B. Schneck ISBN 0-89838-234-4

ASSIGNMENT PROBLEMS IN PARALLEL AND DISTRIBUTED COMPUTING
Shahid H. Bokhari ISBN 0-89838-240-8

MEMORY PERFORMANCE OF PROLOG ARCHITECTURES
Evan Tick ISBN 0-89838-254-8

DATABASE MACHINES AND KNOWLEDGE BASE MACHINES
Masaru Kitsuregawa ISBN 0-89838-257-2

PARALLEL PROGRAMMING AND COMPILERS
Constantine D. Polychronopoulos ISBN 0-89838-288-2

DEPENDENCE ANALYSIS FOR SUPERCOMPUTING
Utpal Banerjee ISBN 0-89838-289-0

DATA ORGANIZATION IN PARALLEL COMPUTERS
H.A.G. Wijshoff ISBN 0-89838-304-8

ANALYSIS OF CACHE PERFORMANCE FOR OPERATING SYSTEMS AND MULTIPROGRAMMING

by

Anant Agarwal
Massachusetts Institute of Technology

with a foreword by

John L. Hennessey

KLUWER ACADEMIC PUBLISHERS
Boston/Dordrecht/London

Distributors for North America:
Kluwer Academic Publishers
101 Philip Drive
Assinippi Park
Norwell, Massachusetts 02061, USA

Distributors for the UK and Ireland:
Kluwer Academic Publishers
Falcon House, Queen Square
Lancaster LA1 1RN, UNITED KINGDOM

Distributors for all other countries:
Kluwer Academic Publishers Group
Distribution Centre
Post Office Box 322
3300 AH Dordrecht, THE NETHERLANDS

Library of Congress Cataloging-in-Publication Data

Agarwal, Anant.
Analysis of cache performance for operating systems and multiprogramming / by Anant Agarwal.
p. cm. — (The Kluwer international series in engineering and computer science ; SECS 69)
Bibliography: p.
Includes index.
ISBN 0-7923-9005-9
1. Cache memory—Evaluation. 2. Operating systems (Computers) 3. Multiprogramming (Electronic computers) I. Title. II. Series.
TK7895.M4A33 1988
005.4'3—dc19 88-36500
CIP

Printed in the United States of America

Contents

List of Figures

List of Tables

Foreword

As we continue to build faster and faster computers, their performance is becoming increasingly dependent on the memory hierarchy. Both the clock speed of the machine and its throughput per clock depend heavily on the memory hierarchy. The time to complete a cache access is often the factor that determines the cycle time. The effectiveness of the hierarchy in keeping the average cost of a reference down has a major impact on how close the sustained performance is to the peak performance. Small changes in the performance of the memory hierarchy cause large changes in overall system performance. The strong growth of RISC machines, whose performance is more tightly coupled to the memory hierarchy, has created increasing demand for high performance memory systems. This trend is likely to accelerate: the improvements in main memory performance will be small compared to the improvements in processor performance. This difference will lead to an increasing gap between processor cycle time and main memory access time. This gap must be closed by improving the memory hierarchy.

Computer architects have attacked this gap by designing machines with cache sizes an order of magnitude larger than those appearing five years ago. Microprocessor-based RISC systems now have caches that rival the size of those in mainframes and supercomputers. These large cache sizes and the need for more accurate simulation have created the demand for new and more ambitious studies of cache performance. Earlier studies of caches used programs that are much smaller than the programs run today. Those earlier studies cannot adequately predict the performance of very large caches, since the benchmarks essentially fit within the cache.

Since small changes in miss rate cause large changes in system performance, our cache performance prediction must be more accurate than ever before. This requirement for accuracy means that factors that were previously ignored or estimated must be carefully analyzed and measured. A primary example of such a factor is the effect of the operating system's references on cache performance of a user program. The emergence of shared-memory multiprocessors has created another demand for accurate modeling of cache performance. These machines are extremely sensitive to cache misses because such misses cause contention for a shared resource (the bus and memory). In addition, multiprocessors cannot be accurately simulated with simple uniprocessor cache traces, due to the presence of invalidation requests and misses arising from those requests, both of which are absent in a uniprocessor trace.

This work addresses these problems by examining the performance of large programs running in large caches and measuring an entire range of effects not examined in earlier work. To conduct these experiments the first challenge was to devise a method for collecting traces of large programs, including the operating system and multiprogramming effects that were neglected in earlier studies. A system for collecting such traces was created and is described herein.

Because of the large domain of possible cache designs and the length of the traces needed to simulate them accurately, analytical modeling techniques that can explore a range of cache organizations quickly are important. These techniques allow a designer to concentrate on a small number of alternatives out of the vast range of possible cache designs. This small number of designs can then be fully simulated to obtain accurate performance estimates.

Finally, exploring the effect of multiprocessing required obtaining traces from a multiprocessor and then constructing accurate simulation models. Since the effects of multiprocessing can have a significant impact on cache performance and an enormous impact on system performance, it is vital to obtain these traces and model these effects accurately.

The research results described here are an important resource for all computer architects. The increasing importance of the memory hierarchy in determining the performance of high speed machines and multiprocessors makes this type of exploration and analysis invaluable if our computer systems are to continue to grow in performance.

John L. Hennessy
Stanford, California

Preface

Advances in high-performance processors continue to create an increased need for memory bandwidth. Migration to multiprocessor architectures exacerbates this need causing the well known Von Neumann bottleneck to main memory. Caches can provide this bandwidth cost-effectively. However, minimizing the performance loss due to caching requires that our analysis and prediction of cache performance become more exact. Although previous studies have shown that operating system and multiprogramming activities affect the cache performance, those studies did not deal with these issues in detail, nor did they address multiprocessor cache performance, largely because of the unavailability of efficient analysis techniques and the difficulty in collecting data for these analyses. To obtain the higher hit rates needed to sustain the effectiveness of caches, we must address these issues completely.

This book investigates the performance of large caches for realistic operating system and multiprogramming workloads. Cache analysis of bus-based multiprocessors is also presented. A suite of efficient and accurate cache evaluation techniques is developed. These include: a mathematical cache model, a trace sampling and a trace stitching procedure, and a trace compaction method. The analyses use a data collection technique called ATUM to obtain realistic system traces of multitasking workloads with little distortion. An extension of ATUM that traces multiprocessors is also described.

Accurately characterizing cache behavior using ATUM traces shows that both operating system and multiprogramming activities significantly degrade cache performance, with an even greater proportional impact on large caches. Multiprocessor interference further reduces cache performance. From a careful analysis of the causes of this degradation, we explore various techniques to reduce this loss. While seemingly little can be done to mitigate the effect of system references, multitasking cache misses can be reduced with little effort. The impact of process migration, virtual versus physical addressing, and the effect of synchronization on large write-back caches in multiprocessors is investigated. We also demonstrate how analytical cache modeling, and trace sampling – with a new approach to cold-start and warm-start analysis – can be used to make large cache studies insightful and efficient.

This book is largely based on my Ph.D. thesis submitted in May 1987 at Stanford University. Chapter 7 contains new material on multiprocessor caches extending the earlier work on uniprocessor cache behavior and represents recent work done at Stanford and also at M.I.T. in collaboration with Dick Sites at Digital Equipment Corporation, Hudson, Massachusetts.

Acknowledgments

I wish to thank Professor John Hennessy for his support, guidance and encouragement, and most of all, for his enthusiasm, throughout the course of my research. Even in his terribly busy moments, he would be happily willing to discuss problems. I am indebted to Professor Mark Horowitz, who was a source of innumerable suggestions and ideas, and to Dick Sites, who was instrumental in getting me going in my research. I am also indebted to Professors Thomas Kailath, Robert Matthews and John Newkirk, who offered me the opportunity for graduate studies at Stanford.

My gratitude to the MIPS-X crew, including Arturo Salz, Paul Chow, Malcolm Wing, Scott McFarling, C. Y. Chu, Steve Richardson, Don Stark, Rich Simoni, John Acken, Steve Przybylski, Peter Steenkiste, Steve Tjiang, and Glenn Gulak, for their suggestions and criticisms, for asking all those questions that motivated my research, and for simply making my experience at Stanford a very enjoyable one.

I must not fail to acknowledge my Indian Institute of Technology clan in the valley, had it not been for whom, I would have completed my thesis far sooner, but with far more of my sanity lost. I am also grateful to Madan Valluri, Sailesh Rao, Barbara and Steve Mckee, and Yvonne and Jim Weiberg for their friendship and affection when I first came to this country.

My research was supported in part by Defense Advanced Research Projects Agency under contract # MDA903-83-C-0335 at Stanford, and under contract # N00014-87-K-0825 at MIT during the preparation of this book. I am grateful to Digital Equipment Corporation, Hudson, for making trace data available for this research.

My wife Anu was a constant source of moral support and encouragement throughout my graduate study, going through some stressful times very patiently and happily.

Finally, I dedicate this book to my parents, for their love, care and sacrifice.

Anant Agarwal
Cambridge, Massachusetts

ANALYSIS OF CACHE PERFORMANCE FOR OPERATING SYSTEMS AND MULTIPROGRAMMING

Chapter 1

Introduction

High-performance processors require a large bandwidth to the memory system. Caches are small high-speed memories placed between the processor and main memory that increase the effective memory bandwidth. They store frequently used instructions and data in high-speed RAMs, providing fast access to a subset of the memory. Cache memories are effective because they exploit the locality property of programs [23]. The property of locality is a program's preference for a small subset of its address space over a given period of time.

In a CPU with a cache, a memory access first queries the cache. If the data is present in the cache, a *cache hit* occurs, and the processor receives the data without further delay. If the data is not present, a *cache miss* occurs, and the data has to be fetched from main memory and stored in the cache for future use. This recent item will usually replace an older item in the cache. Since main-memory accesses typically take an order of magnitude more time than a cache access, the processor is stalled during a cache miss, wasting a number of cycles. A key cache performance metric is the cache *hit rate* (h) or the fraction of processor requests satisfied by the cache. Often, the *miss rate* $(1 - h)$ is a more convenient metric, especially since hit rates often exceed 90 percent.

This book addresses the issue of accurate cache characterization for realistic operating system and multiprogramming environments in single processors and multiprocessors. Accurately estimating cache performance involves investigating better data collection techniques and improved cache analysis methods. In this chapter, we start by briefly reviewing cache design and cache performance evaluation methodologies. Then, after outlining previous cache research, we identify the key problem areas, and summarize how we address these issues. This chapter concludes with some notes on the organization of this book.

1.1 Overview of Cache Design

A cache design selects a set of cache parameters that gives optimal cache performance for the intended workload. The implementor can estimate cache performance using one of several available techniques; the choice of a particular method will depend on the desired accuracy and efficiency. In the following subsection, we will review pertinent cache parameters, and then discuss the various cache evaluation schemes.

1.1.1 Cache Parameters

A memory address submitted to the cache is divided into three fields: a tag, an index, and an offset. Figure 1.1 depicts how these fields participate in a cache access. The *index* first selects a set – a set is composed of one or more blocks each associated with a tag. If the *address tag* matches one of the tags in the set (a cache hit), the *offset* indicates the required word in the block. The cache miss rate depends on several factors:

Cache size: The total amount of memory available in the cache for storage of data.

Block size: The line size, or the number of data words associated with a tag. In Figure 1.1 the block size is four.

Sub-block size: The sub-block size is the amount of data transferred from the main memory to the cache on a miss. The block size and sub-block size are often the same.

Set size: Degree of associativity, or number of columns, or the number of cache locations that any data object can legally be found in. In the figure the set size is two.

Number of sets: Number of rows, or the cache size divided by the product of the set size and block size. There are eight sets in the cache shown in the figure.

Replacement algorithm: Method by which a block in a set is discarded to bring in a new item that maps into the same set.

Write policy: The method by which consistency is maintained between the data in the cache and main memory.

Cache coherence strategy: The method by which consistency is maintained between the data in the various caches.

Finally (and importantly), since a cache exploits the locality in programs, its performance depends on the workload, or the kind of program(s) the processor executes. Smith [76] discusses each of these and their impact on cache performance in detail.

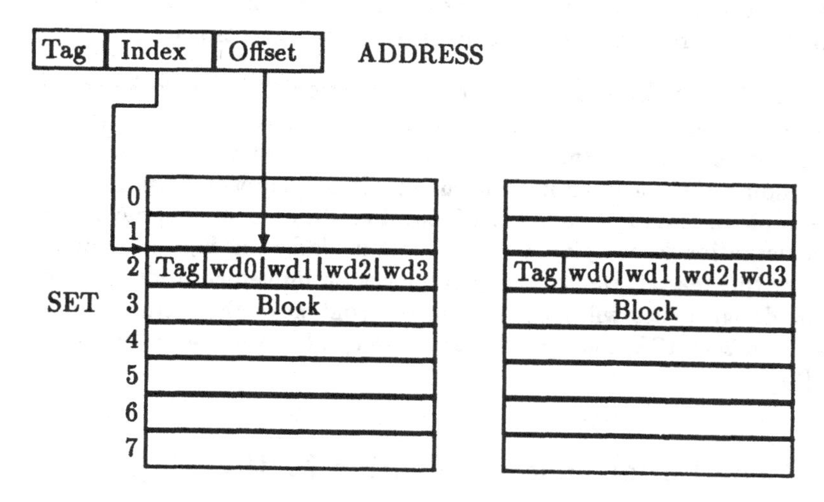

Figure 1.1: Cache organization.

System performance is a decreasing function of the cache miss rate, the cache access time, and the number of processor cycles taken to service a miss. Let T_c and T_m represent the cache access time and the mean cache miss service time, and m the cache miss rate. Then, for a memory bandwidth limited system, performance is inversely related to average memory access time, $T = T_c + mT_m$. A good memory hierarchy design tries to minimize T. Because main memory speeds do not scale up in proportion to processor speeds, both the cost of servicing a miss, T_m, and to a smaller extent the cache access time, T_c, become relatively more expensive as processors achieve greater speeds [36]. Thus, minimizing average memory access time becomes even more important, and to maintain T we must decrease m and T_c. In this book our analyses will concentrate on the miss rate and cache access time because the miss service time, T_m, is primarily a function of main memory and bus architectures.

While most major studies have concentrated on cache miss rate alone, the cache access time is also important because some cache organizations decrease the miss rate at a cost of increased cache access time. The cache access time is the time between a processor request to the cache and the receipt of data from the cache in the event of a cache hit. Although T_c heavily depends on the speed of the RAMs that constitute the cache memory, predictably, the cache access time T_c also depends on many of the other cache parameters. For example, a larger cache size or set size is expected to result in slower speeds.

In cache-based multiprocessors, because the bandwidth to main memory is a precious resource, the bus traffic becomes a major concern in addition to the average cache access time. To first approximation the bus traffic is directly related to the cache miss rate and the average size of a bus transaction.

The miss rate depends both on the cache organization and the workload, and can be easily assessed by a number of methods. The cache access time, on the other hand, is implementation dependent and is harder to assess without actually building the cache or making an inordinate number of assumptions about the implementation. A number of recent studies [36, 60, 65] have shown that implementation issues play a critical role in designing high-performance systems. For this reason, we lay heavy emphasis on implementation in all our discussions; design issues will mostly be in the context of the memory system of MIPS-X – a 20-MIPS, reduced-instruction-set, VLSI processor designed at Stanford [41].

1.1.2 Cache Performance Evaluation Methodology

Cache miss rates can be derived by one of three methods: (1) Hardware measurement, (2) analytical models and (3) trace-driven simulation (TDS). Hardware measurement, an expensive technique, involves instrumenting an existing system and observing the performance of the cache. Naturally, this scheme is inflexible because the cache parameters cannot be easily varied and as such generates only *a posteriori* information on a design. Analytical models and trace driven simulation do not have these drawbacks, although these two methods have their own set of disadvantages.

Analytical models of caches estimate cache performance quickly, albeit at the cost of accuracy. Mathematical models can give more insight into the behavior of caches than other experimental techniques. In addition, models can be used to suggest useful ways of improving cache performance by changing the cache organization or the program structure after studying program-cache interactions.

Trace-driven simulation (TDS) is perhaps the most popular method for cache performance evaluation. TDS evaluates a model of a proposed system using previously recorded address traces as the external stimuli. Address traces are streams of addresses (usually of the virtual address space) generated during the execution of computer programs. TDS involves studying the effects of varying the input trace and model parameters on the behavior of the model outputs.

Chief among its advantages are flexibility, accuracy, and ease of use. Being a software technique, TDS does not require expensive hardware support. The experiments are repeatable and the same data can be used to compare multiple cache strategies. For the past several years trace-driven simulation has been the mainstay of cache performance estimation [76, 31, 38, 80].

The usefulness of trace-driven simulation depends on the integrity of the traces used to drive the simulations. The importance of obtaining traces that provide accurate cache performance predictions motivates a closer look at some tracing methods. Typical tracing schemes include: hardware monitors that watch the address bus for memory transactions; software simulators that can generate address traces by interpretively executing an instruction stream; some hardware assisted methods such as the VAX T-bit [91] technique, which traps every instruction into the operating system when the T-bit is set to enable recording all memory references; and analytical program behavior models that can generate synthetic reference streams. Each of these methods has its own weaknesses, and these will be discussed further in Chapter 2.

1.2 Review of Past Work

The problem of cache memory design and optimization for high-performance computers has occupied researchers for the past two decades. This section highlights some of the research done during this period that is relevant to the material in this book.

The earliest published report on an existing cache was by Liptay [50] for the IBM System/360 Model 85. The cache uses a scheme called sector placement to reduce the amount of data that needs to be transferred on a miss while minimizing tag storage space. Kaplan and Winder [45] presented an early review of cache design parameters and also proposed several new measures of cache performance, including the use of average access time (T) as a measure of cache effectiveness. They recognized the deleterious effect of task switching on cache performance and modeled this effect by assuming the entire cache is flushed when a job resumes. They projected that split user-supervisor caches would be cost-effective in a constantly interrupted environment. Their results were obtained from traces generated by a routine that recorded instruction-by-instruction user-state behavior of various programs onto magnetic tape. Another trace program captured system references and patched them in. Task switching times were handled by separate estimates. The paper has a number of useful trace-driven simulation results on the effect of cache size (up to a maximum of 16K bytes), set size, block size, replacement strategy, and task switching on cache performance.

In early systems, caches were used only in very large-scale high-end machines such as the IBM 360/85. Later, the design of a number of smaller machines also recognized their utility. For example, Bell et al. [11] investigated various cache schemes practical for a minicomputer. In particular, they studied write through and write back caches, and set-associative mapping schemes using trace-driven simulation. This study concluded that simple cache schemes with possible higher miss rates offered a better cost performance tradeoff for minicomputers than the more complex schemes used in larger machines. The decrease in the ratio of the processor cycle time to main-memory access time in minicomputers, and to an even greater extent in microcomputers, increased the importance of caches and encouraged the trend towards simpler cache implementations for enhanced overall performance.

Strecker [84] described the research that led to the design of the cache memory in the PDP-11/70. The studies used trace-driven simulation exclusively. A PDP-11 simulator executed PDP-11 programs interpretively to generate traces of memory references. The paper discusses write strategies: write back and write through. Strecker also investigated the influence of various cache parameters on performance and reported the results for a maximum cache size of 2K words (4K bytes). We summarize the notable results here. The miss rate fell rapidly up to a cache size of 1K words and less rapidly thereafter for his benchmarks. The largest improvement on changing the set size occurred in going from a set size of one to two. A fully-associative organization performed little differently than a four-way set-associative cache, and various replacement strategies (LRU, FIFO, RAND) performed almost the same. The same observation was also made by several later studies. Strecker also studied the impact of context switching by completely flushing the cache of all its references every 300, 3000, and 30000 references.

Unfortunately, in most previous studies the traces excluded operating-system activity. Milandre and Mikkor [55] observed that a large proportion of misses occur in the operating system due to its large working set. Peuto and Shustek [62] also looked at environments where the user code was being constantly interrupted by the supervisor. They presented data on the amount of user data purged by typical operating-system routines in the Amdahl 470 V6 and the IBM 360/168. The method they adopted was a combination of simulation and measurement. Their tracing programs captured only user traces, limiting trace-driven simulation predictions to user-state cache miss rates. The effect of calls to the operating system was later incorporated by timing a loop, first executed without interruption, then interrupted by a supervisor call. Knowing the cache miss penalty in the system and the time difference between the two incantations of the loop, the number of the user loop lines purged from the cache could be determined.

Harding, MacDougall, and Raymond [35] also presented some measured data showing that the supervisor state has a significantly higher miss rate than the problem (or user) state. Rossman [68] evaluated a split user/supervisor cache for the Hitachi 80 and found that the split user/supervisor cache was about as good as a unified cache.

Recent cache performance studies have laid greater emphasis on multitasking, trace accuracy, caches for instructions-only and both instructions and data, and implementation issues. An excellent survey article by Alan Smith [76] thoroughly and systematically analyzes the influence of various cache design parameters on performance using trace-driven simulation. The cache aspects analyzed include cache fetch algorithm, placement algorithm, line size,[1] replacement, main memory update, cold-start versus warm-start effects, I/O, split instruction/data cache, virtual versus real addressing, cache size, and bandwidth issues. The study used a large number of traces of PDP-11 and IBM 360/370 series of computers. Smith accounted for task-switching effects by interleaving a number of traces of individual benchmarks in a round-robin fashion. Although the paper does not present real data on supervisor workloads, it does qualitatively discuss the issue of split user/supervisor caches.

Goodman [31] argued that in a real system, especially in a VLSI implementation, and in multiprocessors, the required bus bandwidth is a critical performance issue. He showed ways of using caches to reduce this bandwidth and proposed using the traffic ratio, defined as the ratio of the total cache-to-memory to the processor-to-cache traffic, as a performance metric. An important conclusion was that block-size variation must be carefully assessed not only in terms of the miss rate but also in terms of the traffic ratio.

Clark [21] presented a set of thorough measurements of caches in real working systems. Clark measured the performance of the VAX-11/780 cache for real workloads. Besides helping in the designs of future systems, these results also helped calibrate and validate previous simulation cache models. The reported miss rates were higher than the miss rates predicted by earlier trace-driven simulation studies. The degradation was attributed to the presence of operating-system references, realistic multitasking, and I/O activity. The failure to capture these affects was recognized as a key drawback of trace-driven simulation and exposed the need for better traces and analysis methods.

Smith's paper [75] on workload selection for cache studies has an excellent discussion on the relative merits and demerits of trace-driven simulation. The paper shows that poor workload selection can lead to severely distorted results. The emphasis is on the choice of realistic traces of large programs that do not fit trivially into the cache. The paper also presents a suite of cache results using

[1] The line size issue is the subject of a later paper by Smith [78].

traces from a wide variety of computer systems including the IBM 370, the IBM 360/91, the DEC VAX, the Zilog 8000, the CDC 6400, and the Motorola 68000, which could be used by a computer architect in designing new machines.

In recent times, microprocessor cache memories became increasingly prevalent, introducing a new set of trade-offs [6, 51]. Alpert [7] analyzed on-chip cache memories; he made a strong case for the inclusion of implementation issues in VLSI cache studies. Some previous studies [76, 45, 84] analyzed caches with a constant amount of data storage. Alpert stressed that for VLSI caches the tag storage must also be considered. His paper discusses cache design and performance given a fixed silicon budget. Alpert recommended that the block size be made larger than the amount of data transferred on a miss to reduce the tag storage space. He called the amount of data transferred the transfer size.[2] Hill and Smith [38] also evaluated on-chip microprocessor cache memories to study the impact of various cache parameters on the traffic ratio and the miss ratio. Their results also indicate that transferring smaller units than the block size (called sub-block placement or sector placement) result in better overall utilization of silicon real estate. Prefetching techniques such as load forward – fetching from the current word to the end of the block – are shown to be advantageous.

Among other VLSI cache studies are a description of a VLSI instruction cache designed to work with the Berkeley RISC-II processor by Patterson et al. [61], and a special VLSI cache for use with a delayed branch for the PIPE processor at Wisconsin-Madison [63].

A recent paper [2] details the design and implementation of a real on-chip instruction cache for the MIPS-X processor designed at Stanford. It analyzes cache organizations ranging from a direct-mapped cache to a fully-associative instruction buffer. The paper advocates the use of average instruction access time as a cache performance metric, particularly for integrated caches, by showing that the miss rate can often be reduced at the expense of the cache access time or the miss service time. The case study of the MIPS-X on-chip instruction cache demonstrates that for a low ratio of processor cycle time to miss service time, cache performance is heavily dependent on implementation; the influence of implementation is much more than the impact of set size, replacement strategy, or block size.

To meet ever-increasing computing needs shared-memory multiprocessors have become popular in achieving high-performance cost-effectively. Per-processor caches are useful in multiprocessors to reduce both the main-memory bandwidth requirements of the processors and the average latency of a memory access. The existence of multiple caches introduces the problem of cache consistency because

[2] The IBM-360/85 used a similar scheme called sector placement.

several cached copies of the same memory block can exist simultaneously. In such a system there must be some mechanism to ensure that two or more processors reading the same address from their caches will see the same value. Most schemes for maintaining this cache coherence use one of three approaches: snoopy caches [31, 88, 28, 46, 69, 59, 53], directories [86, 14, 8, 3], or software techniques [77, 22, 15, 58, 54, 16]. The basic idea behind all these schemes is to ensure that when a block is written into, no other cached copies of that block containing the stale value exist. Maintaining cache coherence requires extra network transactions and increases the bus traffic; most schemes also increase the miss rate.

A few studies estimated the performance of multiprocessors as a function of the bus traffic generated by the various schemes. Dubois and Briggs [24] used analytical models to estimate the performance loss due to cache interference in multiprocessors. They modeled multiprocessor reference streams as the merge of two independent streams, one to private data and the other to shared data. Archibald and Baer [9] used a similar model for the reference streams in multiprocessors. However, they synthetically generated such streams and simulated various snoopy cache coherence protocols. Vernon and Holliday [92] used Petri-Net models to estimate the performance of cache coherence protocols. Only the study by Dubois and Briggs tried to model the impact on the miss rate of caches due to multiprocessor interference.

There were several interesting developments in evaluation techniques during this period. Since trace-driven simulation was the most popular method for cache evaluation, several researchers investigated methods to make it more efficient. Typical simulation studies involved evaluating hierarchies of storage systems (e.g., a cache backed by the main memory) against repeated runs of the same set of address traces. These evaluations were time consuming for reasonable length traces. Mattson, Gecsei, Slutz, and Traiger [52] described new and efficient methods for determining the performance of a large class of multi-level storage systems.

The above techniques allowed the evaluation of several caches in a single run through the trace; similar ideas also formed the basis of a number of useful techniques for reducing simulation time in examining a single level in the memory hierarchy. These include Smith's Stack Deletion and Snapshot method [79], and Puzak's Trace Stripping [64] technique. These are discussed further in Section 4.4.

Some of the problems with earlier evaluation techniques were that the effect of finite trace lengths was not addressed and multitasking was not modeled. Easton and Fagin [25] stressed the need for accurately determining the effect of finite trace lengths by showing that cache miss rates would have significant errors if simulations did not account for these, in particular for large caches. They proposed methods to accurately obtain miss rates for fully-associative caches using their new cold-start and warm-start definitions. Easton [26] further showed how the miss rate of a cache could be efficiently computed in a task-switching environment where the cache is flushed on every context switch.

Haikala [33] assessed the impact of the task switch interval on cache performance. He used a simple Markov chain model to estimate the effect of cache flushes. The LRU stack model of program behavior [82] and geometrically distributed lengths of task switch intervals are assumed. The model is reasonably accurate for small caches where task switching flushes the cache completely and pessimistic for large caches where significant data retention occurs across task switches.

Analytical cache modeling advanced too. Some of the earliest memory hierarchy studies used simple empirical models. Chow [18] assumes a power function of the form $m = AC^B$ for the miss ratio, where C is the size of that level in the memory hierarchy, and A and B are constants. They do not give a basis for this model and do not validate this model against experimental results. Smith [76] showed that the above function approximates the miss ratio for a given set of results within certain ranges for appropriate choices of the constants. However, no claims were made for the validity of the power function for other workloads, architectures, or cache sizes.

The Independent Reference Model [5] is used by Rao to analyze cache performance [66]. This model was chosen primarily because it was analytically tractable. Miss rate estimates are provided for direct-mapped, fully-associative, and set-associative caches using the arithmetic and geometric distributions for page reference probabilities.

Smith [73] focused on the effect of the mapping algorithm and set-associativity using two models: a mixed exponential and the inverse of Saltzer's linear paging model [70], for the miss ratio curve of a fully-associative cache.

The effect of block size was not included in the above studies, and program behavior had to be separately characterized for each block size. Kumar [47] investigated spatial locality in programs. He proposed an empirical technique to estimate the working set of a program for different block sizes. The miss rate calculated as a function of block size is shown to correlate well with the results of trace-driven simulation.

Smith and Goodman [80] analyzed instruction cache replacement policies using a new loop model for instruction behavior. One of the interesting conclusions of the study was that random replacement was often superior to LRU replacement in small instruction caches.

The previous models neglected time dependent effects and multiprogramming issues. Strecker [85] analyzed transient behavior of cache memories for programs in an interrupted execution environment using the linear paging model for the miss ratio function. The analysis accounts for data retention in the cache across interruptions. The form of the miss ratio function used is $(a + bn)/(a + n)$, where n is the number of cache locations filled; a and b are constants obtained by measuring the program miss rates at two cache sizes. Predicted miss rates of several real programs run individually, and interleaved, for various execution intervals compare reasonably well with trace-driven simulation results.

The transient behavior of caches is also studied by Stone and Thiebaut [83]. They calculate the minimum number of transient cache refills necessary at process switch points as a function of the number of distinct cache entries touched by the program, also called the program footprint, for two processes executing in a round robin fashion.

Voldman and Hoevel [93] used a different approach by adapting standard Fourier analysis to the study of software cache interactions. Voldman et al. [94] used fractals to model cache misses.

Improvements in tracing techniques were also reported: Clark [21] reported using hardware monitors, a number of studies at DEC and elsewhere used architectural assists such as the VAX T-bit [91] to gather traces (e.g., [37]), others [20, 57] used microcode to record counts of events.

The research discussed is by no means exhaustive. I have attempted to present a sampling of advances in cache research that have brought us to the current state. For a comprehensive bibliography on cache readings please see [74].

1.3 Then, Why This Research?

Researchers have made great strides not only in identifying an optimal set of cache parameters for a given application, but also in methods for cache performance evaluation and data collection. Many of the problems faced by cache designers such as area-performance trade-offs for on-chip caches, caches for instruction and data, minimizing miss rate while maintaining an acceptable traffic ratio, the effects of the choice of workload on cache performance, physical versus virtual cache issues, replacement strategies and corresponding hardware overhead trade-offs, performance of multiprocessor cache coherence protocols, and a host of other issues have been extensively studied.

Then, why this research?

The key open problems in cache performance analysis can be summarized as:

1. To accurately characterize the performance of large caches for operating system and multitasking behavior in single processor and multiprocessor systems.

2. To capture distortion-free trace data from working systems. Towards this end, tracing techniques that can collect reliable traces to accurately predict cache performance must be developed.

3. To derive more accurate and more efficient techniques for cache performance estimation and analysis.

The remainder of this section discusses the importance of these three issues and why they were inadequately addressed before.

1.3.1 Accurately Characterizing Large Cache Performance

Current high-performance computer systems rely increasingly on large, simple caches to satisfy their high-bandwidth requirements. Large caches also reduce the main memory bandwidth needs of each processor in a multiprocessor configuration. Such reduction allows a more economical shared main memory design. As the number of processors in a configuration grows, this second use of large caches becomes increasingly important. Overall performance of the system bears a strong relation to the performance of its cache, making the accurate characterization of large caches a necessity.

The trend towards large, but simple, cache organizations stems from trying to minimize the average memory access time (T) – dependent on both m and T_c – in these memory-bandwidth-limited, high-performance computer systems. Simultaneously minimizing both cache access time and miss rate is not easy, necessitating a careful tradeoff between the two. At first glance, reducing miss rate may seem more important due to the large miss penalty in fetching data from main memory. Unfortunately, more complex cache organizations, used to reduce miss rates, often result in additional levels of logic and increases cache access times; this access time impacts the clock cycle time of the machine.

Direct-mapped caches, which do not suffer from the complications of associative caches arising from replacement, multiplexing, and associative searches, offer a cost-effective means of keeping T_c small. Because cache access time (T_c) is a major bottleneck in many current high-performance systems, people have chosen to use caches with a low degree of associativity causing an increased miss rate for the same total cache size. The spurt of direct-mapped caches in recent high-performance systems (e.g., VAX 8800 [29]), especially in RISC style architectures (e.g., SPUR [27], MIPSX [40], R2000 [56]), bespeaks the importance of direct-mapped caches and implementation considerations. Since the miss rate must be kept low to sustain performance, large caches become necessary. Although, large caches have an access time penalty, it is less than the penalty for extra chip crossings in the multiplexing logic associated with greater set-sizes, assuming, of course, that large integrated caches will not be available in the near future. Even for non memory-access-time limited systems, large caches are necessary to keep the miss rate as low as possible because the penalty of taking a miss could be tens of wasted processor cycles.

The increased reliance on large caches introduces a number of important questions that have not been adequately addressed so far. For instance, most current research has focused on small to medium sized caches for predominantly single-process user programs. Most studies have either roughly modeled the effects of multiprogramming and system references, or have excluded them altogether. This omission was not significant in the study of small caches as shown by simulation results of Smith [76] and others which correspond reasonably well with actual measurements of systems [21].

However, the same arguments do not apply to large caches in today's powerful systems, where the overall performance of the system is highly sensitive to the performance of its cache. For example, in the design of the Berkeley SPUR processor, performance drops by almost ten percent for every percent increase in cache miss rate [87]; similarly, performance of the MIPS-X processor designed at Stanford degrades by over fifteen percent for the same increase in cache miss rate. The greater penalty in the MIPS-X processor is due to its faster clock cycle which increases the relative cost of main memory accesses. Second order effects that only marginally affect small to medium-size cache performance become critically important now. Because both system references and multitasking significantly influence large cache behavior, analyzing their affects is important.

The high memory bandwidth requirement of multiprocessors makes their performance even more dependent on the performance of their caches. Multiprocessor cache studies are few, and these studies exclusively used analytical modeling or simulations against synthetic reference streams due to the unavailability of real multiprocessor address traces. Without real data from multiprocessor systems, even the parameters in the analytical or simulation models had to be assumed. The performance impact on caches of secondary effects such as process migration, semaphore caching, and virtual address caching versus physical address caching, was largely unknown.

Some of the key questions that we would like to answer are the following: What is the effect of system activity on cache performance? This is an important question since it is known that a significant percentage of CPU time is spent in the operating system (often, over 50%). Some studies have looked at some specific operating system types of workloads, but they do not show the interplay between the user processes and operating-system code. It is also not clear if the workloads used display the typical sorts of activity visible in real working systems.

Another important question is how does multiprogramming affect cache behavior? To quote Alan Smith, "Most machines task switch every few thousand instructions and are constantly taking interrupts. It is difficult to include this effect accurately in a trace-driven simulation and many simulators don't try." Traditionally cache studies analyzed cache behavior for single-user traces. Some took multitasking into account by synthetically slicing together trace segments from multiple user traces; others chose to flush caches every 10,000 instructions (or so) to simulate the effect of interacting processes. However, synthetic methods can be unrealistic, and these simulations cannot be verified until actual multitasking traces are analyzed.

Finally, how do caches behave in multiprocessor environments? What metrics must we use in multiprocessor cache analysis? How do process migration and synchronization behavior impact cache performance? We must answer these questions to determine if the shared-memory model can be efficiently used in multiprocessors and to analyze the limits to performance imposed by the memory bandwidth requirements of these machines.

1.3.2 Obtaining Trace Data for Cache Analysis

Many questions are open mainly due to a lack of good data. Because trace-driven simulation remains the single most popular technique in cache studies, and requires a set of address traces to drive the simulation, address traces of high integrity are crucial. Traditional schemes of obtaining traces such as software simulation of the architecture, hardware monitors, or built-in features, are known to severely distort the traces. Traces currently obtainable lack information on system activity, interrupts, and multitasking. Time-sharing environments are particularly hard to trace. The problem is exacerbated by large caches that require traces of huge hard-to-trace benchmarks to be fully exercised, and multiprocessor traces are non-existent. Computer systems built using predictions based on earlier single processor traces often perform significantly different, and commonly much worse in the real world [21].

1.3.3 Developing Efficient and Accurate Cache Analysis Methods

Ideally, we would like to obtain accurate cache performance statistics with minimal computation. Unfortunately, efficiency and accuracy are two conflicting goals. As stated, *accuracy* is necessary because in high-performance systems, system performance is very sensitive to cache miss rate. *Efficiency* is important because cache simulation becomes computationally expensive when lengthy traces of large workloads must be simulated a number of times to evaluate different cache organizations. The problem arises because most techniques that speed up cache performance evaluation do so at a loss in accuracy.

One method for speeding up simulations and reducing trace storage space uses small samples of program execution. Unfortunately, artificially truncating long execution traces into multiple small samples introduces a considerable amount of start-up distortion in simulations of large caches and gives little insight into the steady-state behavior of the program. Although, other studies (e.g., [76, 31]) have successfully used samples of program traces with similar sample sizes, they did not address the impact of sample size on simulation results. One reason was that the caches under consideration were small (less than 64K bytes) and tended to fill up after a few thousand references in the early portion of the trace; by neglecting trace truncation effects from then on, warm-start or steady-state miss rates could be obtained from the latter part of the trace. Naive extension of this strategy to large caches will require an inordinate number of references for the cache to fill up. Clearly, this model is unsuitable for current cache studies, and in fact, as we will show later, we believe it is incorrect for large set-associative caches where the steady state is reached much before the cache is full.

The other end of the cache analysis spectrum is analytical modeling. Analytical cache models can predict cache performance quickly and yield insights into cache behavior and program-cache interactions. However, analytical models that can predict cache performance with any accuracy for a wide range of cache parameters are non-existent. The program models used and the assumptions made in most studies tailored the analysis to some specific cache parameters limiting the scope of their application. For instance, the models proposed by Rao [66] and Smith [73] need separate characterization of each block size. Kumar's work [47] on the impact of block size used only large caches to exclude the effect of program blocks colliding with each other in the cache. Hence, only start-up effects can be considered to be adequately modeled in this study. In addition, time dependent effects and multiprogramming issues are not addressed.

1.4 Contributions

Our primary goal is to provide insights into the behavior of caches for system references and multiprogramming in uniprocessing and multiprocessing systems with an emphasis on large caches and implementation tradeoffs. We show that system references and multitasking have a significant impact on cache performance with a proportionally greater effect on large caches. Multiprocessor interference degrades cache performance even more severely, especially if process migration is not discouraged. We uncover several issues that are particularly significant in large-cache design, but inadequately addressed before. We also investigate ways of enhancing the performance of caches in multitasking operating-system environments. From the results of our studies on system effects and multiprogramming, stem ideas for designing efficient caches for modern-day computer systems.

We develop new measurement and analysis techniques. These include an analytical cache model, a trace sampling and trace stitching methodology, and an approach to cold-start and warm-start analysis, and a trace compaction method. We also propose an address-tracing scheme called ATUM for single processors, and its extension to multiprocessors called ATUM-2.

Two operating systems, VMS and Ultrix[3], are used for the study of the effect of system references. The results for the two are very similar. We have isolated the effects of the sparse nature and large working sets of system references, and the multiprogramming effect of system and user code. We look at techniques to reduce the deleterious effects of system references on cache performance.

We have analyzed the effect of the multiprogramming level on cache performance and we contrast the various techniques that have been proposed to deal with multiprogrammed caches for both virtual and physical addresses. Earlier models used by previous researchers to account for the multiprogramming effects on caches are scrutinized and shown to be inadequate. We recommend methods to minimize interprocess interference while taking advantage of shared cache space for bodies of common code.

Multiprocessor caches are analyzed using traces of several parallel applications running under the MACH, Ultrix, and VMS operating systems. We study the impact of process migration on cache performance. These traces are also used to contrast the behavior of physical and virtual address caches.

An analytical cache model has been proposed. The model is flexible: it can estimate cache miss rates over a wide range of cache parameter variation. Besides having a significant speed advantage over trace-driven simulation, the

[3] VMS and Ultrix are trademarks of Digital Equipment Corporation.

model also enhances our understanding of cache behavior and program-cache interactions.

We also analyze the transient behavior of caches, and introduce the use of trace sampling and a process called trace stitching to make the study of large caches more efficient. A new approach to cold-start and warm-start analysis yields efficient and accurate cache performance evaluation. We propose a trace compaction method that, in addition to temporal locality, exploits spatial locality in programs.

The tracing method ATUM allows the capture of real working environments, including all operating system activity, interrupts, multiprogramming and multiprocessor activity, with little distortion. These traces are extremely useful in memory studies and, in fact, are now being used by several groups doing cache research. They have also found applications in operating-system performance tuning, system debugging, and basically anywhere where traces are used.

1.5 Organization

This book has three parts addressing the three basic issues: trace data generation, new cache analysis methods, and cache performance analysis.

The second chapter discusses methods to generate accurate trace data for cache studies. It starts with a review of trace-driven simulation and trace generation techniques. Following this is a description of ATUM, a technique we developed to obtain address traces of high integrity using microcode. We contrast ATUM with current tracing techniques and present applications for these new traces.

This is followed by a description of the techniques and tools we developed and used in our caches studies: Chapter 3 proposes and evaluates an new analytical cache model. This chapter also defines a number of terms and describes various aspects of cache and program behavior that are used throughout the rest of the book. Chapter 4 presents a new approach to cache transient analysis and methods to get useful results from small trace samples. A trace compaction strategy is also presented.

Chapters 5 and 6 present our cache performance analysis results for single processors. Chapter 5 studies the effects of operating-system references on cache performance. Cache performance results for both the VMS and Ultrix operating systems are contrasted with the findings of earlier researchers, and methods for enhancing cache performance are evaluated. In the following chapter we look at cache behavior in the light of multiprogramming. Loads ranging from uniprogramming to over ten processes are analyzed. Multiprogramming cache simulation models are validated and methods for improving cache performance, such as using PIDs, hashing and re-hashing techniques, are examined.

Chapter 7 analyzes multiprocessor caches. After a description of ATUM-2, this chapter analyzes the cache performance of physical versus virtual multiprogrammed caches, and evaluates multiprocessor cache interference using a bus-based multiprocessor simulator.

We conclude with a summary of our findings and suggestions for future work.

Chapter 2

Obtaining Accurate Trace Data

Cache simulation studies depend heavily on realistic address traces to drive the simulation; the need for generating reliable traces cannot be overstated. This chapter describes a new method to generate address traces that overcomes many of the limitations of the current tracing methods. By changing the microcode of a computer so that it records the address of every memory location it touches, we can capture complete traces of all programs that run on the computer, including the operating system.

The next section reviews techniques for generating address traces and discusses their strengths and weaknesses. A description is provided on how microcode can be used to generate traces, followed by some details about our implementation for the VAX 8200 processor. The traces generated by ATUM used for our operating system and multiprogramming studies are also described. The multiprocessor extension of ATUM is described in Section 7.

2.1 Current Tracing Techniques

Address traces are currently generated in a number of ways. Some of the more popular techniques of gathering address traces are described below. Table 2.1 shows a number of typical parameters associated with each of the five trace techniques described.

- Hardware monitor. A hardware monitor is a device that plugs onto a working backplane bus to record all bus transactions of a working computer. An example of a hardware monitor is described by Clark [21]. Often these monitors record only counts of events rather than actual addresses themselves, because they have limited memory.

- Built-in tracing mechanisms. An example is the hardware provided T-bit facility in the VAX processor architecture [91]. Setting the T-bit causes a trap to be taken at the beginning of each instruction. These traps are intercepted by the operating system kernel which transfers control to a user-tracing process, whereupon the address of the instruction can be directly recorded. Data references can be determined by interpretively executing the instruction.

- Software simulation of the architecture. There exist a number of simulators that can interpretively execute programs to generate a sequence of addresses, such as MILS: Mips Instruction Level Simulator [19]; and TRACER [37], which is a program that generates address traces for programs executing on a VAX computer under the Berkeley 4.2 VAX/UNIX operating system. In this method, the simulation model of the architecture interpretively executes instructions and writes a stream of virtual addresses.

- Operating system facilities. Traces of page references can sometimes be obtained by adding recording code to page-fault handlers or other such operating system routines. The presence of translation lookaside buffers (TLBs) and the like would filter out many of the references. Unfortunately, traces with coarse granularity (per-page, rather than per-byte) have limited applicability.

- Analytical models. Generative analytical program models, such as the Independent Reference Model (IRM) and the LRU Stack Model [82] can be used to create synthetic address traces. Usually these traces are only used to provide first order insights into the operation of the system.

When a tracing method is unable to record the complete address stream of the running machine, it introduces a distortion into the generated trace. Many techniques suffer from *omission distortion*, the failure to capture some of the addresses of the running system. Common omission distortions are: no record of addresses (data or instruction) generated by the operating system, and no tracing of multiple tasks. These distortions are common because it is quite difficult to write a simulator that takes into account all the operating system activity such as I/O, interrupts, context switching, and time sharing. Even using hardware assisted tracing this information is hard to obtain. On most

Scheme	Cover OS	Multi task	Smpl size	Grnul	Arch/ impl	Slow down	V/P
Soft. sim	no	no	>1M	exact	arch	1000x	V
T-bit	no	no	>1M	exact	arch	100x	V
HW monitr	yes	yes	10K	$2-3$	impl	1x	P
Page ref OS	no	yes	10K	$9-12$	arch	1x	V
Analyticl	?	yes	>1M	exact	arch	–	V
Microcode	yes	yes	>1M	exact	arch	10x	V,P

LEGEND:

Cover OS	- do traces normally include privileged operating sys. code?
Multitask	- do traces normally cover multiple tasks/processes/programs?
Smpl size	- number of address references per coherent sample
Grnul	- address granularity, number of low-order bits dropped
Arch/impl	- architectural trace, or implementation-dependent?
Slowdown	- factor by which tracing slows down execution of workload
V/P	- are the addresses in the trace virtual or physical

Table 2.1: Typical trace-technique parameters

machines, interrupt-handler activity is not interruptible. Thus, any method that relies on some operating system support will not be able to trace interrupt-handler activity.

Another limitation of some tracers is small trace sample size. This problem arises when the tracing mechanism records addresses until a buffer is filled up, then stops tracing until the buffer is written to disk or tape. This problem is most severe with hardware monitors that can only record 1000 to 10000 addresses before filling up. The addresses in each sample are coherent, but two successive samples may be completely unrelated. Many simulation studies show a transient behavior at the beginning of each sample. If the sample size is too small, ***startup distortion*** can unrealistically bias the conclusions.

Some trace techniques truncate addresses, for example turning all byte addresses into aligned memory-word addresses by dropping 2 or 3 low-order bits. This truncation causes ***granularity distortion***, and is acceptable only for simulation studies that use the same or more coarse granularity.

A few techniques capture an address stream that is unique to a particular hardware implementation, and do not represent other implementations. For example, an address trace generated by a hardware monitor on the memory bus captures no data about references that hit in a cache, and a cache bus address trace may capture redundant instruction-buffer prefetches. This bias causes

Technique	OS Omission	Multitsk Omission	Start Up	Granu-larity	Imple-mentation	Time
Software sim	HIGH	HIGH	low	-	-	HIGH
T-bit	HIGH	HIGH	low	-	-	HIGH
HW monitor	-	-	HIGH	low	HIGH	-
Page refs OS	HIGH	low	low	HIGH	low	low
Analytical	HIGH	-	low	low	HIGH	low
Microcode	-	-	low	-	-	low

Table 2.2: Distortions introduced by each trace technique (– implies *none*).

implementation distortion, and only sometimes can be compensated by the programs that use these traces. As shown in Table 2.2, each current technique introduces at least one severe distortion.

Studies using traces generated by the techniques mentioned above have yielded valuable insights into the behavior of computer systems. However, measurements of real working systems often display a different behavior than what is predicted using simulation driven by these traces. The cause of this anomaly can often be found in address traces that are not representative of real working environments. Clearly, there is a need for traces of high integrity.

2.2 Tracing Using Microcode

The basic idea behind Address Tracing Using Microcode (ATUM) is to do the tracing "below" the operating system – in microcode. By making minor changes to the existing microcode of a machine, a trace of all addresses that are touched by the processor can be stashed away in a reserved area of main memory, and periodically written out to disk or tape. These traces represent the addresses generated by the processor with perfect fidelity. While this is not a panacea for all the trace distortions mentioned above, it does have the ability to collect complete address information without the need to build special-purpose hardware.

Microcode tracing is applicable to any machine where modifications to the microcode are possible. Addresses are generated by appropriate microcode routines for macroinstruction fetches and data accesses. At this level, the addresses directly correspond to the addresses that the architecture specification of the machine requires. The addresses are not tainted by implementation-specific resources such as prefetch buffers, caches, or bus sizes. Recording these addresses as they are generated produces undistorted traces.

Our scheme takes advantage of the fact that typically only a small number of microroutines actually generate all memory addresses. These microcode routines can each be modified to record addresses and some type information (such as read, write, or instruction fetch), then continue with their normal work.

In addition to recording addresses, it is possible to record any other activity in the processor that is governed by microcode. This extra information can make a raw address trace much more valuable. For example, a "new process ID" can be recorded at each context switch. This allows later studies to deduce the actual context switch interval directly, and to observe the exact sequence of processes. This can be invaluable in studying the effects of translation lookaside buffer or cache flushing. Similarly, a "new virtual-physical mapping" can be recorded at each TLB miss. Combined with clearing the TLB at the start of tracing, this captures complete information for converting a virtual-address trace to a physical-address one. This can be quite valuable in looking for virtual address synonym use and other mapping anomalies. Processor state information such as interrupt mask or privilege level can also be recorded each time it changes. This allows later analysis of differences in address patterns as a function of processor state.

The ATUM scheme has many advantages over current tracing methods.

- ATUM is independent of the operating system. With the same microcode, all the operating systems that run on the machine can be traced.

- All the system activity can be observed. Even interrupt-handler execution is visible because the microcode used is independent of the interrupt status of the processor. A full multitasking workload can be traced. Thus, there is no operating system omission distortion and no multitasking omission distortion. This makes ATUM a powerful tool for operating system performance tuning and debugging.

- No additional hardware is required, since the processor memory itself can be used to store the traces, and the length of a sample is limited only by the amount of reserved main memory. ATUM is hence extremely cost-effective. Sample sizes of a million references are feasible, and result in very low startup distortion. On some machines, it may be feasible to empty the main-memory buffer as quickly as it fills, or to "freeze" the state of the workload while emptying the buffer. Either technique will yield continuous traces.

- Since full addresses can be recorded, there is no granularity distortion. By recording the instruction-stream and data-stream addresses as each instruction is interpreted, there is no implementation distortion. (Different microcoded implementations of the same architecture could generate identical address traces.)

- Traces contain minimal time distortion. By running about 10x slower than normal, there is some time distortion introduced by ATUM for I/O interrupts, but it is not as severe as that of software simulation running 100x or 1000x slower than normal. For timer-based interrupts, it is feasible in some machines for modified microcode to slow them down by 10x, effectively removing timers as a source of time distortion.

- The trace record contains sufficient information to recreate either the virtual or physical address stream. This has wide applications in large physical cache studies. The traces provide insights into tradeoffs between the use of physical and virtual addressing for some types of system activity. Furthermore, a lot of information on shared data among processes can be derived. This could yield realistic data for multiprocessor cache research.

The microcode tracing scheme is not without its own shortcomings. The major limitation of this method is that only microcode-controlled activities are traced. Thus, I/O activity and hardware-generated memory traffic cannot be observed. Other limitations of this method are time distortion caused by the tracing overhead, and limited trace length. The latter is caused by a limit on the amount of main memory reserved for the trace storage. These limitations will be further discussed in a later section.

2.3 An Experimental Implementation

We built a running implementation of ATUM on a prototype of the VAX 8200 processor at the Digital Equipment Corporation's Hudson, Massachusetts facility [4]. The microcode for this machine is on ROM/RAM chip that allows small modifications to the microcode [12, 13, 42]. Many medium to high end machines have this feature, most often by using RAM for the microstore. In the 8200, the patchable microcode was designed to allow microcode errors to be corrected without the expense of replacing all the ROMs in existing machines. We were able to use this facility to modify the microcode to record all memory traffic.

There are three major tasks in setting up microcode tracing: (1) Reserving a section of main memory in which to record the address trace, (2) making microcode modifications to record addresses of memory references, and (3) providing control of the tracing mechanism from high level computer programs.

Type codes
Read 1, 2, 4, 8, or 16 bytes at address A (five codes)
Write 1, 2, 4, 8, or 16 bytes at address A (five codes)
Modify 1, 2, 4, 8, or 16 bytes at address A (shorthand for R/W)
Read 4-byte indirect address
Instruction starts at address A
New process ID = A
TB fill 1, virtual address = A
TB fill 2, physical address = A
Interrupt vector, value = A
Opcode = A (before postprocessing)
Specifier value = A (before postprocessing)

Table 2.3: Type codes in experimental ATUM output

2.3.1 Storage of Trace Data

The address traces are stored in a reserved part of main memory. Using main memory has the advantage that it is a large, high speed storage medium, and standard microinstructions can be used to write data into it. This memory must be inaccessible to normal VAX computer code (specifically, the operating system). In our experimental implementation, the hardware design includes starting and ending address registers on each memory board. These registers are loaded by power-up microcode, and each board responds only to addresses within its range. A simple change to the power-up microcode shortens the address range in the last board, reserving that memory for tracing.

Each VAX computer operating system determines the size of memory and builds page tables by reading successive addresses until no memory board responds. After this has been done, it is safe to restore the last board to its full size, so tracing microcode can write to the reserved area.

The operating system has no knowledge of the trace memory. Hence, all accesses to this memory have to be via physical addresses. There also has to be some special way to transfer data from the trace memory to some mass storage device. The method we adopted is explained later. We reserved two megabytes of main memory for the ATUM traces, enough to contain 400K trace records. Each trace record is a five-byte entry: one byte of type code and four bytes of address. The type codes are shown in Table 2.3.

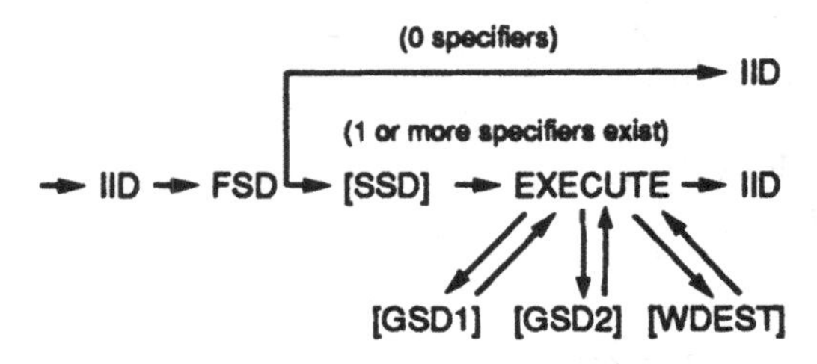

LEGEND:

IID	- Initial Instruction Decode
FSD	- First Specifier Decode
SSD	- Second Specifier Decode
GSD1, GSD2	- General Specifier Decode
WDEST	- Write Destination

Figure 2.1: Typical VAX computer microcode flows.

2.3.2 Recording Memory References

The VAX instruction set [91] is fairly complex and patches in a number of micro routines are needed to record all the memory addresses. Each macro instruction consists of an opcode and 0 to 6 operand specifiers. The overall microcode flow typical of many VAX processor implementations is given in Figure 2.1. Shared subroutines (FSD, SSD, GSD1, GSD2, WDEST) are used to parse the 0-6 operand specifiers, and to do the reads and writes involved. Individual "execute" microroutines exist for each opcode. For the majority of VAX computer instructions, the only memory activity is the explicit read/write of the operands; hence the common microcode that parses all specifiers can record these addresses. For some instructions, such as CALL or MOVE CHARACTERS, the operand specifiers only calculate addresses, and the instruction-execution microcode does individual data references. Each such instruction-execution microroutine must be modified to record the address trace. In addition, some important non-instruction microcode routines access memory, such as the microcode to take an interrupt or to handle a translation-buffer miss. Each such routine must also be modified.

The initial microcode branch for decoding instructions goes to one of about 30 locations. Each of these is modified to record the I-stream address, then continue execution. D-stream addresses can be gathered by patching all those locations in the microcode that do a memory reference. Patching the shared specifier routines detects most memory activity. Patching the individual "execute" flows records the rest.

Unfortunately, due to limitations imposed by microcode RAM size, it was impossible to modify all the necessary execute flows. A large number of the execute-flow memory accesses are for opcodes that reference character, decimal, or bit strings whose addresses and lengths are given in the specifiers. So when recording the instruction address, we also do a quick table lookup to identify such string opcodes. For each string opcode, we record the opcode itself, and the VALUES of all the specifiers. This is enough information to postprocess the trace into a full sequence of memory references. Except for a few very low-frequency paths (e.g., using 16 bytes of scratch data on the stack for DIVP), all the "execute" memory-access locations were modified to record the address trace.

2.3.3 Tracing Control

To obtain maximum flexibility and ease of use, it is beneficial to allow complete control of tracing from a high-level user program. To do this, the "microcode extension" opcode, XFC, is used. This allows control of the starting and stopping of tracing, or a data word transfer from an offset in the trace memory to a VAX processor general purpose register. From this register, the user program can transfer the data to user memory and then to disk. We wrote a Pascal program to enable tracing, wait for the buffer to fill (tracing is disabled automatically when the buffer fills up), dump it to disk, and re-enable tracing.

The entire facility took about 1000 words of microcode, consisting of about 80 distinct modifications. For this implementation, no attempt was made to record the partial progress of a string instruction that takes an interrupt or page fault in the middle of its execution. This is one of the small distortions we allowed when faced with a shortage of microcode space. Similarly, no attempt was made to "freeze" the machine when the trace buffer got full, so two samples are not contiguous in time. This introduces startup distortion every 400,000 references.

2.4 Trace Description

We traced both Ultrix and VMS operating systems running on a VAX 8200 processor and gathered a comprehensive set of traces covering a wide range of workloads and multiprogramming levels. Each ATUM trace, roughly 400,000 references long, is a half-second snapshot execution on a machine the speed of a VAX-11/780. Of the four to eight samples taken for each application, one to four are used for this study. In all, thirty traces are used.

For the effect of system references we concentrated on traces that had just one or two processes to exclude multitasking behavior. Twenty traces of eleven programs running under VMS and Ultrix are used.

ALLC – a trace sample of a microcode address allocator (VMS);
DIA0 – a diagnostics program for the VAX computer (VMS);
IVEX0, IVEX3 – two samples of a DEC program, Interconnect Verify, checking net lists in a VLSI chip (VMS);
UMIL2 – MIPS instruction level simulator running TLB, a TLB simulator (VMS);
DEC0, DEC1 – trace of DECSIM, a behavioral simulator at DEC, simulating some cache hardware (VMS);
FORL0, FORL1 – FORTRAN compile of LINPACK (VMS);
PASC0, PASC1 – PASCAL compile of a microcode parser program (VMS);
SPIC0, SPIC1 – SPICE simulating a 2-input tri-state NAND buffer (VMS);
LISP0, LISP1 – LISP runs of BOYER (a theorem prover) (VMS).
NMLST – produces a name list from an executable (Ultrix);
SAVEC0, SAVEC1, SAVEC2, SAVEC3 – samples of the C compiler (Ultrix).

In the VMS traces between 5 and 50 percent of the references are due to system activity, with an average of about 20 percent. In the Ultrix workloads, about 50 percent of the references in NMLST are system, while the SAVEC traces show about 75 percent system references.

We used nine VMS trace samples of multiprogramming levels three, six, and ten – three trace samples at each multiprogramming level – to study the impact of process switching. The trace samples for a particular multiprogramming level shown the same component processes. The three samples of each multiprogramming level were concatenated to form three large traces called **MUL3, MUL6,** and **MUL10**. The processes active in **MUL3** are a FORTRAN compile of LINPACK, the microcode address allocator, and a directory search; those in **MUL6** are two FORTRAN compiles of LINPACK and a program called 4x1x5, the microcode address allocator, a SPICE run, a PASCAL compile of a microcode parser, and LINPACK; and those in **MUL10** include the six programs in MUL6, a numerical benchmark JACOBI, a string search in a file, MACRO – an assembly level compile, an octal dump, and a linker. For multiprogramming under Ultrix, we concatenated the four samples of the SAVEC traces – calling it **SAVEC** – which, besides the C compiler, also show two other tasks, or a multiprogramming level of three.

In addition to the above traces, we will use a VMS trace of Interconnect Verify stripped of all extraneous processes – called **IVEX** – for some of the examples. Table D.1 in Appendix D summarizes benchmark trace characteristics.

2.5 Applications in Performance Evaluation

Besides the performance evaluation of caches, ATUM has also been successfully used as a powerful debugging and performance tuning tool. In a few cases, it has been used to understand anomalously-slow program performance for which standard software tools gave no insight. With address traces, the problems were quickly revealed to be unusually low cache or TLB hit rates, due to specific memory-addressing patterns. In another instance, ATUM has been used to find the operating-system code paths that resulted in long measured interrupt latency. An operating system algorithm performance bug was understood by capturing the exact sequence of table accesses used.

In general, using the ATUM technique to performance-tune a user program is overkill, akin to using a microscope where a magnifying glass would do. However, it gives valuable insight in a few special cases of performance-tuning operating system code or hardware algorithms (cache, TLB, interrupts).

2.6 Extensions and Summary

In the current ATUM scheme, the maximum size of memory allocated for traces limits the length of any coherent trace sample. As memory boards grow denser the limiting value becomes proportionately larger. Other than waiting for denser memories, there are a few techniques one could use to record data over much longer intervals of time.

The first technique involves compacting the traces. A small filter cache [79, 64] can be implemented in microcode to filter out recurring addresses on the fly. The degree of compaction can be increased by neglecting some lower order bits at a cost in granularity in the traces. Another method is to focus attention on only those activities that are of immediate interest. For instance, recording only page references and page faults for paging studies, opcode counts to obtain distributions of opcode use, etc. Clark [20] reports the use such event count monitors.

The above methods sacrifice detail to achieve length. An alternate technique can be adopted to generate large traces without giving up fine-grain effects. It is possible to trace a specific process along with all the associated system activity. After choosing some workload, one can record just a *summary* at each process switch point, e.g. the new process identifier and the number of references since the last switch. Then for the same workload, one can use multiple runs to record traces of individual processes. A postprocessor can then synthesize a large multiprocess trace from the process-switch summary and the individual traces.

In summary, we have described the theory and an experimental implementation of a cost-effective method to gather address traces with very low distortion. The traces capture complete operating system and multitasking activity. Our experiments using the ATUM traces have yielded a better understanding of computer systems. Should various processor groups adopt this technique and make the resulting traces available to the general research community, significant improvements in our understanding of the dynamics of memory systems will result.

Chapter 3

Cache Analyses Techniques – An Analytical Cache Model

Once accurate traces have been obtained, their efficient analyses is an important issue. Brute-force simulations to derive cache performance figures are time consuming and may not yield much insight into cache behavior. Three methods are presented in the following chapters for efficient and insightful analyses of caches.

This chapter discusses the first of these: an analytical cache model that uses parameters extracted from address traces of programs to provide estimates of cache performance and shows how various parameters affect cache performance. By representing the factors that affect cache performance, we generate an analytical model that gives miss rates for a given trace as a function of cache size, degree of associativity, block size, sub-block size, multiprogramming level, task switch interval, and observation interval. The estimated values closely approximate the results of trace-driven simulations while requiring only a small fraction of the computation cost.

Our approach differs from some of the earlier memory hierarchy modeling efforts that tended to focus on some specific aspect of cache performance but did not adequately address the issue of a comprehensive cache model. The early portion of this chapter defines some cache and workload terminology that will also be used in our empirical cache studies in later chapters. We then present a basic cache model to introduce some of the key principles and ideas. A comprehensive cache model, model validations against real address traces, and our results follow.

3.1 Motivation and Overview

In this section, we first discuss why mathematical cache models are necessary. We then present the rationale behind our modeling strategy, and briefly overview some of the key concepts that the cache model is based on.

3.1.1 The Case for the Analytical Cache Model

Two methods predominate for cache analysis: trace-driven simulation and hardware measurement. The survey article by Smith [76] uses the former technique extensively, while a comprehensive set of hardware measurements is presented by Clark [21]. Other examples of cache studies using the above methods include [7, 20, 31, 38, 81, 75, 78, 2]. These techniques provide an accurate estimate of cache performance for the measured benchmarks. The problem is they cannot be used to obtain quick estimates or bounds on cache performance for a wide range of programs and cache configurations. Simulation is costly and must be repeated for each possible cache organization, although stack processing techniques can sometimes be used to reduce the number of simulations [52]. Large caches requiring longer traces for simulation exacerbate the problem. Multiprogramming effects are seldom studied using simulation due to the lack of multitasking traces; the availability of such traces (e.g., ATUM traces) introduces additional dimensions over which simulations must be done. Hardware measurement, which usually involves costly instrumentation, requires an existing cache and gives data for only one cache organization (sometimes with limited size variations [21]). Furthermore, simulation and measurement inherently provide little insight into the nature of programs and the factors that affect cache performance. Analytical models on the other hand, if simple and tractable, can provide useful "first cut" estimates of cache performance. Simple models provide more intuition, but may lack the accuracy of more complex models. Therefore, if more detailed results are needed, simulations can be carried out to fine-tune the cache organization.

There are added advantages to having a simple model for cache behavior. For example, an understanding of the exact dependence of cache miss rate on program and workload parameters can identify those aspects of program behavior where effort would be best justified to improve cache performance. Cheriton et. al. [16] suggest that building caches with large blocks (cache pages), in conjunction with program restructuring to exploit the increased block sizes, could yield significant performance benefits. A cache model that incorporates the spatial locality of programs would be useful in analyzing the effects of various program restructuring methods. In addition, this model could be incorporated into optimizing compilers to evaluate tradeoffs in decisions, such as procedure merging, that affect cache performance. Also, in a multiprogramming environment, the tradeoff between higher resource utilization and degradation in cache performance with the level of multiprogramming can be easily assessed with a simple analytical cache model.

3.1.2 Overview of the Model

Our cache model is hybrid in nature, involving a judicious combination of measurement and analytical techniques yielding efficient cache analysis with good accuracy. Since the intended application of our model is to obtain fast and reliable estimates of cache performance, the time spent in measurement of parameters from the address trace and, more importantly, in model computations must be significantly less than simulation. To minimize the number of parameters that have to be recorded and stored, average quantities are often used instead of detailed distributions. Mean Value Analysis (MVA), an example of this approach [49], gives accurate predictions of computer system performance using average measured system parameters to drive analytical models. MVA has been a key motivating factor in our cache modeling efforts.

Cache performance data for a given address trace is derived in two steps. First, we analyze the reference stream and record a few parameters. The model parameters, which are extracted from an address trace, are meaningful by themselves and provide a good indication of cache performance. In the second step, we vary cache and workload characteristics and project cache performance from the model. The model includes cache parameters such as cache size, degree of associativity, block size and sub-block size; and workload characteristics such as multiprogramming level and the time between process switches.

Cache miss rates can be derived by representing the following factors that cause cache misses:

Start-up effects: When a process begins execution for the first time on a processor, there is usually a flurry of misses corresponding to the process getting its initial working set into the cache. In the early portion of any trace, a significant proportion of the misses in a large cache can be attributed to start-up effects. This effect is also observed when a program abruptly changes phases of execution. Since miss-rate statistics for different phases of the same program are often widely uncorrelated, just as those of different programs are, each phase has to be separately characterized for maximum accuracy. However, for simplicity, or if the phases are short or if phase changes are small, their effects can be smoothed into the non-stationary category. Start-up effects are excluded when warm-start (or steady-state) miss rates are needed [25]. Inclusion yields cold-start miss rates.

Non-stationary behavior: This is caused by the slow change of a program's working set over time. The misses that occur when references are fetched for the first time after the start-up phase are included in this category. Any program performing the same sort of operation on each element of a large data set shows this behavior. Subtle changes of phase over small intervals of time, corresponding to change in cache working set, can also be modeled as a non-stationary effect. Often all phase behavior within a trace can be conveniently treated as non-stationary. While the overall miss rate might not be in error, the resulting transient miss rate, as predicted by the model, would show a smoother variation than in practice.

Start-up and non-stationary behaviors are evident from working set plots [23] of programs. Working set plots have a roughly bilinear nature with a sharply rising initial portion corresponding to start-up, and a gradual slope thereafter denoting non-stationarity. The misses caused by the above two effects are dependent on the block size – assuming that a block is fetched from the main store on a cache miss. Increasing the block size (up to a limit) takes advantage of the spatial locality in programs and reduces cache miss rate. A model of spatial locality is proposed to account for this effect.

Intrinsic interference: Due to finite cache size multiple memory references of a process may compete for a cache set and collide with each other. If the number of cache sets is S, then all addresses that have the same index (i.e., a common value for the address modulo S) will have to be in the same cache set. Interference misses occur when these references have to be fetched after being purged from the cache by a colliding reference of the same process. This effect depends both on how the addresses are distributed over the address space – a static effect, and the sequencing of references, a dynamic effect. The static characterization is based on the assumption that any reference has a uniform probability of falling into any cache set. The hashing operation (e.g., bit selection) that maps the large address space of programs to the much smaller cache space effectively randomizes the selection of any given cache set. Our results, and also those of Smith [73], show that this assumption is quite reasonable. The dynamic component is represented using a measured parameter from the trace called the collision rate. Unlike the distribution of blocks in the cache, which is dependent on the cache size, the collision rate is shown to be reasonably stable over a wide range of cache and block sizes.

Extrinsic interference: Multiprogramming is an additional source of misses because memory references of a given process can invalidate cache locations that contained valid data of other processes. The impact of multitasking, not widely considered in previous cache studies, is particularly important for large caches where a large fraction of the misses tend to be clustered near process switch points. Extrinsic interference will increase with the level of multiprogramming and decrease with the quantum of time that a process executes before being switched out. Other causes of extrinsic interference such as I/O and cache consistency invalidations are not included in this study but could be added. Extrinsic interference is modeled in the same manner as intrinsic interference with only the static characterization being necessary. The dynamic component, characterized by the collision rate in intrinsic interference, is not needed because a collision can happen only once per colliding reference after a process switch.

All the above effects are included in our comprehensive model of cache behavior. Start-up effects and extrinsic interference characterize the transient behavior of programs, and non-stationary effects, intrinsic and extrinsic interference determine steady-state performance. The extent to which each effect contributes to the miss rate is a strong function of the cache organization and workload. In small caches misses are predominantly caused by intrinsic interference, whereas in caches large enough to hold the working set of the program, non-stationarity and extrinsic interference are the important sources of misses.

In the following section, we first describe a basic cache model taking into account start-up, non-stationary, and interference effects for a direct-mapped cache with a fixed block size. We then extend the model by including the effect of set size, block size and multitasking. A discussion of the results of our experiments and model validations against several address traces are then provided.

3.2 A Basic Cache Model

This section describes a model for direct-mapped caches with a fixed block size. The total number of misses is calculated as the sum of the misses due to start-up, non-stationary, and intrinsic-interference effects. Only one process, i, is assumed to be active. In general, all parameters associated with this process will be subscripted with the letter i. However, for simplicity, we will bring in this subscript only when necessary to distinguish between processes.

A notion of time in the context of a reference stream is necessary to study the transient behavior of caches. We assume that each reference represents a time step. We also define a larger time unit called a *time granule (tg)* for use in the model. A time granule is sequence of τ references. Average parameter values are calculated over a time granule. Processes are assumed to execute on the processor for an integral multiple of time granules and process switches occur on a *time granule* boundary. This may not be the case in real life, but, as we shall see, this approximation is still useful in predicting average cache performance and has little effect on the actual results. In the analytical model, all sizes are specified in words, where a word is four bytes.

Cache organization, C, is denoted as a triple (S, D, B), where S in the number of sets, D is the set size or degree of associativity, and B is the block size or line size in four-byte words.

The cache size, in terms of blocks, is the product of the number of sets and the set size. It is assumed that a block of data is transferred between the main store and the cache on a cache miss.

We have tried to validate the basic model at every step against simulation results. For intermediate results, we use an address trace of Interconnect Verify (IVEX) of length 400,000 references. Interconnect Verify is a program used at Digital Equipment Corporation's Hudson site to compare two connection net lists. Our trace is a sample of Interconnect Verify operating on a processor chip.

First we need some definitions:

τ: The number of references per time granule. A typical value is 10,000. As we shall see in the discussion on sensitivity analysis in Appendix A, the choice of τ is not critical to the analysis. Ideally, τ should be bounded below by the average time spent in start-up activity, as defined in Appendix A.

T: Total number of time granules of a process i, or the trace length in number of references divided by τ.

t: Represents a particular time granule. t varies from one to T.

$u(B)$: The average number of unique memory blocks accessed in a time granule by the process. Clearly u is a function of block size. u is similar to the working set with parameter τ as defined by Denning [23].

$U(B)$: The total number of unique memory blocks used in the entire trace. In the basic cache model, we drop the use of B and use the notation U since the block size is kept constant. In practice, U is less than $T * u$ because many references are common across time granules.

$m(C,t)$: The miss rate for process i up to and including its tth time granule for cache $C : (S, D, B)$. This is the total number of misses divided by the total number of references in the first t time granules.

3.2.1 Start-Up Effects

The initial filling of the cache causes start-up misses. Let us assume for a moment that all these misses happen in the first time granule. Then, for the first time granule, the miss ratio due to start-up effects is the ratio of the number of unique references accessed in that time granule to the total number of references:

$$m(C,1)_{startup} = \frac{u}{\tau}$$

The start-up component decreases monotonically with time because the number of start-up misses is constant:

$$m(C,t)_{startup} = \frac{u}{\tau t} \tag{3.1}$$

The above formula shows that even if the cache filling takes more than one time granule, the miss rate will be in error only as long as cache filling due to start-up takes place. This term becomes vanishingly small for large traces. For the IVEX trace, with a block size of one word (four bytes), and τ chosen to be 10000, the average number of unique memory blocks accessed in a time granule, $u(1)$, is 1624.

3.2.2 Non-Stationary Effects

Equation 3.1 considered the misses that occur in fetching blocks for the first time during the initial time granule and did not take into account the fact that in each time granule the process could be renewing parts of its working set. For example, this behavior is seen when a program is operating at any instant on a small segment of a large array of data. As the program moves to new portions of the array, these new references will give rise to an added component of misses.

In our model, the first time granule has a large number of new blocks, which is the initial working set u. In subsequent periods, only a fraction of these will be renewed. Let f_u be the fraction of unique references, u, that are new in every time granule. In keeping with our assumption of the average being a good predictor of the actual value, we can estimate the total number of non-stationary misses as the number of unique blocks in the entire trace minus the initial start-up misses. On dividing by T, the total number of time granules, the average number of non-stationary misses in a time granule is obtained. The ratio of this quantity to u gives f_u:

$$f_u = \frac{U - u}{T\,u}$$

where, U are the number of unique blocks in the entire trace and T are the total number of time granules represented by the trace. Thus the cumulative number of misses up to the tth time granule due to non-stationary effects, is

$$f_u\, u\,(t-1)$$

and the corresponding miss rate is obtained by dividing the number of non-stationary misses by the number of references, $t\tau$,

$$m(C,t)_{nonstationary} = \frac{u}{\tau}\,\frac{f_u\,(t-1)}{t} \tag{3.2}$$

IVEX, with a block size of one word (four bytes), has, $u(1) = 1634$, $U(1) = 7234$, $T = 40$, and $f_u = (7234 - 1624)/(40 * 1624) = 0.0863$. Note that the non-stationary component of misses over the entire trace is over four times the start-up component.

3.2.3 Intrinsic Interference

Some cache misses are caused by multiple program references competing for the same cache block. This effect lessens as cache size grows larger because fewer references on the average compete for any given cache block. To include this effect in the model, we need to estimate the number of collision-induced misses that will occur as a function of cache size. In general, the set size or associativity plays an important role, but for the present, the analysis assumes a direct-mapped cache. As mentioned before, estimation of interference misses involves both a static and a dynamic factor.

Static Characterization

For the static characterization, the distribution of program blocks into cache sets will be modeled. From this model, we will estimate the number of blocks that collide with each other.

We define a *collision set* as a set that has more than one block mapped to it, and, a *colliding block* (or an interfering block) as any block that maps into a colliding set. In other words, a colliding block is one that could be potentially displaced from the cache by another block. As an illustration, Figure 3.1 shows a direct-mapped cache with 8 sets, $S0$ through $S7$. A program block is denoted by a shaded rectangle. The cache set $S3$ contains block $B1$, while blocks $B2$ and $B3$, which also map into the same set, are not cache resident. By our

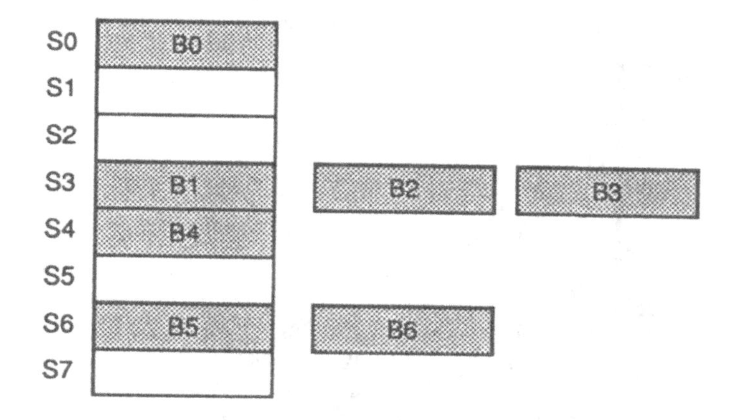

Figure 3.1: Collision in a direct-mapped cache. Shaded rectangles represent blocks.

definition, the number of collision sets are two ($S3$ and $S6$), and the number of colliding blocks are five ($B1$, $B2$, $B3$, $B5$, and $B6$).

The key assumption we make in our derivations is that a program block has a uniform probability of being in any cache set. Many factors contribute to the validity of this assumption. The hashing operation that maps the large process address space to the smaller number of sets in the cache randomizes the selection of any given set. In physical caches, virtual pages can be mapped to an arbitrary physical page. In virtual caches, the Process Identifier (PID) is sometimes hashed in with the address used to index into the cache causing references of different processes to be uncorrelated with each other. Also, since code and data for user and system tend to reside in different segments of the address space, they are mutually independent with respect to the cache sets they occupy.

Assuming random placement in the cache, the probability, $P(d)$, that d blocks fall into any given cache set (depth of overlap d) has a binomial form. As usual, we leave out the dependence of this probability on B for notational brevity.

$$P(d) = \binom{u}{d} \left(\frac{1}{S}\right)^{d} \left(1 - \frac{1}{S}\right)^{u-d} \tag{3.3}$$

The probability that a block maps into a given cache set is $1/S$, and that d

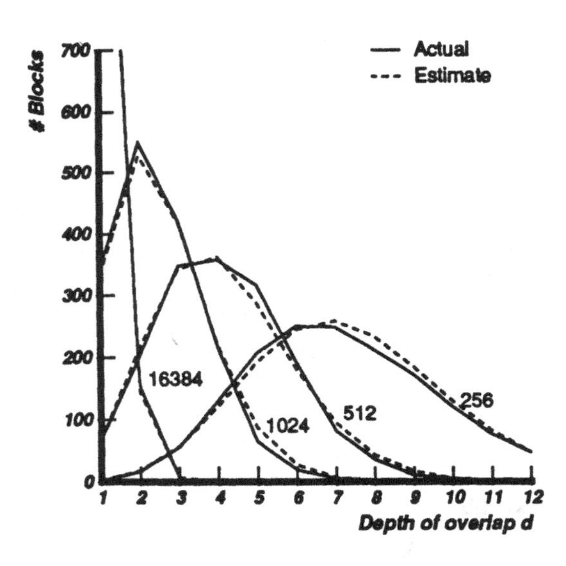

Figure 3.2: Number of blocks of size one word (4 bytes) that map into a cache set with depth of overlap d. Values on the figure indicate cache size in number of sets.

blocks map into this cache set is $(1/S)^d$; $(1 - 1/S)$ is the probability that a block does not map into the given set.

To validate this model, the number of blocks that map into a set at a depth of overlap d is calculated for IVEX. The correspondence between calculated and observed values (Figure 3.2) for a wide range of cache sizes (256 to 16K sets) is very close. Considering depths of up to seven, which includes 99% of the references, the mean and maximum errors in estimation are less than 15% and 42% respectively for a $1K$-set cache. There are two caveats to this error presentation. First, in our mean value modeling approach, only the mean error is important, and second, noting that errors in the tail of the function do not significantly affect the predictive capability of the model, a better indication of performance is provided by focusing on depths less than five which corresponds to 95% of the references. The mean and maximum errors in this range are 2% and 4% respectively. The component of error in the intrinsic interference dominated miss rate attributable to inaccurate calculation of the number of overlapping blocks for the 4K byte cache is only 2.6%, which further corroborates our argument.

The number of interfering blocks can be calculated straightforwardly from Equation 3.3. Collisions will not occur in any cache set that has at most one program block. Hence, in a direct-mapped cache, the probability that a cache set has no

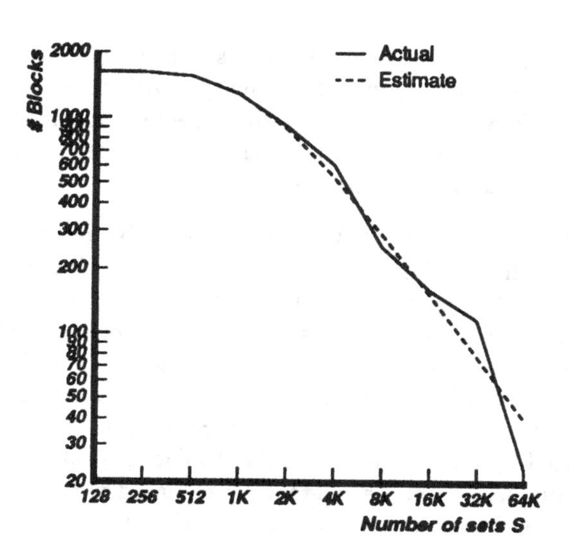

Figure 3.3: Number of collision blocks as a function of the number of sets. Block size is one word (4 bytes).

colliding blocks is $P(0) + P(1)$, and the number of such non-colliding blocks is $S * [0 * P(0) + 1 * P(1)]$, which is $SP(1)$. In general, for any number of sets S, we can compute the number of interfering blocks to be the difference between the number of unique memory blocks and the number of blocks that do not collide, or,

$$Number\ of\ interfering\ blocks = u - S\ P(1) \tag{3.4}$$

Figure 3.3 shows colliding blocks as a function of the number of sets. For small caches, all the blocks collide yielding a maximum of u colliding blocks, and for large caches this number approaches zero. Again the correspondence between estimated and actual values is quite good with average the error 14% and the maximum error 72%. The large error in $64K$ sets is of little consequence because the miss rate is predominantly start-up dominated; the impact of incorrectly estimating the number of colliding blocks on the miss rate for a cache with 64K sets is less than 9%. The mean and maximum errors excluding 64K sets are 8% and 33% respectively.

Dynamic Characterization

The above formula gives just the number of colliding blocks, or the static portion; it does not indicate when colliding blocks actually induce misses, nor does it tell us anything about the number of times that the blocks actually purge each other from the cache (the dynamic component), which is what we need to compute the miss rate. First, we will derive some loose bounds on this number and on the miss-rate component due to intrinsic interference, then present a more accurate characterization of the miss rate.

We define a *dead block* to be one that is not going to be referenced in the future. A *live block*, on the other hand, is still active. The minimum number of misses occur if every colliding block that is brought into the cache lands on top of a *dead* one. For example, if two variables that compete for a cache block are live only in alternate halves of a time granule the number of collision induced misses due to these two blocks will be zero. However, if colliding references are very finely interleaved, then these will cause thrashing in that cache block. Thus, a miss is induced by a collision only if the displaced block is live. In our model, the average number of times a reference is repeated per time granule is τ/u giving rise to a possible maximum of τ/u intrinsic interference misses per colliding reference.

Let the *collision rate, c*, be the average number of times a live colliding block in the cache is purged due to a collision in a time granule. In other words:

$$c = \frac{Number\ of\ times\ live\ variables\ are\ purged\ in\ direct\ mapped\ cache\ per\ tg}{Number\ of\ colliding\ references} \quad (3.5)$$

The actual miss rate due to intrinsic interference is given by,

$$\begin{aligned} M(C,t)_{intrinsic} &= \frac{c * Number\ of\ colliding\ references}{\tau} \\ &= \frac{c\,[u - S\,P(1)]}{\tau} \end{aligned} \quad (3.6)$$

We now need a characterization for the collision rate, c, which is bounded as

$$0 \leq c \leq \frac{\tau}{u}$$

The high value is attained when the cache has only one set and every reference is a miss. The collision rate, c, will depend on a number of factors including the number of times loops are executed in the given program and the time interval between the live periods of colliding blocks. Intuition leads us to believe that c will be approximately the same for different cache sizes for any given program up to the point where the cache becomes small enough that all cache sets are filled. Beyond this ceiling point, c will monotonically increase until it reaches its maximum, τ/u, for $S = 1$. Our experiments (presented in Appendix B) show this to be true. Thus, we can measure a value for c from the given trace for a representative direct-mapped cache with a block size of one and number of sets S_0. We will use this value of c in miss rate projections for most other cache sizes and organizations as well.[1] Hence, we derive c as follows:

$$c = \frac{Number\ of\ times\ live\ variables\ that\ are\ purged\ in\ a\ tg\ when\ S = S_0}{Number\ of\ colliding\ references}$$

For our example we choose $S_0 = 1024$. Total number of live blocks (of size four bytes) purged in IVEX per time granule is 2391; the probability that only one block maps into a given cache set, $P(1) = 0.32$; number of unique references in a time granule, $u = 1624$; the number of colliding references $=$ $1624 - 1024 * P(1) = 1291$. The collision rate

$$c = \frac{2391}{1291} = 1.9$$

We need to verify whether c is stable over different numbers of sets. Table 3.1 displays the actual values of c for IVEX, and we see that c is reasonably stable and the variations do not seem to show any pattern.

No. sets	c measured
1K	1.9
2K	2.0
4K	2.1
8K	1.6
16K	1.9
32K	2.2
64K	1.2

Table 3.1: Collision rate for various cache sizes.

Summarizing, the basic cache model for direct-mapped caches gives the miss rate as a sum of start-up (Equation 3.1), non-stationary (Equation 3.2), and intrinsic interference effects (Equation 3.6):

$$m(C,t) = \frac{u}{\tau t}\left[1 + f_u(t-1)\right] + \frac{c}{\tau}\left[u - SP(1)\right] \tag{3.7}$$

[1] The exceptions are discussed in Appendix B.

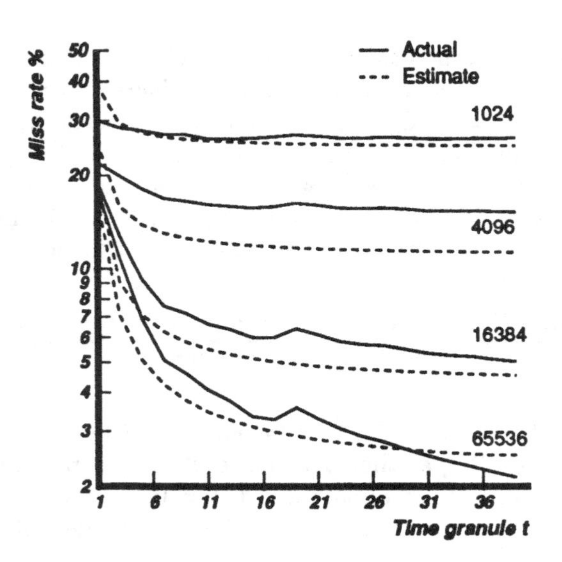

Figure 3.4: Miss rate versus time granule for direct-mapped caches with 1024, 4096, 16384, and 65536 sets. Block size is 4 bytes. Actual values represent simulated miss rates.

In the steady-state (as t tends to ∞) the miss rate becomes independent of start-up effects:

$$\frac{u\,f_u}{\tau} + \frac{c}{\tau}\left[u - SP(1)\right].$$

This simple cache model predicts miss rates for direct-mapped caches with a fixed block size both as a function of time and cache size. Figures 3.4 and 3.5 compare the results of the simple model with trace-driven simulation results using the benchmark IVEX. Further validations against other traces are provided after the following section. The IVEX trace has 400,000 references. Block size is chosen to be four bytes. S_0 for parameter extraction was 1K.

Miss rates for various cache sizes as a function of time granules are in Figure 3.4. Prediction is quite accurate for caches of size 1K sets (mean error 6%, maximum error 30%), 16K (17% and 30%), and 64K sets (13% and 35%). In the 4K-set cache (mean error 25%, maximum error 28%) the estimated values are lower than the actual values because both c and the number of colliding blocks are underestimated. Miss rate is substantially overestimated for small caches in the first time granule ($1K$ and $4K$ caches in Figure 3.4) because the model assumes that intrinsic interference is uniform over time. In practice, the initial portion of a trace has a relatively few intrinsic interference misses since most of the

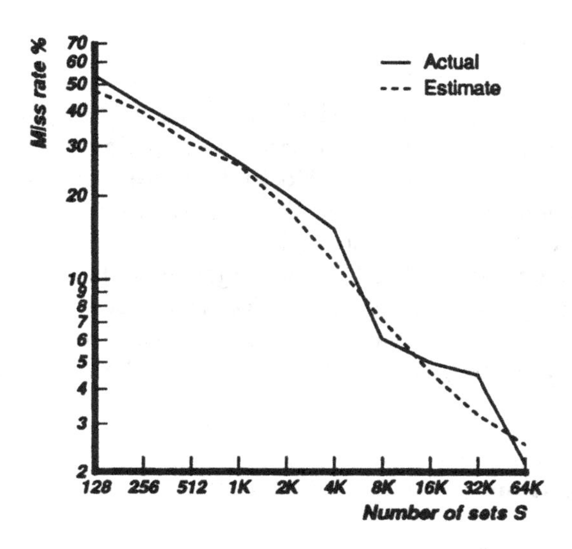

Figure 3.5: Miss rate versus number of sets S. Caches are direct mapped and block size is 4 bytes.

misses are attributable to start-up activity. Prediction suffers more in smaller caches because the intrinsic interference miss rate component is higher. This problem is easily fixed by only including intrinsic interference misses from the second time granule onwards. Prediction for the 64K-set cache is quite good despite c being off by almost 60% because the number of colliding blocks is so small as to make intrinsic interference an insignificant component in the miss rate. IVEX shows a subtle phase change near the 20th time granule, which the model cannot detect because of its averaging property.

Figure 3.5 shows miss rates as a function of the number of sets. Estimated miss rates are very close to actual for caches ranging from 128 sets to 64K sets. The estimated curve yields a good overall fit to the actual curve even though individual miss rates may be in error.

3.3 A Comprehensive Cache Model

In the previous section we derived miss-rate estimates for a single process using a direct-mapped cache and a given block size. We now extend the model to include set size (degree of associativity), block size, sub-block size and multiprogramming.

3.3.1 Set Size

The intrinsic interference term is affected when set size is changed. If the set size is D, only those cache sets with more than D competing blocks will have collisions. Thus, the number of colliding blocks decreases monotonically with increasing degree of associativity D when the number of sets, S, is constant. The effect of set size on the collision rate, c, is more subtle. Recalling that in a collision set a miss is induced if a live block is purged, more blocks can co-exist in a set without purging each other if the set size is increased, thus decreasing c. Clearly, both the static and dynamic components that comprise intrinsic interference depend on set size. As before, we first derive the static component, followed by the dynamic part.

Static Characterization

To estimate the number of colliding blocks for any set size D, we start with the probability, $P(d)$, that d blocks fall into any given cache block as in Equation 3.3.

$$P(d) = \binom{u}{d} \left(\frac{1}{S}\right)^{d} \left(1 - \frac{1}{S}\right)^{u-d}$$

The number of sets that have d competing blocks is therefore $S\ P(d)$. The number of blocks that collide, for a cache with degree of associativity, D, is obtained by subtracting the total number of blocks that overlap with depth less than D from the total number u:

$$u - \sum_{d=0}^{d=D} S\ d\ P(d)$$

Figure 3.6 shows the number of colliding blocks in the Interconnect Verify trace (IVEX) for caches with set sizes one through 16. The number of colliding blocks decreases with set size for most caches. The correspondence between observed and predicted values in Figure 3.6 is good. The mean and maximum errors for a 4K-byte cache are 1% and 2% respectively, for a $8K - byte$ cache 5% and 16% respectively, and 38% and 88% respectively for a cache of size $16K$ bytes. As stated before, the tail portion of the curves can be off by a large relative amount and do not contribute significantly to the final result. In this case, the relative error in our colliding block estimate for set size 16 is unimportant because the miss rate is start-up dominated, and in fact, the corresponding errors in miss rate for a 16K-byte cache is less than 5%. Hence, the mean and maximum errors for a 16K-byte cache not including set size 16 become 25% and 33% respectively.

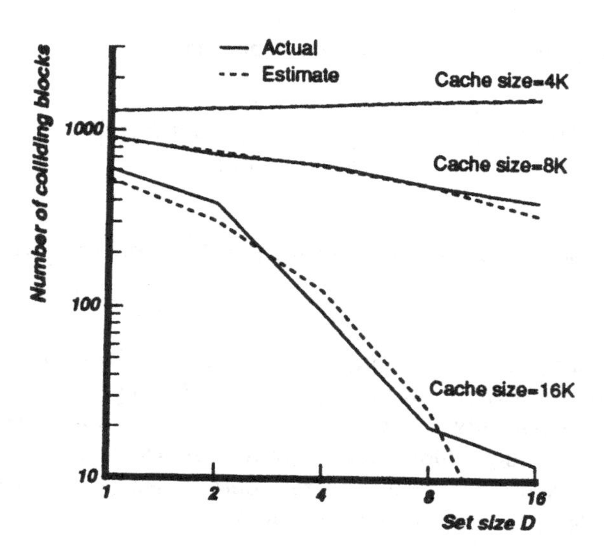

Figure 3.6: Number of colliding blocks vs. D. Cache size is specified in bytes.

Dynamic Characterization

We need the collision rate, or the average number of times a block collides, in addition to the static factor. For caches with set size greater than one, the *replacement algorithm* has to be considered in determining the average number of times a block collides. Since we do not have use information, modeling LRU replacement is hard. Appendix B shows how $c(D)$ can be obtained for set sizes greater than one from the value of c measured from a direct-mapped cache (please see Equations 3.5 and B.2). This method approximates random replacement. The results can be used as a good estimate for the miss rates given by other non-usage-based replacement schemes such as FIFO [76]. Smith also shows that random replacement has about ten percent worse cache miss rate than LRU replacement on average, and we believe this difference will decrease with increasing cache size. Thus, our predicted miss rates can be used as a loose estimate on those with LRU replacement also.

The total number of collisions in a time granule due to intrinsic interference is the number of colliding blocks weighted by the collision rate, $c(D)$. The aggregate number of misses per time granule due to intrinsic interference in a cache with S sets and set size D is therefore

$$c(D)\left[u(B) - \sum_{d=0}^{d=D} S\ d\ P(d)\right] \tag{3.8}$$

and the corresponding intrinsic miss rate component is

$$m(C, D)_{intrinsic} = \frac{c(D)}{\tau} \left[u(B) - \sum_{d=0}^{d=D} S\, d\, P(d) \right] . \tag{3.9}$$

3.3.2 Modeling Spatial Locality and the Effect of Block Size

The derivations in the previous sections assume that the block size is kept at some constant value throughout all measurements and analysis. By increasing the block size, we can take advantage of the spatial locality in address streams because the number of unique blocks is a decreasing function of the block size. The dependence of u and U on the block size is determined by two factors: the distribution of run lengths and the distribution of space interval between runs.

The *distribution of run lengths* is needed to estimate the effect of changing block size, where a *run* is defined as a maximum stream of sequential references. As an example, if some data objects are isolated words, then we will need one block for each of these data items for most reasonable block sizes. Runs of length B aligned on block boundaries will be contained in blocks of size B. Further, if blocks cannot be aligned on arbitrary word boundaries then the alignment of the given run within a block will also matter.

The distribution of space intervals accounts for the capture of multiple runs by a single block. While run lengths usually range from one to ten words, empirical cache studies have shown that block sizes far in excess of ten words can still capture additional localities. This effect can be explained by the fact that a large enough block can capture more than a single run. Thus, we need *the distribution of space intervals between runs* to predict the usefulness of increasing block sizes beyond average run lengths.

The ensuing discussion uses the distribution run lengths to characterize spatial locality in programs. From this characterization the miss rate dependence on block size is determined. Appendix C extends the discussion by considering the effect of capturing multiple runs in a single block.

Run Length Distribution

Direct measurement of run-length distributions is difficult for two reasons. First, typical address traces contain interleaved streams of instruction and data addresses. Even after separating these streams, the data addresses from the stack and the heap could be interleaved. For example, a VAX trace can contain a sequence starting with an instruction address, followed by addresses of the first, second, and third operands. Sequentiality of this nature[2] has to be detected in the address traces to derive run length statistics. An efficient method (albeit approximate) of separating these streams and identifying runs is to sort the references in successive segments of the trace.

The second problem is that an accurate characterization of run lengths mandates the use of a large number of parameters – one for every possible run length. To keep computation and the number of parameters to a minimum, we propose a simple Markov model to depict the spatial locality in programs. We can use this model to approximate the distribution of run lengths using two average parameters measured from the address trace.

In general, an n stage Markov model is required (see Figure 3.7(a)) to characterize run lengths, where n is the largest run length in the trace. In the figure, state $R1$ corresponds to the beginning of a run; state Rk is reached if the first k addresses are sequential. f_{lk} is the probability that the next address will be sequential given that the first k addresses are. Since the longest run is of length n, the probability of a sequential reference in state Rn is zero, and a new run is begun with probability one.

In practice, the complication of a n stage model is not actually necessary; we can make a good approximation using a two-stage model. The reason is quite simple. Addresses typically fall into two categories: those that form part of a run of unit length and those that do not. The former are called singular references. Addresses (in particular data) have a reasonably high probability $(1 - f_{l1})$ of being a singular address[3]. Further, given that an address is non-singular, it has a high probability of having a sequential successor (f_{li}, $i = 1, 2, 3, \ldots, n$). Instruction streams, and clustered accesses in data structures display this behavior. We have observed that non-singular addresses show a memoryless property to some extent: the probability that a non-singular address has a sequential successor does not depend strongly on the number of preceding addresses in the run.

The values of f_{lk} for IVEX are: $f_{l1} = 0.56$, $f_{l2} = 0.72$, $f_{l3} = 0.70$, $f_{l4} = 0.84$, $f_{l5} = 0.86$, $f_{l6} = 0.90$, and $f_{l7} = 0.80$. The values of f_{lk} for $k > 1$ are quite close. This confirms that we can approximate the n stage Markov model by a two stage model as in Figure 3.7(b). f_{l1} remains the same. f_{l2} is chosen to be the weighted average of the other f_{lk}s. For IVEX, $f_{l1} = 0.56$ and $f_{l2} = 0.85$.

[2] Rau presents an interesting discussion on this issue [67].

[3] This is the reason why a two stage model is chosen; a one stage model would fail to capture the dichotomous nature of reference patterns.

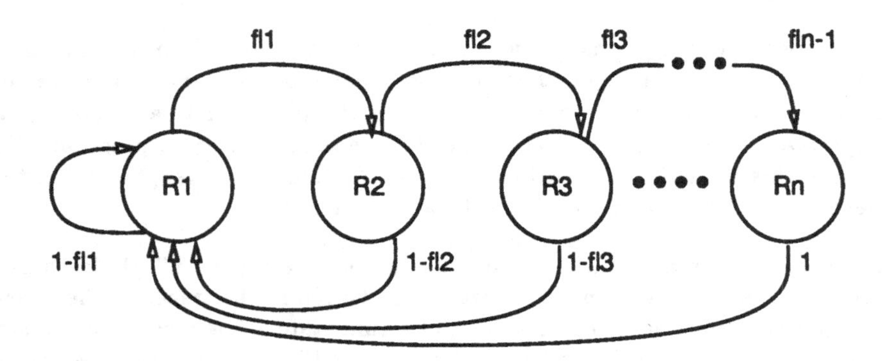

(a) An n stage Markov model

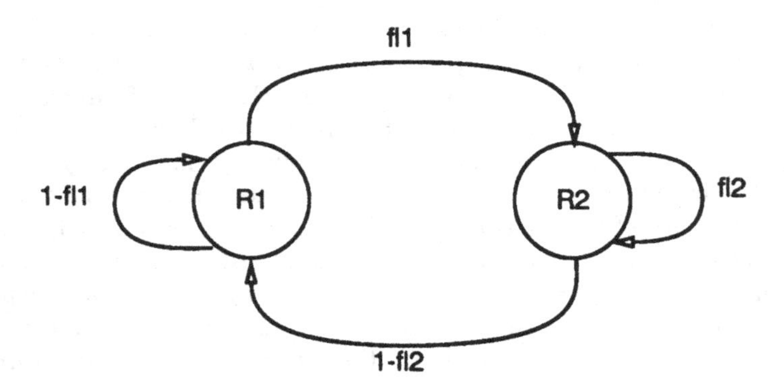

(b) A two-stage Markov model

Figure 3.7: Markov models depicting spatial locality in programs.

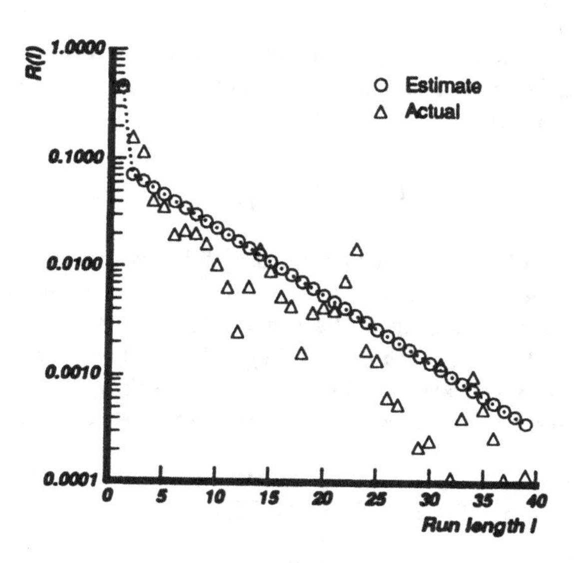

Figure 3.8: Distribution of run lengths for the benchmark IVEX. $R(l)$ is the probability that a run is of length l.

The probability of any run being of length l is given by,

$$
\begin{aligned}
R(l) &= 1 - f_{l1}, \quad l = 1, \\
R(l) &= f_{l1}\, f_{l2}^{l-2}\, (1 - f_{l2}), \quad l > 1.
\end{aligned}
$$

Furthermore, the probability of being in state R_1 in the steady state [90, 39] is the fraction of references that begin a new run, the reciprocal of which gives the average run length:

$$l_{av} = \frac{1 + f_{l1} - f_{l2}}{1 - f_{l2}} \tag{3.10}$$

and the number of unique runs is the number of unique references divided by the average run length, that is $u(1)/l_{av}$. Figure 3.8 shows the distribution of run lengths for IVEX. The dotted line is the approximation using the above simple two stage model.

The next step is to calculate $u(B)$, the number of unique blocks contained in the trace. We define the *cover* for a run to be the set of blocks that have to be fetched on average to bring the entire run into the cache. Note that a reference to any word in a block causes the whole block to be fetched. We start by assuming that a cover for a run can contain at most one run. Then, for a run of length l with ideal alignment (the run starts on a block boundary), at least $\lceil l/B \rceil$ blocks are needed. In general, the alignment is random and the average number of blocks needed to contain a run of length l, or the *cover size*, is given by the following equation:

$$Cover\ size = 1 + \frac{l-1}{B} \tag{3.11}$$

For example, assuming a block size of four words (16 bytes), exactly one block is needed for a run of length one. For a run of length two we need at least one block. Two blocks are used up if the run is aligned such that it crosses block boundaries. This happens with probability 1/4. So, the cover size, or the average number of blocks allocated to the run is 1.25. Lacking the inclusion of multiple runs in a cover, each cover will waste a fraction of a block given by the following formula:

$$\left(1 + \frac{l-1}{B}\right) - \frac{l}{B} = \frac{B-1}{B}$$

In the above example three words are unused.

Hence, the total number of unique program blocks for a given block size B corresponding to $u(1)$ unique words is the average number of blocks needed to cover a run of length l times the number of runs of length l, summed over all l:

$$\begin{aligned} u(B) &= \frac{u(1)}{l_{av}} \sum_{l=1}^{l=\infty} R(l) \left(1 + \frac{l-1}{B}\right) \\ &= u(1) \frac{\left(1 - \frac{f_{l1}}{B} + f_{l2}\right)}{(1 - f_{l1} + f_{l2})} \end{aligned} \tag{3.12}$$

Figure 3.9 compares predicted and actual values of $u(B)$ as a function of block size for IVEX. The mean error in the estimated values is 33% and the maximum is 115%. However, the mean and maximum errors are less than 5% and 8% for block sizes up to 8 words (32 bytes). Thus, the above simple model is sufficient for block sizes less than about 8 words. For greater block sizes, the model incorrectly predicts that $u(B)$ is insensitive to block size. The cause of this error lies in our assumption that a block can capture only a single run. Because average run lengths are of the order of four, larger blocks will be mostly empty having little impact on $u(B)$ in the model.

Actually, the probability of a block capturing more than a single run is non negligible if the distance between the runs (inter-run interval) is small, as is often the case, and it becomes necessary to include inter-run intervals in our discussion. For a detailed characterization of spatial locality please refer to

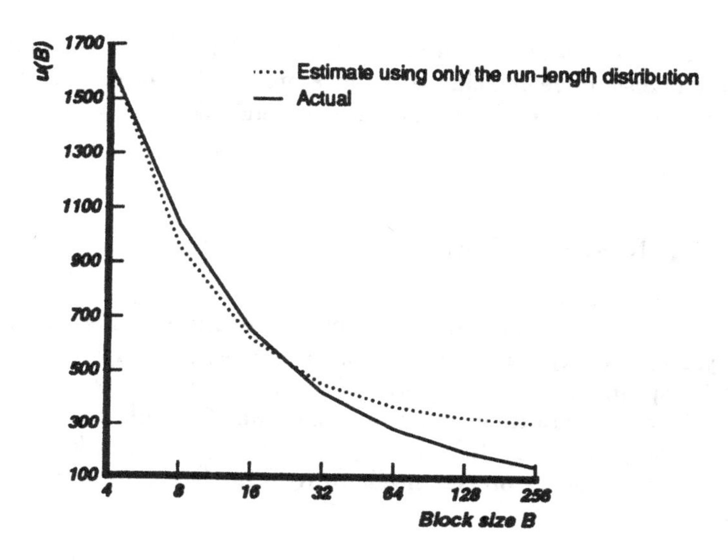

Figure 3.9: Average number of unique blocks, $u(B)$ in a time granule, τ, vs. the block size B in bytes.

Appendix C. Basically, the cover size for a given run, as calculated in Equation 3.11, includes a fraction of a block that could presumably cover neighboring runs. The portion of the block utilized for other runs, determined from a measured average inter-run interval and the run-length distribution, is subtracted from the cover size to yield the actual number of words allocated to the run. $u(B)$ is then computed as in Equation 3.12.

The miss rate can now be estimated using $u(B)$ and $U(B)$ calculated as shown above. The relevant miss rate formulation (as in Equation 3.7) is repeated here including the dependence on the block size B.

$$m(C,t) = \frac{u(B)}{\tau t}[1 + f_{i,u}(B)\,(t-1)] + \frac{c(D)}{\tau}\left[u(B) - \sum_{d=0}^{d=D} S\,d\,P(B,d)\right] \tag{3.13}$$

For sub-block placement, where the block size is B and sub-block size is B_s, the miss rate is approximately $u(B_s)/u(B)$ times the miss rate given by the above equation.

Appendix B provides a discussion on the impact of block size on the collision rate c. Basically, the collision rate is not significantly affected by a change in the block size for most cache sizes. Note that the collision rate reflects the dynamic sequence of referencing to various program localities (blocks), and a locality can be expected to have a similar dynamic behavior as its component words.

3.3.3 Multiprogramming

The discussion thus far assumed single process execution. Because workloads of real systems usually consist of multiple processes, and single process models tend to be optimistic, multiprogrammed cache models are necessary to accurately depict cache performance. Large caches can often hold the entire working set of a single process. In this case most misses occur immediately following a process switch when a process needs to refill its data purged by intervening processes.

The following discussion assumes round robin scheduling with constant duration time slices; in general, time slice lengths can be measured, or picked from an appropriate distribution with the constraint that each time slice equals an integral multiple of time granules. Let *mpl* represent the multiprogramming level and t_s represent the number of time granules in a time slice. Our derivation assumes that the cache is physically addressed, or in the case of a virtually addressed cache assumes that each process has a unique process identifier (PID) that is appended to the cache tags to distinguish between the virtual addresses of different processes. Flushing the cache on every process switch can also be modeled in an even simpler manner. We concentrate on the miss rate for a process i. Let $m_i(C, t_i)$ be the aggregate miss rate for process i after the t_i time granule, and, as before, let the average number of blocks of process i used in a time granule be u_i.

Let *carry-over set* denote the set of references that a process leaves behind in a cache on being switched out and reuses on its return, and $v_i(B)$ be the average number of blocks in the carry-over set. The notion of a carry-over set yields an accurate characterization of the transient nature of cache misses due to multiprogramming. It is easy to see that the maximum number of misses that can occur after a process resumes execution after being switched out is $v_i(B)$. The number of blocks in the carry-over set is bounded above both by cache size and program working set size. Thus, in a small cache multiprogramming induced misses are smaller in number than in a large cache.

Using the notion of a carry-over set the effect of multiprogramming on cache performance is computed as follows. Suppose that a process i has been scheduled to run on the processor after being switched out. There would have been

$mpl - 1$ processes between instances of process i. Due to these $mpl - 1$ intervening processes some fraction, $f_{i,v}(mpl)$, of the blocks in its carry-over set gets purged. The resulting additional misses will be equal to the product of $f_{i,v}(mpl)$ and the number of blocks in the carry-over set. The number of blocks in the carry-over set in a cache with number of sets S, set size D, and block size B, is approximately given by the sum of all the blocks in cache sets that do not collide:

$$v_i(B) = \sum_{d=0}^{d=D} S\, d\, P_i(d). \tag{3.14}$$

This is not strictly true because we have excluded cache entries that could potentially be purged due to intrinsic interference. The implicit assumption is that a colliding variable is more likely to be purged due to intrinsic interference than due to the intervening processes. This makes the miss rate estimates slightly optimistic. $v_i(B)$ could also be computed by summing all cache resident blocks of process i to give pessimistic miss rate estimates. To arrive at a more accurate estimate of the carry-over set, a fraction, equal to the ratio of the size of the time granule and the time slice, of the program blocks in the cache that are more likely to be purged by intrinsic interference can also be included in the carry-over set.

Then, the equation for the miss rate component due to multiprogramming, as shown below, is similar in form to Equation 3.2 which was derived for non-stationary behavior. The main differences are: (1) the working set size is replaced by the size of the carry-over set, $v_i(B)$; (2) $f_{i,u}$, the fraction of references renewed, is replaced by $f_{i,v}$, the fraction of references purged; and (3) the time parameter is adjusted to add in the extrinsic misses once every time slice, t_s.

$$m_i(C, t_i)_{extrinsic} = \frac{v_i(B) f_{i,v}(mpl)}{t_i T} \left\lfloor \frac{(t_i - 1)}{t_s} \right\rfloor \tag{3.15}$$

We need to derive an expression for $f_{i,v}(mpl)$, the probability that any reference in the carry-over set is purged due to extrinsic interference. To model flushing the cache on every process switch, we can set $f_{i,v}(mpl)$ identically to one. For physical caches, or virtual caches with process identifiers, $f_{i,v}$ can be estimated by applying Binomial statistics to the carry-over set of process i and the set of references of all intervening processes. Denoting the number of unique blocks of all intervening processes as $u_{i'}(B)$,

$$u_{i'}(B) = \sum_{j=1, j \neq i}^{j=mpl} u_j(B)$$

and applying binomial statistics we derive the probability, $P_{i'}(d)$, that d blocks fall into any given cache set:

$$P_{i'}(d) = \binom{u_{i'}}{d} \left(\frac{1}{S}\right)^{d} \left(1 - \frac{1}{S}\right)^{u_{i'}-d}$$

Before proceeding with the derivation, a discussion of the replacement issue in the multiprogramming context is necessary. The intrinsic interference model uses random replacement because the order of use of blocks required to model LRU replacement is not available . However, for multiprogramming, LRU replacement is the natural choice, because the order of execution of processes determines the reference order. Consider the case where process i having just relinquished the processor is followed by $mpl - 1$ intervening processes. Clearly, if LRU replacement is used, the references of process i will be purged before those of the intervening processes. In the ensuing derivation, LRU replacement is first used for simplicity, followed by a discussion on how random replacement can be modeled.

Continuing with the model of process i followed by $mpl - 1$ processes, a block of process i can get purged from a given cache set only if the sum of blocks of processes i (say d) and all intervening processes i' (say e) exceeds the set size D. Also note that the number of blocks of process i purged in any cache set is the minimum of (1) the number of blocks of process i in that set, d, (2) the set size D, and (3) the difference between the sum of the number of blocks of process i and i', and the set size D, or $(e+d-D)$. Cases (1) and (2) are trivial, while case (3) deserves comment. This handles the situation where $d <= D$. As many as $D - d$ blocks out of e of the intervening processes can co-reside in the set. The remaining, $e - (D - d) = e + d - D$, will collide with the blocks of process i. The number of blocks of process i that get purged in any one set is therefore

$$\sum_{d=0}^{d=D} P_i(d) \sum_{e=0}^{e=u_{i'}(B)} MIN(d, D, e + d - D) P_{i'}(e),$$

which is simplified to yield

$$\sum_{d=0}^{d=D} P_i(d) \sum_{e=D+1}^{e=u_{i'}(B)} MIN(d, e + d - D) P_{i'}(e).^4 \tag{3.16}$$

The total number of blocks of process i that get purged is the number purged per set times the number of sets S. The fraction of the blocks that are purged

[4] A similar equation for two processes was derived simultaneously and independently by Stone and Thiebaut [83].

out of the carry-over set of process i is then,

$$f_{i,v}(mpl) = \frac{S\sum_{d=0}^{d=D} P_i(d) \sum_{e=D+1}^{e=u_{i'}(B)} MIN(d, e+d-D) P_{i'}(e)}{v_i}, \qquad (3.17)$$

which is substituted into Equation 3.15 to yield the miss rate component due to extrinsic interference.

Random replacement, modeled in slightly different fashion, assumes that all blocks in a fully occupied cache set are equally likely to be purged, irrespective of which process they belong to. Hence, a block of process i in a collision cache set is displaced with probability d/D by random replacement, as opposed to probability one by LRU. Thus the inner summation in Equation 3.16 will now include an additional factor, d/D. Contrary to intuition, the extrinsic interference miss rate component with random replacement can actually be smaller than that due to LRU replacement. The explanation is that unlike the LRU scheme random replacement can cause extra collisions amongst blocks of the executing process itself before the blocks of previous processes are completely purged from a set, which shifts misses from the extrinsic category to intrinsic. Therefore, even if the expected number of extrinsic interference misses for the given process decreases, the the total number of misses induced by collisions (intrinsic and extrinsic) is still expected to increase. We also conjecture that shifting misses from the extrinsic to intrinsic category will reduce the bursty nature of misses particularly at process switch boundaries.

This concludes the derivation of the cache model in the multiprogramming environment. The overall miss rate is the sum of the four components calculated in Equations 3.1, 3.2, 3.9, and 3.15:

$$m_i(C, t_i) = \frac{u_i(B)}{\tau t_i}\left[1 + f_{i,u}\,(t_i - 1)\right] + \frac{c(D)}{\tau}\left[u_i(B) - \sum_{d=0}^{d=D} SP_i(d)\right] + \frac{v_i(B)}{\tau t_i}\, f_{i,v}(mpl)\, \left\lfloor \frac{(t_i - 1)}{t_s} \right\rfloor \qquad (3.18)$$

3.4 Model Validation and Applications

Our cache model has been applied to study a number of cache organizations; the results are compared with those of trace-driven simulation. Three benchmark traces are used in the uniprogramming cache study: interconnect verify (IVEX), which is a DEC program to compare two interconnection net lists in VLSI circuits; a microcode address allocator (AL1); and MILS, an instruction level simulator for the MIPS processor designed at Stanford (TMIL1). The first two traces were obtained using the ATUM address tracing scheme, and TMIL1 was obtained by tracing a VAX-11/780 using the T-bit technique. For the multiprogramming case, MUL10, a trace obtained using ATUM showing ten active processes is used (for trace details see Appendix D).

Figures 3.10 through 3.12 show plots of miss rates versus cache size for a variety of block sizes and degrees of associativity for the three uniprogramming traces, IVEX, AL1, and TMIL1. Corresponding cache performance figures obtained through trace driven simulation for both LRU and random replacement are also shown to assess the accuracy of the model. Analytical model results are shown in solid lines, LRU replacement results in dashed lines, and random (or FIFO) replacement in dotted lines. All cache sizes are in bytes. Mean and maximum errors in miss rate estimates over all cache sizes for random replacement are shown in Table 3.2. We also present the error in hit rate because for very low miss rates the percentage error in miss rate can be very high, but may not significantly affect performance.

Figures 3.10(a), 3.11(a), and 3.12(a) show the miss rate as a function of cache size for direct-mapped caches with block sizes of 4 and 16 bytes. Prediction is quite good for all the benchmarks and block sizes for a direct-mapped cache. The mean error in miss-rate estimates is about 15%.

The miss rates for caches with a set size of two are shown in Figures 3.10(b), 3.11(b), and 3.12(b). Interestingly, the intrinsic interference component of the miss rate becomes insignificant (miss-rate curve bottoms out) after a cache size of 32K bytes for two-way set-associative caches, while it is important for direct-mapped caches even as large as 128K bytes.

Figures 3.10(c), 3.11(c), and 3.12(c) show the variation of miss rate with cache size for a block size of 4 bytes and set sizes of one and two. For benchmarks AL1 and TMIL1, the miss rate does not drop below one percent for caches larger than 32K bytes, implying that most misses are due to start-up and non-stationary effects. In Figures 3.10(d), 3.11(d), and 3.12(d) the block size is 64 bytes and set sizes are one and two. Note that associativity is not particularly useful for small caches.

Figure 3.13 summarizes the model validations for multiprogramming workloads. To keep our analysis simple, we exclude the effect of shared system code and data between processes. As before, dotted curves represent simulated miss rates and solid curves show estimates. For this experiment, we focus our attention on one process in the trace. The curve with the triangle symbol shows the miss rate for the process assuming that the process has its own separate cache. This is the uniprogramming miss rate for that process. The diamond symbol corresponds

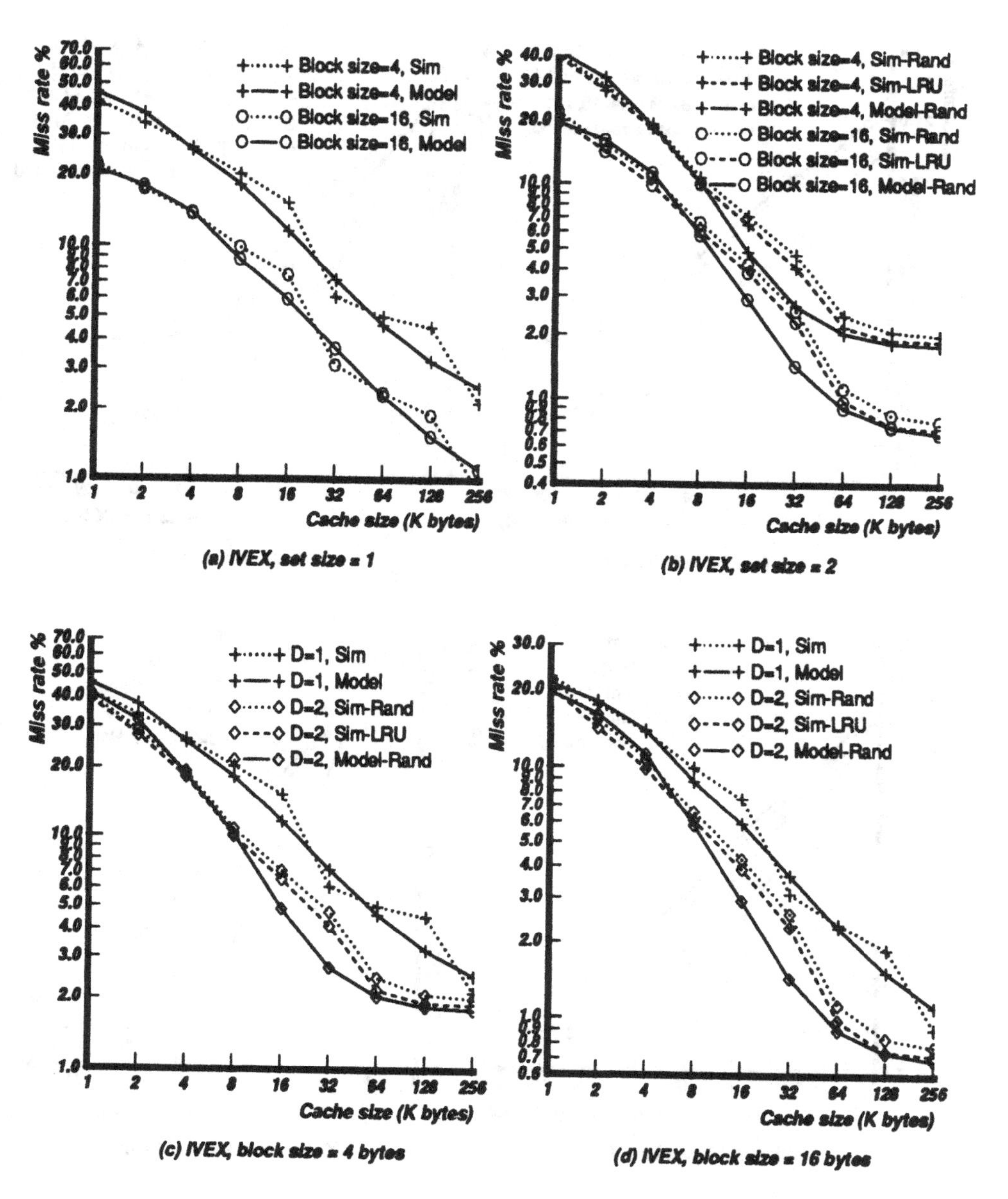

Figure 3.10: Miss rate vs. cache size for IVEX. In (a), (b) set size is constant, and in (c), (d) block size is constant. Solid lines are model, dotted lines are simulation with random replacement, and dashed lines are simulation with LRU replacement. All sizes in bytes.

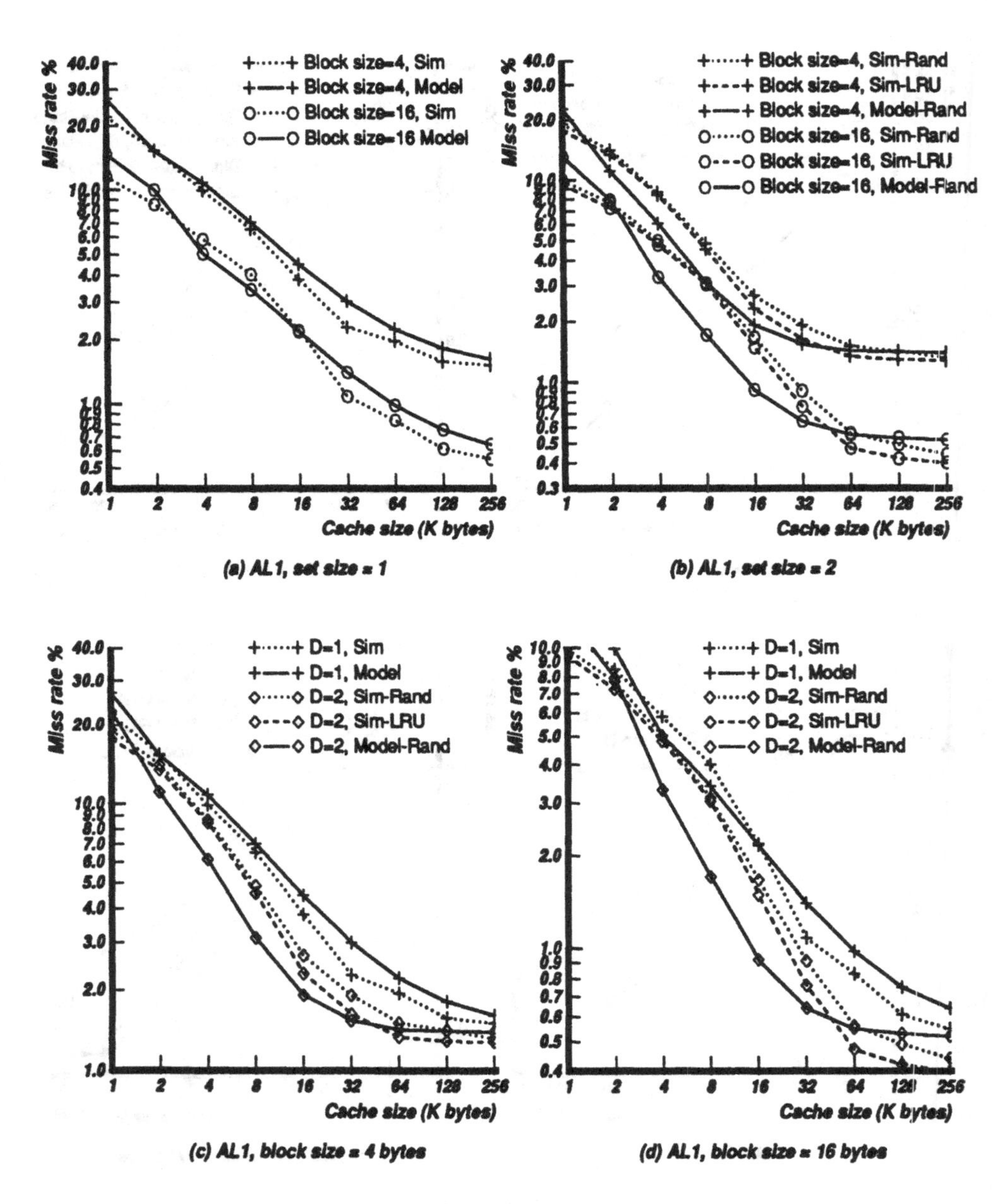

Figure 3.11: Miss rate vs. cache size for AL1. In (a), (b) set size is constant, and in (c), (d) block size is constant. Solid lines are model, dotted lines are simulations with for random replacement, and dashed lines are simulations with LRU replacement.

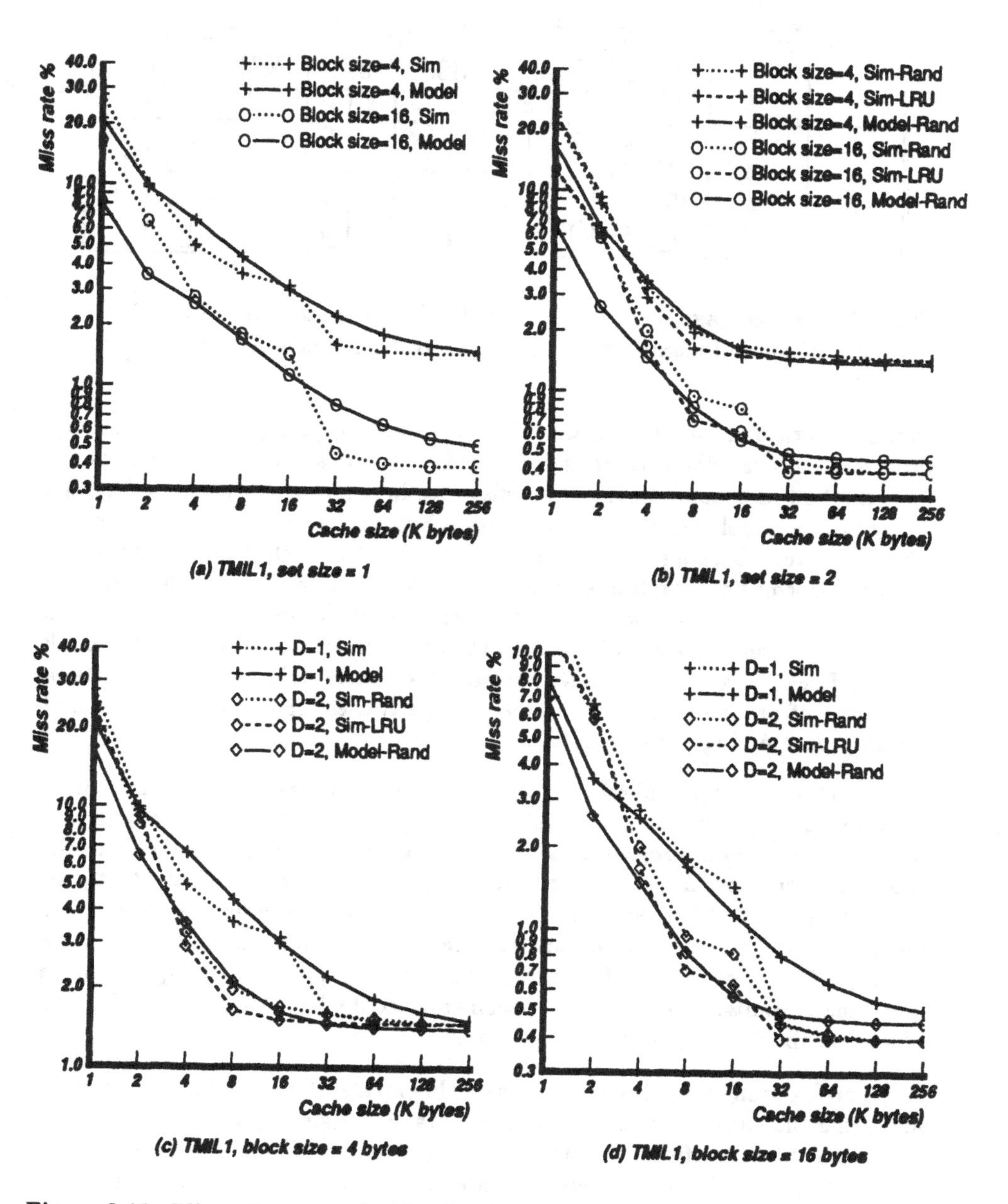

Figure 3.12: Miss rate vs. cache size for TMIL1. In (a), (b) set size is constant, and in (c), (d) block size is constant. Solid lines are model, dotted lines are simulations with random replacement, and dashed lines are simulations with LRU replacement.

Setsiz	Blksiz	IVEX				AL1				TMIL1			
		MISS		HIT		MISS		HIT		MISS		HIT	
		$\bar{e}$	$\hat{e}$	$\bar{e}$	$\hat{e}$	$\bar{e}$	$\hat{e}$	$\bar{e}$	$\hat{e}$	$\bar{e}$	$\hat{e}$	$\bar{e}$	$\hat{e}$
1	4	14	28	2	7	14	32	1	6	18	38	1	9
1	16	13	22	1	2	19	30	1	4	38	76	2	10
2	4	15	42	1	4	18	36	2	4	11	27	1	8
2	16	19	45	1	3	26	45	1	3	26	55	1	7

Table 3.2: Percentage error in estimated miss rates and hit rates. $\bar{e}$ and $\hat{e}$ represent mean and maximum errors respectively. Block sizes are in bytes.

to the miss rate of the process assuming that each process is assigned a unique process identifier (PID) which is appended to the tag portion of the address. This method also approximates the miss rate in a physically addressed cache. The bullet symbol depicts the miss rate when the cache is flushed on every process switch. Lacking PIDs, a virtual cache that is flushed on every process switch performs poorly relative to the other schemes for cache sizes greater than 32K bytes. This is because a significant fraction of the references of a process are reused across process switches. All the schemes perform the same for small caches. Because very large caches can simultaneously hold the working sets of a number of processes, the miss rates of large caches for the PID scheme and for uniprogramming are very similar.

In general, the model predictions are similar to those of trace-driven simulation. However, the model does not capture the sharp and often abrupt changes in miss rate that many programs display. For example, in Figure 3.10(a), IVEX shows a sharp drop in miss rate in going from a cache size of 16K to 32K bytes, while the predicted behavior shows a smooth trend. The estimated results are most accurate if the trace parameters are measured from a cache in a close vicinity of the cache types of interest. This provides a useful strategy to obtain fine tuned results. For example, parameters could be measured keeping the block size fixed throughout the analysis.

In general, parameter extraction is reasonably straightforward, but may require analyzing the entire trace if maximum accuracy is desired; parameters can otherwise be extracted from sample segments of the trace. While u and U – the average number of unique references in a time granule and in the entire trace respectively – are easily measured, some of the other parameters deserves more comment. The collision constant, c, is obtained by simulating a typical cache. If the cache is small enough, the entire trace need not be necessary because once steady state is reached only a few more references need be simulated to give a good indication of c. The spatial locality parameter, f_{l1}, is simply the fraction

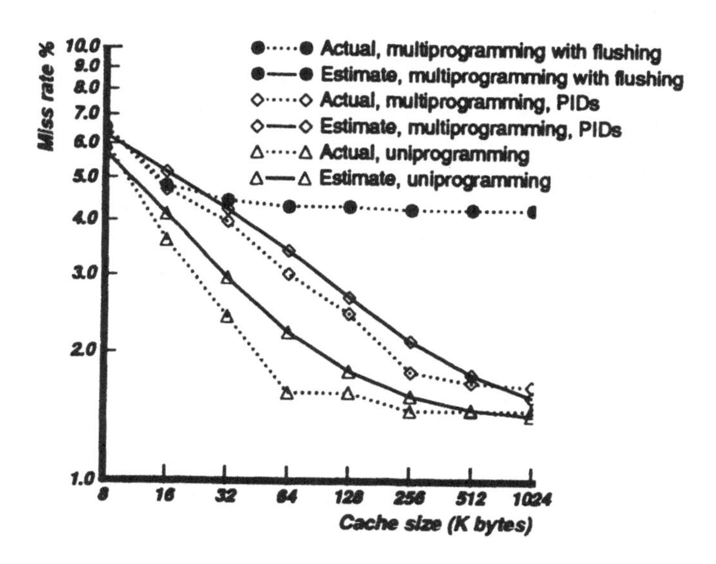

Figure 3.13: Miss rate vs. cache size (K bytes) for multiprogramming. Block size is 16 bytes and cache is direct-mapped.

of singular addresses in the trace; f_{l2} can be derived using Equation 3.10 and the measured average run length (ratio of the number of runs to the number of references in the trace). Depending on the desired accuracy in multiprogramming results, either an average time slice parameter or a distribution (measured or assumed) can be used.

3.5 Summary

An analytical model for caches based on a judicious combination of measurement and analytical techniques reduces computation time without significantly sacrificing accuracy. Cache performance due to start-up effects, gradual locality changes in program execution, contention for a cache block, and multiprogramming can be quickly estimated for most cache parameters of interest, including cache size, block size, degree of associativity, trace size, and multiprogramming level. In addition to the models predictive capability, the categorization of the program-cache interactions yields valuable insights into cache transient analysis, and will be used in the next chapter to obtain efficient cache simulation techniques.

Chapter 4

Transient Cache Analysis – Trace Sampling and Trace Stitching

Despite its expensive nature, trace-driven simulation is necessary if more than first-cut estimates as provided by analytical models are desired. In the following two chapters, efficient techniques of trace-driven simulation for cache performance evaluation are presented. This chapter first analyzes cache transient behavior, and then presents a trace sampling methodology.

4.1 Introduction

One of the chief aims of cache performance evaluation is to obtain a "steady state" miss rate for a given cache organization. While it is hard to define steady-state cache miss rate precisely, generally speaking, it is the average miss rate of the cache over a long period of time – long enough that a good cross section of the intended workload is seen. Unfortunately, only measurement over this period can yield an exact steady-state miss rate. While we will not actually simulate the cache against an entire execution trace of a program to get the steady-state program miss rate, we will examine more practical techniques – trace sampling and trace stitching – to obtain good estimates from several small trace samples.

Trace sampling is a method by which finite segments of a trace, relatively small in size compared to the entire trace generated by a program, are used to estimate steady-state cache performance accurately for the program. Studying trace sampling is important because enormous potential exists for reducing the simulation time required to characterize large caches, and because ATUM traces are of finite length (typically a half-million references) it could be argued that artificial truncation of long execution traces into multiple small samples introduces start-up distortion in simulations of large caches. The need to study sampling effects and the transient behavior of caches is even greater in operating system and multiprogramming simulations, where start-up effects are more pronounced due to larger working sets and context switching. We will describe a technique to overcome these difficulties and show how trace sampling can be used to obtain accurate estimates of cache performance efficiently.

This chapter deals primarily with trace sample size. The number of samples required, an important consideration, will depend both on the desired accuracy and on workload characteristics. Non-uniformly behaved programs will need more samples that well behaved ones. In general, a simple statistical analysis will yield confidence limits on the accuracy of the mean miss rate obtained from a number of samples (see [48] on a related topic).

In the next section, after motivating the study of cache transient behavior, we provide a set of working definitions for the transient behavior of caches to assess start-up effects. We describe how to find the minimum trace length necessary to obtain steady-state cache miss rates for the given workload. From the results of this transient behavior analysis of caches, we then show how small trace samples can be effectively used to obtain accurate steady-state cache performance statistics. In the concluding section of this chapter, we examine the benefits of trace stitching, a technique to obtain sufficient length traces when a single sample does not yield accurate cache performance estimates.

4.2 Transient Behavior Analysis and Trace Sampling

We examine the transient nature of the miss rate to motivate studying start-up behavior and finite trace-size effects, especially for large caches. Figure 4.1 shows a plot of miss rate versus time for cache sizes 4K and 64K bytes for the benchmark IVEX.[1] While the dependence of miss rate on time is not strong for small caches, it is a decreasing function of trace length for large caches implying that start-up cost can dominate cache behavior. Use of a short trace (say

[1] Please refer to Section 2.4 and Table D.1 in Appendix D for trace details.

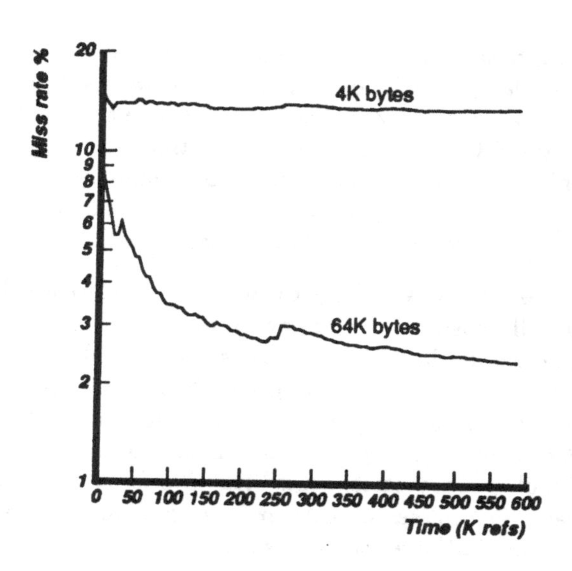

Figure 4.1: Miss rate vs time for benchmark IVEX. Set size is 1; block size is 4.

150,000 references for the above benchmark) for the large cache will introduce severe start-up distortion. On the other hand, one may have to wait a long time for the curve to bottom out to a steady-state value. Clearly, an understanding of the exact dependence of miss rate on trace length is essential to obtain steady-state performance data from short trace lengths.

Easton and Fagin [25], and Strecker [85], also stress the need to accurately analyze transient effects in caches. Easton and Fagin define two types of miss rates for fully-associative caches to address this issue: cold start and warm start. Their definition yields the cold-start miss rate by simulating an initially empty cache, and warm-start (or steady-state) miss rate by first allowing the cache to fill up. Many previous cache studies did not need to address this issue because either only small caches were being considered, or trace length was not an issue since arbitrarily long traces (albeit typically only for single-user programs) could be generated using simulation. Other papers that used small trace samples (e.g., [76, 30]) applied Easton and Fagin's fully-associative cache related cold and warm-start terminology for set-associative and direct-mapped caches as well. Although these definitions are satisfactory for small fully-associative caches (where the cache fills up quickly), they become inadequate for large set-associative caches because one might have to wait an arbitrarily long time for the cache to fill up.

The basic problem with these definitions is the implicit notion of reaching steady state when the cache fills up. This notion is based on the assumption that a large proportion of cache misses in the steady state is due to *interference*. An interference miss is caused by a reference to a block that was purged from the cache by an intervening reference. Interference is predominantly seen in small caches where multiple simultaneously-active, program-blocks map into the same cache block causing strong contention for limited cache resources.

The same situation does not apply to large caches. A new reference that purges a valid cache entry will cause an interference miss only if the purged block is still *live*. In other words, interference misses are caused only by purged blocks in the current working set of the program. Program working sets tend to be much smaller that overall program size owing to the locality property of programs [23]. Consequently, large caches, which can comfortably sustain the working sets of multiple processes, show little interference because purged blocks are often dead. The misses that occur in such a large cache are those caused by bringing in the initial working sets into the cache for the first time, called *start-up misses*, and from then on, in fetching additional blocks for the first time due to changing program localities, or *non-stationary* misses.[2]

The need for a modified definition of steady state becomes apparent from the following hypothetical example. Consider an infinite cache. Previous definitions based on cache fill-up would imply that such a cache would never reach steady state. But, clearly, a program would reach steady state after an initial transient. Recalling that our aim is to obtain the miss rate of the program, the desired steady-state miss rate of the trace sample should correspond to program miss rate. Our definition will yield precisely this steady-state miss rate.

4.2.1 Definitions

We define cold start and warm start using the more general notion of steady state. Let the *warm-start region* be the portion of a trace after the point where: either the cache has filled up, or the initial[3] working set of the program or workload is cache resident. The former effect is called *cache saturation* and the latter *trace saturation*. The *steady-state miss rate* or *warm-start miss rate* is the miss rate in the warm-start region. As before, the *cold-start miss rate* is for the entire trace assuming an initially empty cache. We also define a *cold miss* as a miss in an empty (or invalid) cache location, and *cumulative cold misses*

[2] For a detailed characterization of start-up, non-stationary, and interference misses please refer to Section 3.1.2.

[3] When programs show multiple short-phase behavior, start-up is limited to fetching the working set of the initial phase into the cache. Fetches of subsequent-phase working sets fall into the non-stationary category and represents steady-state behavior.

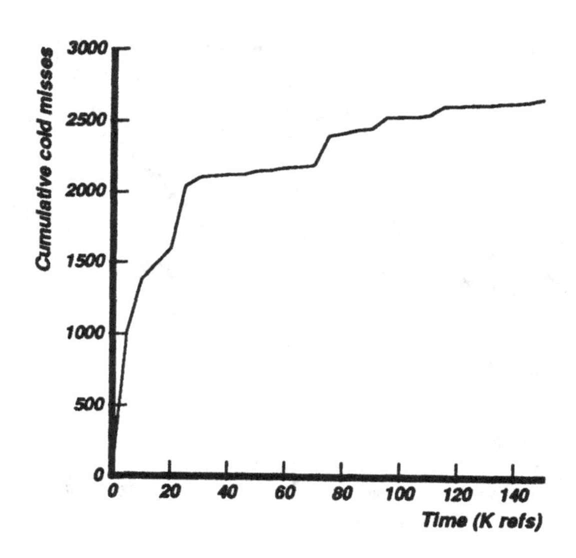

Figure 4.2: Cumulative cold misses for IVEX for a 16K-byte cache (block size is 4 bytes).

as the aggregate number of cold misses in an initially empty cache. A nice feature of our warm-start definition is that it gracefully degenerates to Easton and Fagin's for a small fully-associative cache.

The mechanism by which steady-state is reached is different for small and large caches. In small caches, cache saturation occurs first, and in large caches trace saturation sets in earlier. A uniform and convenient method of detecting the onset of the warm phase for both cases is to observe when the rate of cold misses in a cache drops sharply. Alternatively, if we plot the cumulative cold misses for a given trace and a given cache as a function of time, the knee of the curve suggests the beginning of the steady-state region.

Consider this curve for a 16K-byte cache and the IVEX trace depicted in Figure 4.2. The figure shows the *bilinear* nature of the cumulative cold misses curve. The initial high slope portion corresponds to the cache acquiring parts of the program working set. In a small cache the knee occurs when there are no more empty cache blocks, or the cache saturates, while in a large cache, the knee arises when the rate of new references drops sharply, or the trace saturates. The inclusion of trace saturation distinguishes our steady-state definition from earlier ones, which considered just cache saturation.

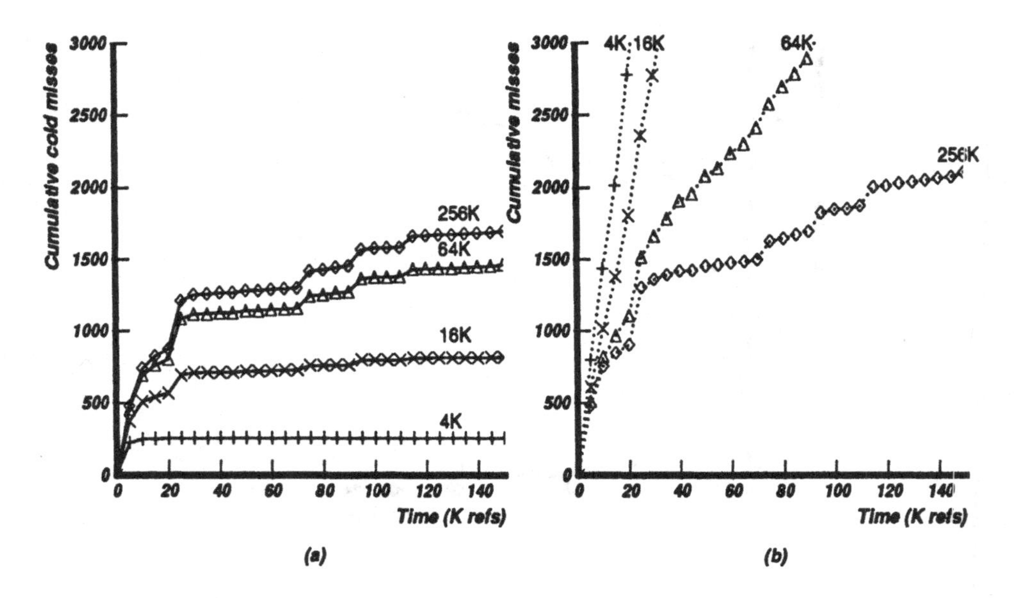

Figure 4.3: (a) Cumulative cold misses and (b) cumulative misses for direct-mapped caches.

4.2.2 Analysis of Start-up Effects in Single Process Traces

We will first address start-up effects in uniprogrammed traces. The goal is to obtain steady-state miss rates for the program from minimal length traces and to ascertain whether the length of ATUM traces is sufficient for this purpose. Since we know that steady-state behavior is reached after the knee of the cumulative cold misses curve, trace length must be much longer than the cold-start period to obtain useful steady-state cache miss rates.

We will use the trace IVEX as an example to analyze how cache organization affects start-up behavior. Figure 4.3(a) shows cumulative cold misses for a number of cache sizes. In small caches, the cold-start portion increases as the cache grows: from about 5K references in a 4K-byte cache, to 10K references in a 16K-byte cache. The length of the cold-start portion ultimately attains a fixed value of about 25K references irrespective of cache size. The dotted curves representing cumulative misses in Figure 4.3(b), which correspond to all types of misses, corroborate the above argument. The number of cumulative misses is very close to the number of cold misses for large caches, showing that most of the misses occur in bringing in the program references for the first time. In small caches, because cold misses account for a very small portion of the overall number of misses, most misses are caused by interference.

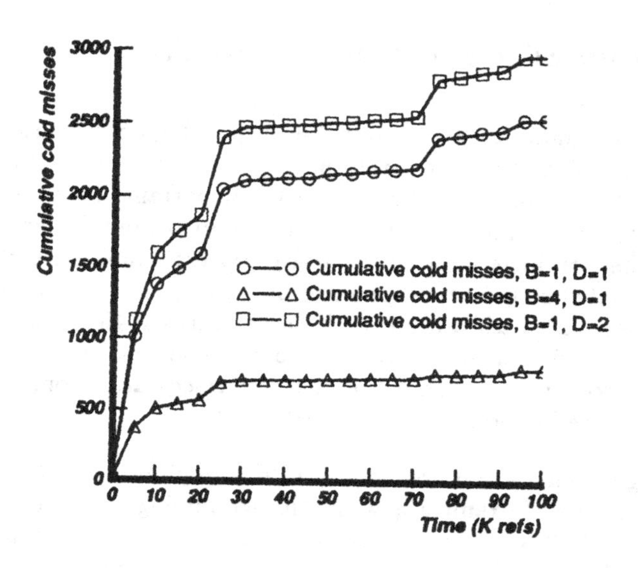

Figure 4.4: Cumulative cold misses for a 16K-byte cache for various block and set sizes.

The length of the cold-start phase also depends on the other cache parameters such as block size and associativity. Figure 4.4 depicts cumulative cold misses for two block sizes and set sizes. The start-up period is longer for a higher degree of associativity because of reduced interference; it is shorter for larger block sizes, because a small cache can fill up with fewer misses, and in a large cache the working set can be brought in with fewer misses (assuming that the entire block is fetched on a miss.) Workload characteristics are also important because start-up is longer in programs with large working sets.

For IVEX, the longest cold-start region, equal to about 25K references, is for caches bigger than 64K bytes. The start-up region will only decrease if the block size is increased from its current value of 16 bytes or if the cache size is decreased. Therefore, in general, a good steady-state estimate of miss rate can be obtained by letting the cache warm up on the initial 25K references from the trace provided the block size is not decreased. Clearly, an IVEX trace must be much longer than 25K references to give adequate cache performance results. Note that if the caches under consideration are small (less than 16K bytes) then the miss rate for the entire trace will be very close to the steady-state value.

Since small caches saturate early, trace-size issues are relevant only to large caches, where trace saturation determines warm start. Trace saturation is in turn related to program working-set size.

4.2.3 Start-up Effects in Multiprocess Traces

Start-up behavior is more severe in traces that display large working sets. Multiprogram traces, which often have over ten processes active, fall into this category, and trace length issues become much more important. In the worst case (for large caches), one would expect that start up period would be as long as it takes to fetch the working sets of all the active processes into the cache. This situation is alleviated somewhat in practice because the references of various processes interfere with each other even in large caches (64K to 256K bytes) causing cold-start period to end earlier due to cache saturation. However, increased interference just postpones the onset of trace saturation, and trace length becomes more important for large caches.

In the following figures we will first concentrate on *a given process* in the multiprogrammed trace and examine how multiprogramming affects the start-up period. Figures 4.5(a) and (b) compare the start-up portion of a process in MUL3 and MUL10 for a 16K-byte cache with and without multiprogramming. The multiprogramming level of three does not cause any significant change in the start-up portion of the process, implying that in large caches, interference between processes for low multiprogramming levels is not appreciably increased; the trace saturation point is consequently expected to be proportional to the sum of the working sets of all the processes in that trace. For a multiprogramming level of ten, however, start-up is reduced drastically (in fact start-up is almost non-existent) due to interference from other processes or early cache saturation.

We now extend our discussion to all the processes in the trace. Figure 4.6 displays cumulative cold misses for all the active processes in MUL3 and MUL10. Cache saturation dominates in caches up to a of size 64K bytes. Trace saturation sets in thereafter, causing the cold-start period to be bound above by about 600K references. The cold-start period for the multiprogramming level of ten is only slightly greater than that for level three, even though the sum of working set sizes for MUL10 is much larger, because of the greater interference component in MUL10.

Since, both MUL3 and MUL10 display cold-start behavior for very large caches (256K to 1M byte) until almost 600K references, trace lengths in the neighborhood of a million references are necessary to obtain estimates of steady-state cache performance for these multiprogrammed workloads. This length is expected to increase less than linearly as the level of multiprogramming increases because the cold-start period (for a given cache size) is a slowly increasing function of the multiprogramming level due to a corresponding increase in the interference component of misses.

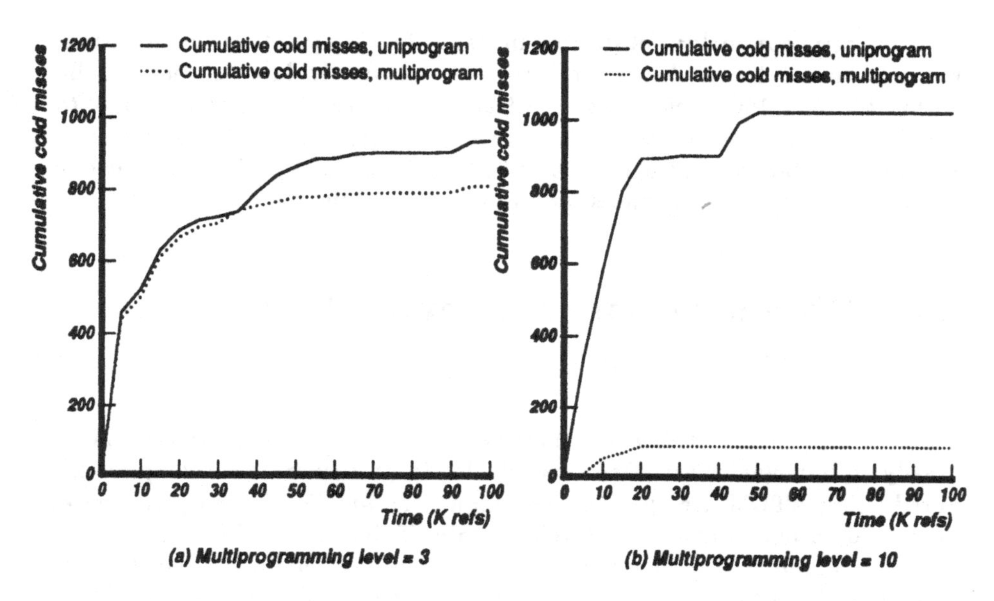

Figure 4.5: Comparing cumulative cold misses for uniprogramming and multiprogramming. Cache size is 16K bytes, block size is 16 bytes and set size is 1.

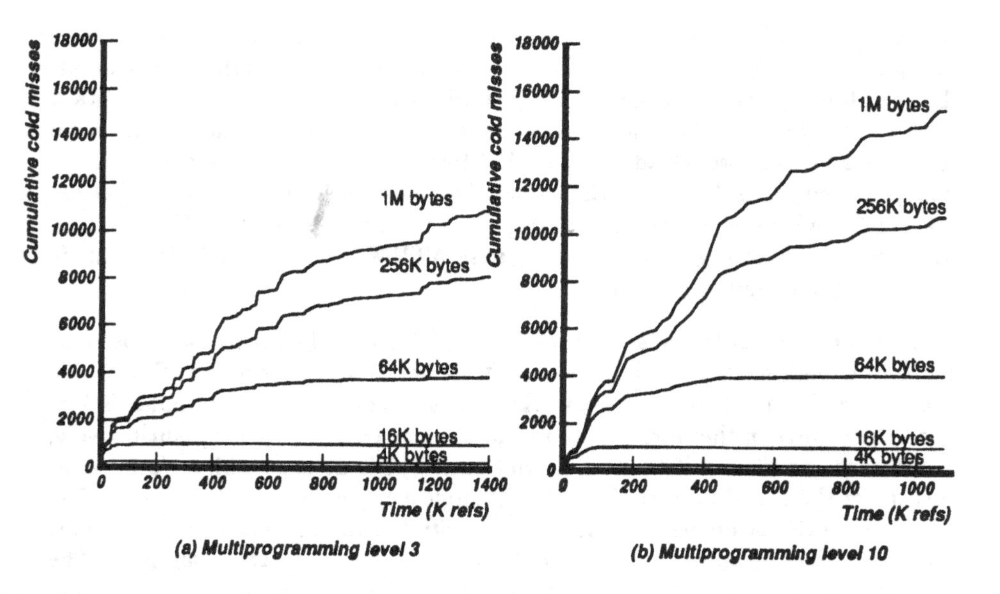

Figure 4.6: Cumulative cold misses for various cache sizes, block size 16 bytes, set size 1.

To summarize our analysis of start up in traces, two key points are noted. First, uniprogrammed traces display steady-state behavior in large caches usually within the first 100K references in a trace. Trace lengths of about 200K to 400K references are thus adequate. Second, multiprogrammed traces show a much longer start up phase, often over 600K references, requiring trace lengths greater that a million references for steady state simulations.

4.3 Obtaining Longer Samples Using Trace Stitching

Realistic trace samples that are always long enough to satisfy our criteria for steady-state behavior are often unavailable. In particular, trace samples captured using ATUM are typically less than a half-million memory references each, and do not yield steady-state miss rates if simulated individually. As an example, Figure 4.7(a) shows cumulative cold misses for three adjacent trace samples of MUL10 simulated individually. In other words, the cache is flushed at the beginning of each trace sample. Observe while each of the three samples shows a long warm phase for a 16K-byte cache, they never reach the warm phase for the 256K-byte cache.

To meet the minimum length constraint with smaller trace samples, we use *trace stitching* – a method of obtaining adequate length traces for warm-start studies. Trace stitching is simply concatenating *similar* adjacent trace samples to obtain longer ones when one sample alone is insufficient to predict steady-state cache miss rates for that workload. We say that two traces A and B are *similar* if the concatenated trace AB yields the same miss rate statistics as the hypothetical trace AB', where A and B' are contiguous in time. (Note that ATUM trace samples are not contiguous in time because ATUM loses some activity while it is dumping a sample to disk.)

It is hard to predict the miss rate statistics of the hypothetical contiguous sample B'. Instead, we will try to determine if the two traces are similar. Two traces are *similar* if the change in the working sets of the two trace samples is less than the change in the working set within any one trace sample. Quantitatively, two traces are similar if their similarity ratio (ρ) is at least unity. (ρ is reminiscent of the correlation coefficient, although ρ can be greater than one). The *similarity ratio* is defined as the *co-similarity* between the two trace samples divided by the mean of the *auto similarities* of each of the trace samples. The *co-similarity (cs)* is simply the number of the unique common references in the two trace samples, and the *auto-similarity (as)* of a trace is the co-similarity between each half of the trace.

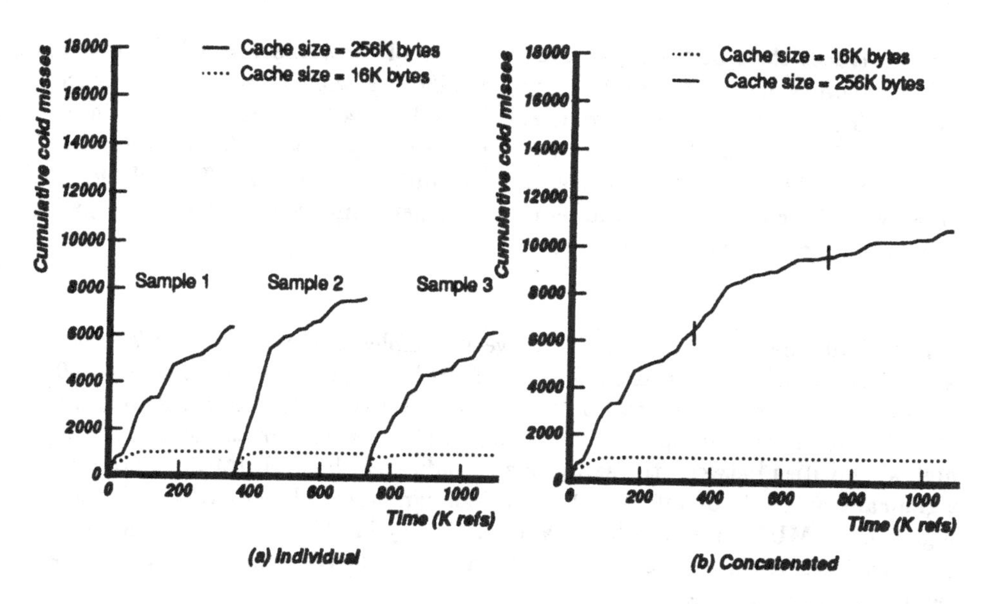

Figure 4.7: Cumulative cold misses for three MUL10 traces, with Block size 16 bytes. (a) Individually simulated (b) Concatenated.

As an example, let us test two hypothetical traces A and B for similarity.

A: 1,2,3,4,5,3,4,5,6,7
B: 6,7,8,3,4,5,3,4,5,6,7,8,3,4
as(A) = 3
as(B) = 6
cs(AB) = 5
$\rho = 1.1 \Longrightarrow$ A and B are similar.

Why can ρ be used to test the effectiveness of concatenating traces? When the working set of a given workload follows a perfect non-stationary pattern (i.e., the working set is renewed at a constant rate), all the similarity definitions will be equal, yielding unity for the similarity ratio. Consequently, concatenating the two traces will cause a proportionately smaller change in working set size than in the total trace length, thus increasing the likelihood of reaching steady state. The second case is for a rapidly changing environment, where the co-similarities and auto-similarities are all expected to be near zero, and still yield unity for ρ. For the latter case each sample itself will yield a good steady-state estimate of the miss rate. ρ can be greater than one if the total number of unique references is an increasing function of time in the first sample because there is the potential for a greater number of references to be common between the two traces than between two halves of one of the traces. ρ will be much less than unity if two traces have widely differing working sets, while each individual trace has the same working set in each of its two halves. In this case, concatenating the two traces will not improve the quality of the steady-state simulations. Trace Stitching of dissimilar samples that are insufficiently long to individually characterize steady-state cache performance can be used to give only an upper bound on the miss rate.

For MUL10, the similarity ratio ρ between samples one and two is 1.79, and is 1.88 for samples two and three. The MUL3 samples have ρ equal to 1.30 for samples one and two, and 1.19 for samples two and three. Clearly, the MUL3 and MUL10 samples are suitable candidates for concatenation. The high similarities between the samples also indicates that ATUM does not lose significant amounts of information between samples. The MUL10 ratios are higher than MUL3 due to a lower auto-similarity in MUL10 samples. MUL10 samples have lower auto-similarities because the larger number of processes reduce the repetitiveness within a sample.

Figure 4.7(b) – the *cumulative cold misses* curve for the same three concatenated MUL10 trace samples – shows a knee point at roughly 400K references for a 256K byte cache signaling the beginning of the warm portion. Thus, start-up dominates over two thirds of the combined trace; warm-start miss rate can be obtained from the latter third of the trace. Note also that the total number of cumulative cold misses for the combined trace (from Figure 4.7(b)) is much less than the sum of the three corresponding numbers for each sample (from Figure 4.7(a)).

In our experiments, steady state miss rates are obtained from uniprocessing traces by first letting the cache warm up on the initial 100K references in the trace of 400K references. It turns out that due to the short start-up portion in uniprogramming traces the warm-start miss rates are very similar to cold-start rates and we will present only the cold-start numbers.

For multiprogramming traces, we concatenate three adjacent traces, each of length 400K references, and obtain warm-start miss rates by using the first 600K references for warming up. All concatenations are with $\rho > 1$. The cold and warm-start miss rates are usually different and we shall present warm-start miss rates for the most part.

4.4 Trace Compaction – Cache Filtering with Blocking[4]

Since the cost of trace-driven simulation is directly related to the trace length, reducing the number of references in given trace has a tremendous impact on simulation time. Trace sampling methods described in the previous sections reduce the number of references by using several discrete samples of program execution instead of a single, long, continuous, trace without significant loss of accuracy, but at a much reduced cost. However, individual trace samples that are hundreds of thousands of references long are necessary to simulate large caches and multiprogramming workloads. Therefore, if the trace samples could be compressed, the benefits would be proportionally greater. Compacting traces has the added advantage that trace storage space requirements are eased.

The key idea behind trace compaction is that not all references carry the same amount of useful information. By retaining only those references that contribute some new information, traces can be stripped down in size by an order of magnitude or more. Program references display the property of locality [23] by repeatedly reusing references from a working set over a given period of time. Discarding repeat references in some time interval can retain most information necessary for cache studies.

Two earlier studies used this property of programs in their trace compaction efforts. Smith [79] described two methods of reducing trace length. The first scheme, called ***stack deletion***, discards all references that are hits to the top D levels of the LRU stack of data. Because the hit rate to the top stack levels is very high, and because any reasonable memory management scheme will succeed in retaining these frequently used references in main memory, little if any information is lost by discarding these repeated references for memory management studies. The second scheme is the ***snapshot method***, which records the set of references in memory at regular time intervals. The rationale for this scheme is that the set of references in use does not change rapidly with time. So, recording the set every T references will not result in significant information loss. Unfortunately, Smith's scheme is not flexible because its assumes that the page size (or block size) is fixed throughout the analyses. Furthermore, the schemes are primarily suited for paging studies and no data is provided on the suitability of the schemes to cache studies.

Puzak [64] proposed a scheme called ***trace stripping*** with particular application to cache studies. A direct-mapped cache (called a cache filter) is simulated and a trace of the references that miss is generated. This method has the appealing

[4]The reader can skip this section without compromising comprehension of the rest of the text.

property that compaction does not introduce any error in cache simulations if the number of sets in the given cache is not less than the number of sets in the cache filter, provided the block size is kept constant. As in Smith's techniques, the constant block size requirement limits the scheme's flexibility. Although it is mentioned that the stripped trace can be used to derive rough miss rate estimates for block sizes larger than the cache filter block size, smaller block sizes are not considered. This is a problem because when the number of sets of the final cache organizations cannot be less than the corresponding cache filter parameter, a small direct-mapped cache must be used as the filter for maximum flexibility, which results in poor compaction. Consequently, one uses large block sizes in the cache filter to improve the compaction, but this precludes the simulation of smaller block sizes. It is also not possible to derive sub-block statistics. (A sub-block is the portion of a block that is fetched into the cache on a miss.)

The reason why earlier schemes failed to achieve significant compaction while allowing flexibility in cache studies was that compaction was achieved primarily by exploiting the *temporal* locality of program blocks, and not providing a model for the *spatial* locality. Spatial locality is the property by which programs tend to reuse references that are in a close spatial neighborhood in a given time interval. As we demonstrate later, obtaining results for smaller block sizes requires explicit knowledge of the compaction components due to both temporal *and* spatial locality.

Our technique uses separate models for temporal and spatial locality to yield increased compaction and allows caches with arbitrary parameters to be simulated. The key assumption is that the properties of the spatially proximal references are correlated just as the properties of references in a temporal locality are. (We will provide supporting empirical evidence.) In our scheme a trace is compressed in two steps. First, a cache filter compresses the trace by eliminating a large proportion of the references in each temporal window, a block filter then compacts the trace by discarding a large fraction of the references in each spatial neighborhood. While our experimental data concerns caches, the techniques can be used for TLB and paging studies also.

The ensuing discussion begins with some definitions and a brief review of how a cache filter compresses traces, followed by an analysis of how a block filter can be used to compact traces further. This section describes the rationale behind our blocking scheme, the implementation of the block filter and miss rate estimation. Section 4.4.5 presents our results and an analysis of the sensitivity of the various block and cache filter parameters on the miss rate estimates.

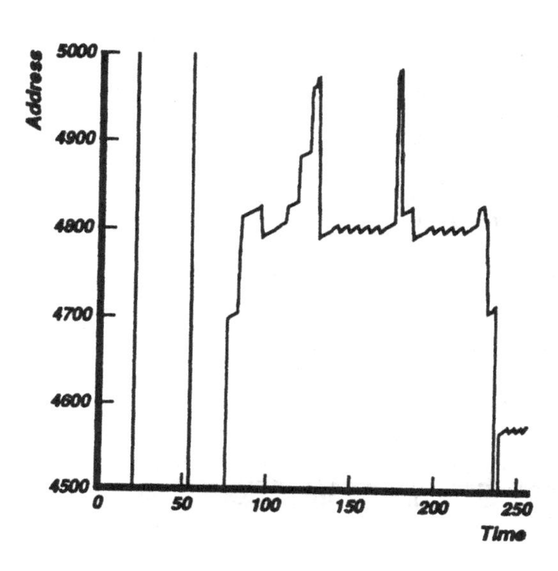

Figure 4.8: Addressing pattern in a trace segment.

4.4.1 Cache Filter

Consider the segment of a raw instruction-only address trace shown in Figure 4.8. The segment represents 250 references, most in the address range 4500 to 5000. This trace segment displays a large amount of temporal and spatial locality. A diagonal line segment represents a stream of sequential references, called a *run*, epitomizing the spatial locality in the program. A run is defined as a maximal stream of sequential references. The saw-toothed segment made up of repeated runs depicts the temporal locality in the program.

Let us first consider a cache filter. We define *compaction ratio* of a cache filter (c_f) to be the number of references in the compacted trace (T_f) divided by the number of references in the original trace (T), or $c_f = T_f/T$. A cache filter eliminates redundant references from the trace by recording only those references that miss in the cache. Puzak [64] proves the following theorem to show that a cache filter retains complete information for cache studies: the filtered trace generated using a direct-mapped cache with 2^s sets preserves the number of misses over all caches with $2^{s'}$ sets, for all $s' \geq s$, provided the block size remains constant. The proof uses the property that a reference that hits in a cache with 2^s sets is guaranteed to hit in a cache with $2^{s'}$ sets, if $s' \geq s$. In this scheme, if the miss rate of a cache simulated against the compacted trace is m_f, the actual miss rate of the cache is $m = c_f m_f$.

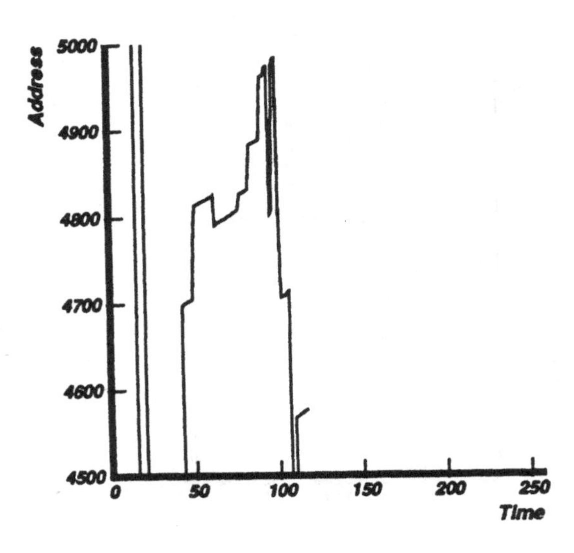

Figure 4.9: Addressing pattern of a trace segment after cache filtering.

As an illustration, Figure 4.9 shows the trace segment displayed earlier after filtering with a cache of block size one and 256 sets. Notice the absence of any repetitive patterns. To ensure maximum flexibility, all our filter cache studies will assume both a set size of one and a block size of one. Typical traces yield a compaction ratio between 0.2 and 0.5 after this stage. The example in Figure 4.9 shows a compression ratio of about 100 : 250 or 0.4.

4.4.2 Block Filter

Figure 4.9 shows that the filtered reference stream has a considerable amount of spatial locality which can be exploited to obtain further compaction. Figure 4.10 shows the same trace, but with only the first reference in any run represented, which reduces the overall compression ratio to 40 : 250 or 0.16.

The blocking technique uses a representative reference from each run to predict the performance of the entire run by assuming that all the references in the run have similar properties. Blocking, which is also referred to as stratified sampling [43], comes from an established statistical technique [44], and can be explained as follows. Consider a large population of data over which the mean of some parameter is desired. Assume the population can be divided into strata (in our case the strata are runs) within which the value of the parameter of interest is more nearly constant than it is in the population as a whole. Then,

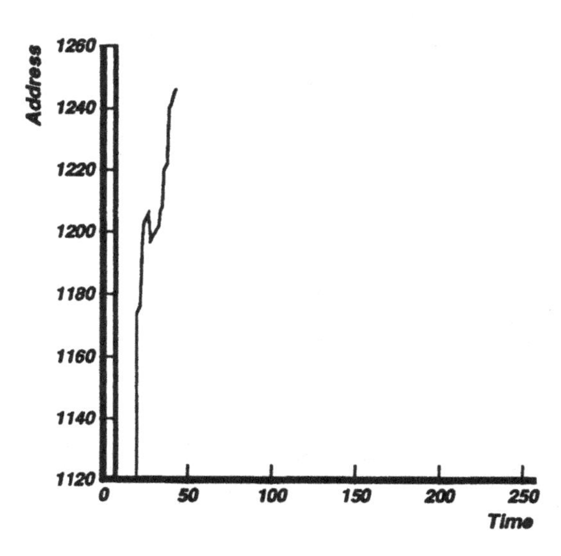

Figure 4.10: Addressing pattern of a trace segment after cache filtering and block filtering.

blocking draws small unrelated samples from each of the strata separately to estimate the value of the given parameter. Blocking is statistically superior to taking a single sample of the same size from the entire population, or, conversely, for a given accuracy in the estimate of the required parameter value, blocking requires a smaller number of samples, which can result in marked savings in the computation cost.

As an intuitive example, consider a population that has S strata of exactly N items each. Let some parameter of interest be *constant* within each strata i. Then the population mean is equal to the mean of representative values from each strata. However, the mean of a random sample from the population might not yield the exact mean. The former method also requires much less computation than the latter for a given accuracy.

A proof of the success of blocking in predicting the population mean accurately from a sample that is a fraction of the population size is easily derived by computing the variance in the calculated mean for blocking and is presented in [1].

The effectiveness of blocking depends on the availability of samples with smaller variances within the sample than in the whole population. We performed several experiments to evaluate the potential of applying blocking to trace compaction.

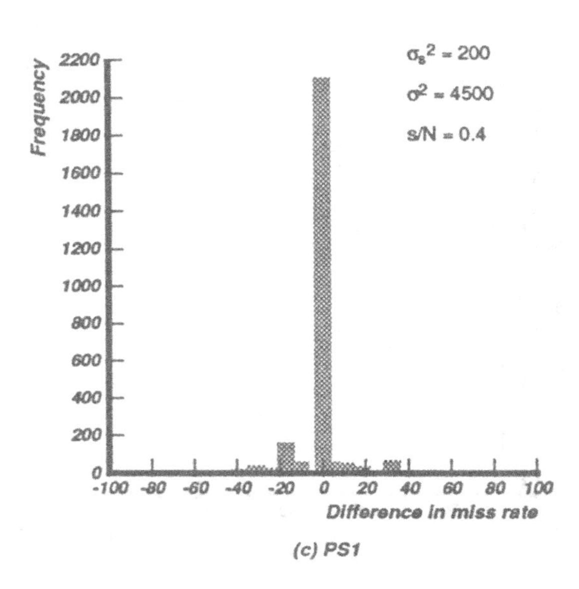

(c) PS1

Figure 4.11: Distribution of the difference between the mean miss rate within a run and the miss rate of a representative reference from that run for PS1. σ_s^2 is the intra-run variance of the miss rate (percent), σ^2 is the miss-rate variance in the entire trace, and s/N is the compaction ratio.

For our studies concerning address traces, N is the length of the original trace, the parameter of interest M is the miss rate, s is the trace sample length obtained by applying the blocking technique to the original trace, and n is the number of references in a random sample from the original trace. The miss rate computations assume a cache with 16K sets, block size one, and set size one. Three benchmark traces PS1 (also called IVEX), AL1, and TMIL1, are used for this study (see previous chapter for a description of these traces). Strata sizes or run lengths in the block filtered trace are limited to a maximum of four for reasons discussed later. For example, a run of length of 11 will be partitioned into three strata of sizes 4, 4, and 3.

Figure 4.11 displays the correlation between the miss rates of references within a run by plotting the distribution of the difference between the mean miss rate within any run and the miss rate of a representative reference. By miss rate of a reference we mean the proportion of times the reference suffers a miss. Figures 4.11 shows the distribution for PS1 when the representative reference is the leading reference in the run. (See [1] for additional data.)

It is easy to see that the mean miss rate for the run and the representative miss rate are nearly identical. Minor variations, if at all, are randomly distributed around zero, and their effect cancels out to first order. The choice of the representative also does not matter because distributions for the three positions of the selected reference are also similar. Quantitatively, for all benchmarks the intra-run variance in the miss rate is substantially smaller than the variance over the whole trace. For example, in PS1 σ_s^2 is 200 and σ^2 is 4500 (miss rate is in percent). Blocking with a maximum strata size of four yields a compaction of about 0.4 and a miss rate variance less than 0.002. (Compare this with the variance of 0.03 in a random sample of the same size). The small variance in the miss rate estimate from the compacted trace displays the effectiveness of blocking.

Our goal is to reduce the compaction ratio s/N while minimizing the variances in the blocking mean. Because the variance within runs, σ_s^2, is very small, theoretically, we expect that s/N can be made very small without significantly sacrificing accuracy by choosing larger strata sizes. For instance, in the PS1 trace, a compression of 0.15 can be achieved if the maximum strata size is relaxed to 16. However, in practice, we cannot arbitrarily reduce the blocking sample size because our assumption of equal strata sizes is violated. By choosing just one reference from each strata, the results get biased towards small sized strata which have a higher miss rate on average. For instance, we have observed that runs of length one, typically composed of data, have a higher miss rate as compared to relatively long runs, typically formed by instructions. One solution is proportional sampling, where the number of samples chosen from each strata is proportional to the strata size [43]. We propose a simple and more practical solution to the strata size inequality problem by limiting the maximum size of any stratum. By this method, a stratum that exceeds the maximum size is split up into smaller strata, thus decreasing the bias against large strata.

4.4.3 Implementation of the Cache and Block Filters

Our trace compaction set-up is depicted in Figure 4.12. Let us denote a cache with S sets, set-size D, block size B, and sub-block size B_s, as $C : (S, D, B, B_s)$.[5] The original trace is first passed through a *cache filter* $C_f : (S_f, 1, 1, 1, 1)$, which emits only the references that miss in the cache. The number of references is reduced from T to T_f, which gives a cache filter compaction ratio of $c_f = T_f/T$.

The trace of size T_f is subsequently passed through a *block filter* characterized by two parameters called the window size (w) and filter block size (b). The block filter scoops up a window of w references and sends out a reference from each spatial locality contained within the window. References are said to

[5] Note that this notation is slightly different from our earlier notation in that it includes the sub-block size.

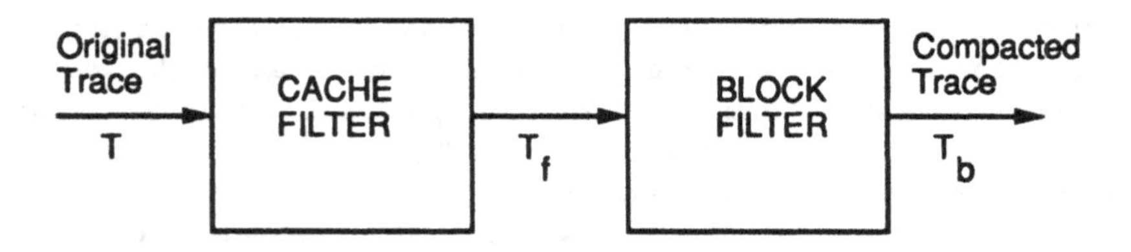

Figure 4.12: Trace compaction steps.

belong to the same spatial locality if they have the same *address div b*, and runs that straddle block boundaries of size b are split up into multiple runs of maximum size b. The above procedure is repeated until no more references remain. Because the emanated references represent the given locality, the low order $log_2 b$ bits are dropped from the output reference. We limit the search for runs within time intervals of w references because spatially local references that are temporally unrelated are unlikely to have similar properties. Furthermore, looking for sets of spatially proximal references within a given time window is also necessary to overcome the practical difficulty of isolating possibly interleaved runs in a stream of references. The block filter reduces the trace length to T_b for a blocking compression ratio $c_b = T_b/T_f$, and an overall compaction of $c_{fb} = c_f c_b$.

For example, consider a cache filtered trace that consists of the following addresses: (1, 199, 2, 198, 4, 196, 6, 194, 7, 3000, 8, 9, 10). This trace is input to a block filter with parameters $w = 10$ and $b = 4$. The block filter outputs the references (0, 49, 1, 48, 750) from the first window, and outputs (2) from the second window, yielding $c_b = 6/13$.

Before the compacted trace can be used for simulations, we need to go through one more step. Because the block filter transforms the trace by dropping the low order $log_2 b$ bits, the cache under consideration C must also be transformed correspondingly. Let the cache under consideration be $C : (S, D, B, B_s)$, with the only constraint $S \geq S_f$. The transform on the cache can be derived by observing how the low order bits are used in a normal cache access. Bits $< 0 \; : \; log_2 B >$ choose a word within the block, and bits $< log_2 B \; : \; log_2(S + B) >$ index into some cache set; of these, the operations corresponding to the low order $log_2 b$ bits must be dropped. Therefore, the original cache is transformed to the cache denoted as $C^* : (S^*, D^*, B^*, B_s^*)$, or

$$C^* : \left(\frac{S}{\lceil \frac{b}{B} \rceil}, D, \lceil \frac{B}{b} \rceil, \lceil \frac{B_s}{b} \rceil \right)$$

For example, the cache $C : (16K, 1, 4, 4)$ is transformed to the cache $C^* : (16K, 1, 1, 1)$ for $b = 4$, and to the cache $C^* : (4K, 1, 1, 1)$ for $b = 16$. As can be seen from the latter case, the above transformation often reduces the amount of memory required to simulate the cache.

4.4.4 Miss Rate Estimation

We now describe how the miss rate of the trace sample can be derived from the miss rate of the cache filtered and block filtered trace. Let the miss rate of the cache C^* simulated against the block-filtered trace be m_b, and as before, let the cache filter compaction ratio be c_f. Because the references in each spatial locality are expected to behave similarly, the miss rate can be calculated using only one representative from each locality in the compacted trace. Thus, assuming that only one reference is fetched on a miss ($B_s = 1$), the estimated miss rate is simply

$$m^* = c_f m_b$$

For larger sub-blocks we must include the effect of prefetching, and the formula for the miss rate becomes:

$$m^* = \begin{cases} c_f c_{B_s} m_b & \text{if } B_s^* = 1 \\ c_f c_b m_b & \text{if } B_s^* > 1 \end{cases}$$

The factors c_b and c_{B_s} are the block filter compactions with parameter b and B_s respectively. To explain why the miss rate is of the given form, consider the following two cases.

1. When B_s^* is one ($B_s \leq b$), the effect of fetching B_s references on a miss must be included and c_{B_s} represents the fractional miss rate decrease.

2. When B_s^* is greater than one ($B_s > b$), the sub-block size B_s is composed of two factors: B_s^* and b. The prefetch benefits due to B_s^* are already included in the miss rate m_b, and the remaining fraction of prefetch benefits due to b is represented by the factor c_b.

A noteworthy feature of our scheme is that explicitly splitting the filter cache and block filter compressions allows estimating the miss rates of caches with

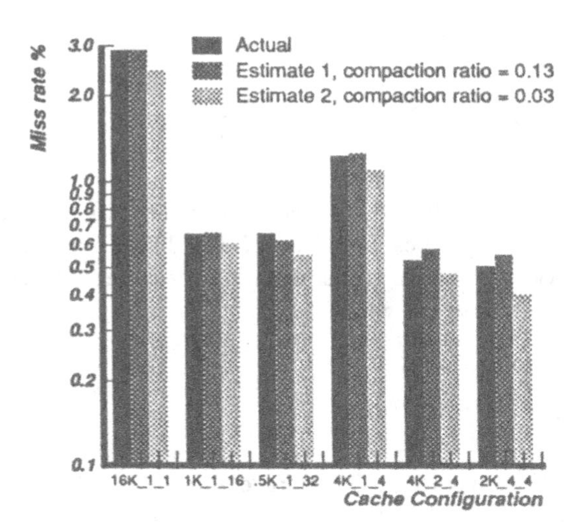

Figure 4.13: Comparison of actual and estimated miss rates for various compactions. The results for benchmarks PS1, AL1 and TMIL1 are averaged. Estimate 1 uses a cache filter $C_f : (256, 1, 1, 1)$, and the block filter parameters are $w = 128$ and $b = 4$; estimate 2 uses $C_f : (1K, 1, 1, 1)$, $w = 128$ and $b = 16$.

$B < b$, possibly with sub-block placement, which was not possible in earlier schemes. The drawback is that caches with $B_s < b$ require the computation of an additional compaction ratio c_{B_s}, but the negative effect of this extra computation is mitigated because the trace that is used to derive the compaction ratio is itself compressed by a factor of c_f, the extra computation is much smaller than the computation needed to generate the cache filtered trace.

4.4.5 Compaction Results

Figure 4.13 summarizes the average performance of our compaction algorithm for the three benchmarks, PS1, AL1 and TMIL1. The miss rates of the three benchmarks are averaged to obtain the depicted miss rates. It is easy to see that reliable cache performance estimates for a variety of cache organizations can be obtained with a compaction of about an order of magnitude in trace length; the results are less accurate in absolute terms when the compaction is close to two orders of magnitude. Nevertheless, the relative performance of the various caches is still reliably predicted.

An interesting question that one would like to answer is: How sensitive are the cache performance estimates to the choice of blocking parameters? Answering these questions is important because for trace compaction to be useful the estimated cache performance results must be robust with respect to filter parameters. A sensitivity analysis identifies such robust regions in the parameter space. We investigated the robustness of the block filter parameters for the three traces and the results can be found in [1].

In summary, our experiments show that a block filter window size w in the range 64 to 256 gives the best tradeoff between accuracy and compaction, and a large blocking parameter b can yield significant compaction while introducing few distortions in the compacted trace. As an indication of the power of the compaction technique we can routinely compact traces by nearly two orders of magnitude while introducing less than 10% – 15% error in the miss rate estimate.

Chapter 5

Cache Performance Analysis for System References

The previous chapters laid the groundwork for accurate and efficient cache performance analysis by describing techniques for data collection and cache analysis. The next two chapters analyze cache performance using both cold-start and warm-start trace-driven simulation of the ATUM trace samples.

This chapter discusses the effect of system references on cache performance. From the VMS and Ultrix traces described in Section 2.4 we chose traces with low levels of multiprogramming to exclude multitasking effects. The VMS traces have 20% system references on average, while the Ultrix traces contain about 50% system references. System and user references occupy distinct portions of the address space (determined by the value of the most significant address bit) in the VAX architecture [91]; the system space is shared between all processes, while the user space is distinct for every process. For our system reference studies, we tag every user address with a process specific identifier (PID) to distinguish between the references of the user processes. The PID is also appended to the cache tag. We will discuss other methods of handling multitasking in the next chapter.

5.1 Motivation

The significant cache performance degradation caused by the operating system motivates a thorough characterization of the effect of system references. Figure 5.1 contrasts the performance for system and non-system traces for direct-mapped, two-way, and four-way set-associative caches for the VMS and Ultrix operating systems. The first observation is that the inclusion of system references degrades cache performance considerably for all our benchmarks and all our cache organizations. The miss rate often increases by almost a factor of two. For a 32K-byte two-way set-associative cache, the miss rate degrades from 1.05% to 1.93% for VMS benchmarks. For the same 32K-byte cache, Ultrix system references cause the miss rate to increase from 2.04% to 3.60%.

The effect of system references is even more dramatic when viewed from the perspective of the cache size needed to achieve a targeted miss rate. For small caches (less than 64K bytes), to keep the user+system miss rate comparable to the user miss rate, the cache size must be doubled. For larger caches the effect is more severe. For example, in Figure 5.1(a), a 32K-byte cache has a miss rate of 2% if only user references are considered, but a cache four times larger is needed to ensure a similar miss rate for user and system references due to the asymptotic nature of the miss rate versus cache size curve. Both system and user curves bottom out at a cache size of about 256K bytes implying that large caches tend to capture a significant fraction, if not all, of the user and system working set.

The *relative* impact of system references on the miss rate shows an increasing trend as cache sizes grow from 1K to about 64K bytes; after 64K bytes, the relative impact begins to decrease. That is, the increase in miss rate due to system references as a percentage of the total miss rate increases with cache size up to a cache size of 64K bytes. From Figure 5.2, the increase is roughly 20% (from 17.55% to 20.65%) for a 1K byte direct-mapped cache, while for a 16K-byte cache the increase is over 50% (from 3.11% to 4.67%).

5.2 Analysis of the Miss Rate Components due to System References

The cache miss rate for combined user and system workloads is made up of three components: user alone, system alone, and user-system interference. The miss rate due to user references alone is the miss rate without system references weighted by the fraction of user activity in the trace; the system component is

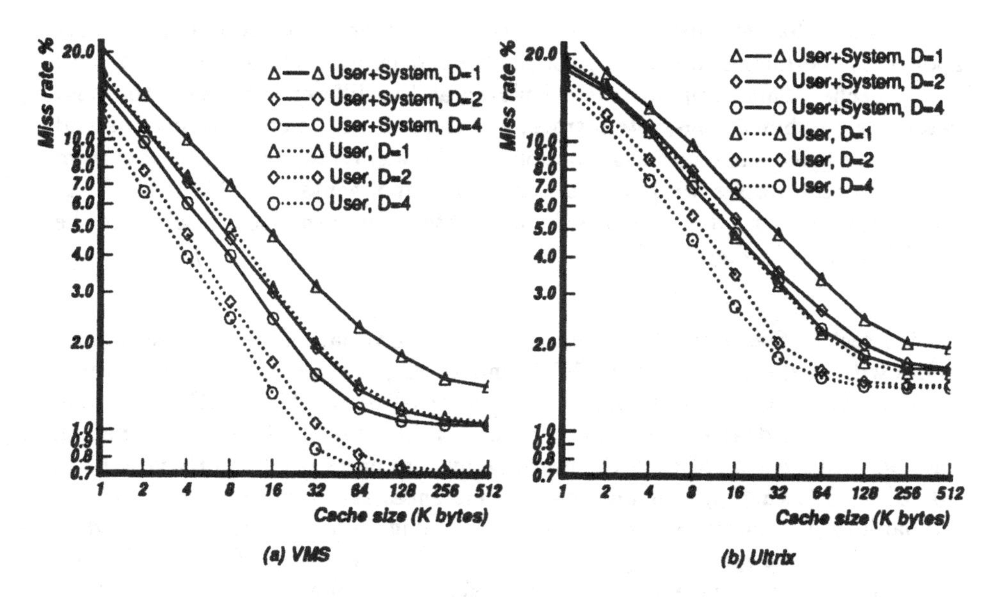

Figure 5.1: Effect of system references on cold-start cache miss rate. Cache block size is 16 bytes. D is set size or degree of associativity.

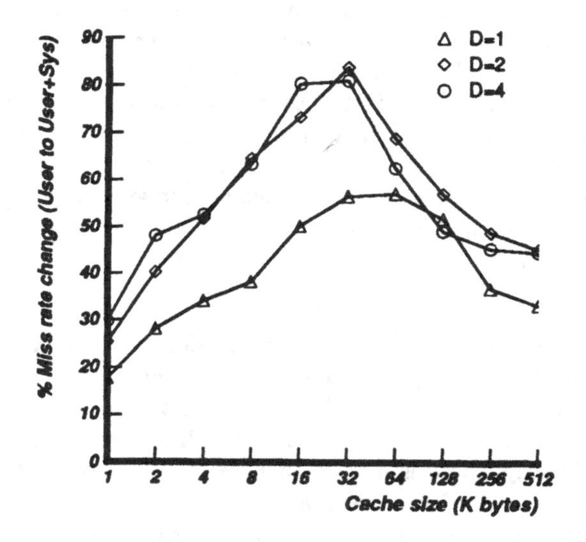

Figure 5.2: Relative increase in cache miss rate due to system references for VMS. Block size is 16 bytes, and D is set size.

computed in like manner; and the user-system interference component corresponds to the misses induced by collisions between user and system references in the cache. This component is calculated as the difference between the miss rate for a combined user-system trace, and the sum of the components one and two above (user alone and system alone). To understand the nature of system induced cache misses we plot the miss rate components for VMS and Ultrix workloads in Figure 5.3, and also the miss rate components as a fraction of the total miss rate in Figure 5.4.

An interesting feature of the graphs is the relative variation in the three components with cache size. For both VMS and Ultrix, the user-system interference component becomes a small fraction of the total miss rate in both very small (less than 2K bytes) and very large caches (128K bytes and above). For small caches, the miss rate of both the user and system parts is inherently very high, while in large caches, user and system references rarely interfere because the probability of collision is very small. The combination of these effects, leading to a peak in the system caused miss rate, is clearly visible when the relative increase in the miss rate due to system references is plotted as in Figure 5.2.

For VMS traces, the user component of the misses always predominates due to its higher frequency, and the user component is significantly greater for small caches. While the user miss rate drops sharply with cache size, the system and interference components show a slower decline, and their sum soon equals the user miss rate for a cache size of 16K bytes. As the cache grows bigger, the user and system components remain almost the same, but the user-system interference component reduces. The miss rate for user-system worsens because the interference component is non-zero, and because the system component is roughly half the user component even though the fraction of system references in the trace is only one-fifth.

The miss rate components due to system related effects in Ultrix traces are much more pronounced than for VMS traces due to the higher incidence of system references in our Ultrix traces. However, the net user-system miss rate increases less than the VMS miss rate because the Ultrix system miss rate is relatively smaller. Clearly, there is a tradeoff here. The more the fraction of system references in the trace, the higher the overall miss rate is expected to be, since system references have an inherently higher miss rate than user; however, one would expect a higher frequency of system references to lower the inherent system miss rate. The following section further analyzes the inherent system miss rates in Ultrix and VMS and the dependence of the overall miss rate on the ratio of operating system references in a trace.

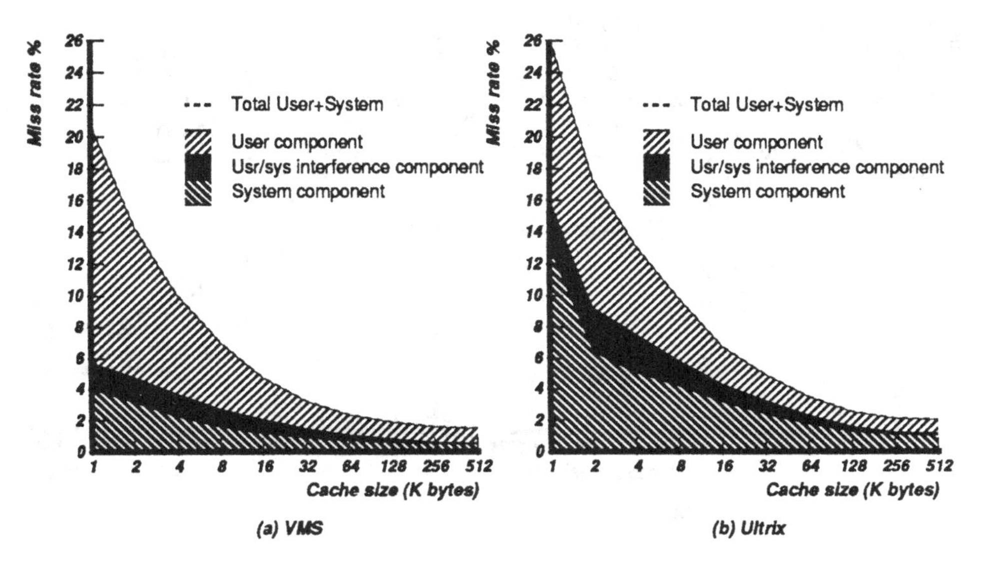

Figure 5.3: Components of system and user miss rate. Set size is 1, block size is 16 bytes.

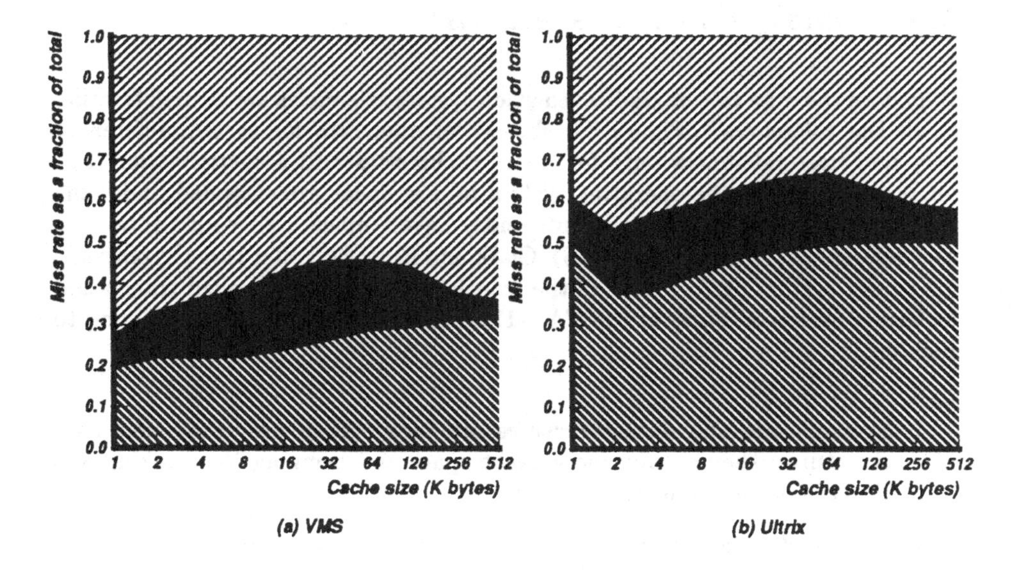

Figure 5.4: Components of system and user miss rate as a fraction of the total miss rate. Set size is 1, block size is 16 bytes.

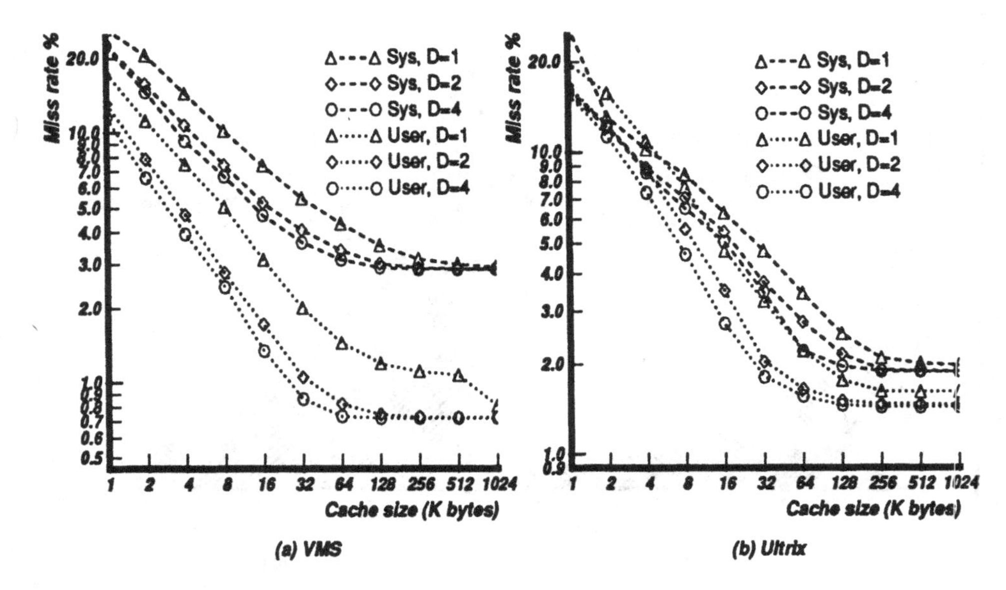

Figure 5.5: Comparing inherent system and user miss rate for VMS and Ultrix traces.

5.3 Analysis of System Miss Rate

Why does the miss rate degrade even when system references are a small fraction of all the references? Figure 5.5 shows the miss rate for system references only and user references only for many cache sizes and associativities. The references made by the operating system in user space are classified under the user category. System references inherently have a much higher miss rate than user references (especially for VMS). Clark and Emer [20] offer three hypotheses for poorer system performance of the translation buffer (also called translation lookaside buffer or TLB) in the VAX-11/780, which we restate as applying to caches:

1. System code and data structures are bigger than user code and data structures; they occupy more cache space and bringing the working sets into the cache needs more misses.

2. System data structures are more complex and more pointer rich than process data structures. Consequently, they are more scattered across the address space, and show lower spatial locality than user.

3. System-code loops have fewer iterations than user-code loops.

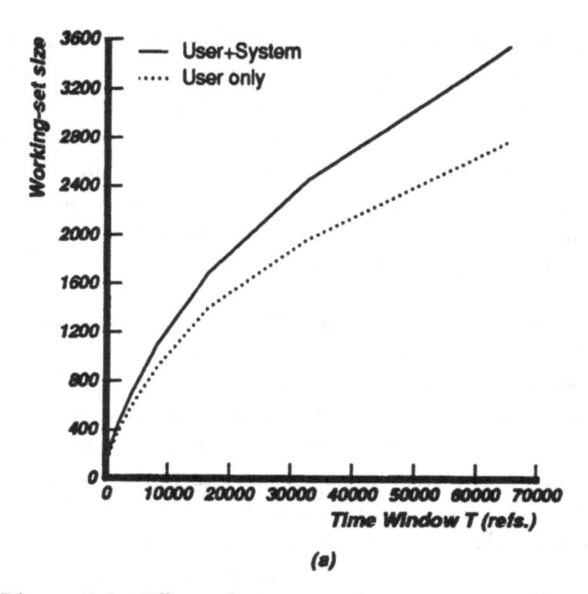

Figure 5.6: Effect of system references on working-set size.

We concur with hypotheses one and three as applied to cache performance. Below, we show some experimental evidence for these two hypotheses. However, we believe hypothesis two is not significant in caches. System structures occupy more pages than user structures *for a given amount of data* because of their extra complexity, and thereby degrade TLB performance. However, we have some evidence indicating that system structures do not display the same complexity at the finer granularity level of a cache block (assuming that a cache block is much smaller than a TLB page). In other words, we have observed that given the same amount of data, system structures do not occupy significantly more cache blocks than user structures.

To verify hypothesis one, we compared the sizes of the code and data structures of both system and user by computing the working sets [23] of several programs. We estimated the working set with parameter T – a quantity independent of trace length – by averaging the number of unique references found in all segments of length T in the trace. Figure 5.6 displays the average user and user+system working set sizes for the VMS benchmarks. Tables D.2 and D.3 in Appendix D tabulate the individual benchmark working sets. For example, the IVEX3 working-set size, for time window parameter 16K references (see Appendix D for trace details), increases from 1332 (user only) to 1832 (user+system), or by 38%. Clearly, the average user and system working sets are larger than user-only working sets.

The working-set experiments also justify hypothesis three in an indirect manner. Because the relative increase in working-set size when the system references are included is greater than the relative increase in the trace length, it follows that system references must be reused less often than user on average. Compare, for example, the 38% increase in working set (from Tables D.2 and D.3 in Appendix D) with the 10% increase in trace length (from Table D.1 in Appendix D) on including system references in the IVEX3 trace. This indicates that system code is less repetitive than user.

Larger working sets and fewer loops suggest that the system miss rate will be more influenced by start-up and non-stationary behavior than the user miss rate. That is, a larger fraction of the system miss rate will be caused by fetching system references into the cache for the first time. Because the ratio of system-only and user-only miss rates becomes progressively larger with cache size (Figure 5.5), start-up and non-stationary effects must comprise a greater proportion of system cache miss rate. Of these, non-stationary effects are more evident, as can be graphically seen from the scatter diagram in Figure 5.7. This figure plots the system miss rate versus the percentage of system references in several traces. A high start-up component would have been possible only if the inherent system miss rate was a decreasing function of the number of system references. It is easy to see that the graph shows little negative correlation, and hence lower start-up as compared to non-stationary effects.

The dominance on the system miss rate by start-up and non-stationary behavior also affects the relationship between cache associativity and miss rate for user and system references. We will return to a discussion of hypothesis two, which is related to the issue of block-size, after we look at the effect of associativity.

5.4 Associativity

A noteworthy feature of the curves in Figure 5.1 is that associativity reduces the miss rate of large user-only caches by a greater fraction than the miss rate of user-plus-system caches. For example, for VMS traces, the miss rate of a 32K-byte user cache decreases from 2.01% to 1.05% (a 48% improvement) when the associativity is increased from one to two, whereas the combined user-system miss rate decreases from 3.14% to 1.93% (a smaller relative improvement of 39%). One might expect the reverse, i.e., associativity to be relatively more beneficial to user-plus-system caches because it would reduce user-system interaction. The reason for this behavior is that associativity does not benefit system references.

Figures 5.8(a) and (b) show the system component and the user-system inter-

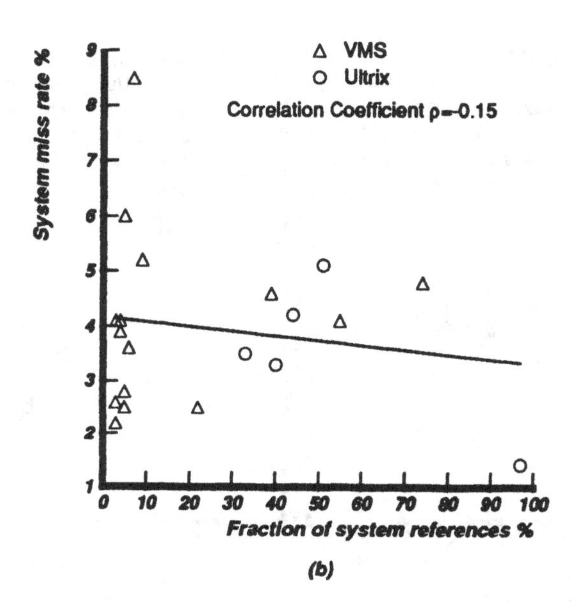

Figure 5.7: The relationship between the fraction of system references and the system miss rate.

ference component of the miss rate in VMS and Ultrix traces for associativities of one, two, and four. Predictably, the interference component is strongly dependent on associativity. However, for large caches, interference misses are an insignificant fraction of the overall misses, which decreases their relative impact, and the impact of associativity on the miss rate.

Furthermore, associativity has a smaller impact on the system miss rate component than on the user component. Unlike the user miss rate curves in Figure 5.5, the system miss rate curves only show a weak dependence on associativity. For the VMS workload, and a 32K-byte direct-mapped cache, for instance, the relative change in the user miss rate on doubling the associativity is over twice the relative change in the system miss rate. This is because most system misses are simply to bring in the references for the first time.

Most of the benefits of associativity are achieved by a two-way set-associative cache; associativity of four yields little additional performance. For a 32K-byte user-system (VMS) cache the miss rates for set sizes one, two, and four are 3.14%, 1.93%, and 1.56% respectively. The two-way set-associative cache miss rate is 39% lower than direct mapped, while the four-way set-associative cache is just 19% lower than the two-way set-associative cache miss rate. Because associativity buys relatively less for system references than for user references, increasing associativity to improve overall system performance must now be

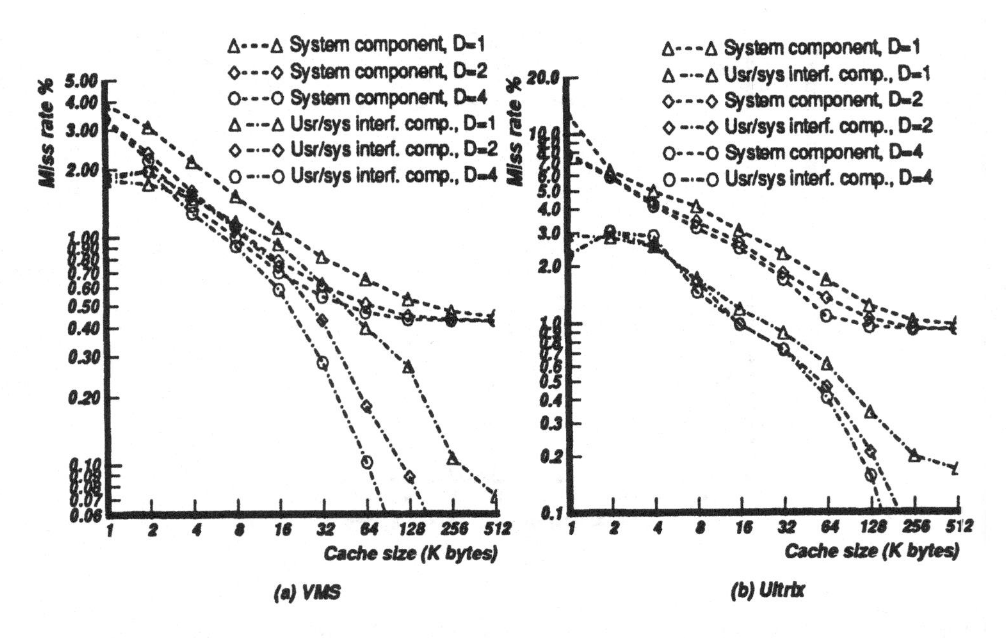

Figure 5.8: Effect of associativity on system and interference components of the miss rate (a) VMS (b) Ultrix. Block size is 16 bytes.

scrutinized even more carefully to analyze if the access time penalty is justified by the performance gain.

5.5 Block Size

We now study the effect of block size on the miss rate to see if system references behave any differently than user. The question we would like to answer is: Are system structures more complex than user structures at the cache block level? We showed earlier how a large portion of system misses in big caches are caused by start-up and non-stationary effects. This means that the miss rate for an arbitrarily large cache with any choice of associativity will be bounded below by the start-up and non-stationary components of the miss rate, which may be unacceptably high. A method of decreasing these components is to fetch more words from the main store on a cache miss, i.e., by increasing the block size. The block size is strongly affected by implementation constraints and bus bandwidth limitations. Although, this section deals primarily with isolating the effect of block size on system references, a more detailed discussion on block size effects is presented in the multiprogramming section.

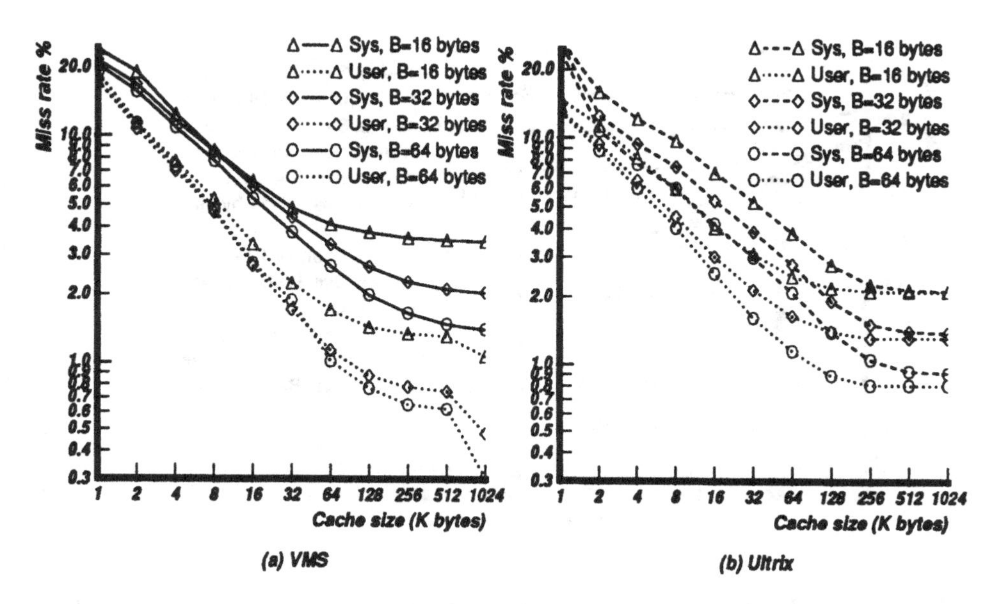

Figure 5.9: Effect of block size on user and system miss rates. Caches are direct-mapped.

Figures 5.9(a) and (b) show the variation of the miss rate with cache size in VMS and Ultrix for a number of block sizes for both user-only and system-only workloads. The unique feature of these graph is the lack of any special system behavior. For example, the VMS, system-only miss rate of a 512K-byte cache decreases from 3.5% to 1.48% (by 58%) by increasing the block size from 16 to 64 bytes, which is similar to the corresponding user-only miss rate decrease from 1.31% to 0.62% (by 53%). Because block size affects both system and user miss rates roughly equally, we feel that system structures are no more complex than user when observed at the granularity of a cache block. Therefore, we conjecture that Clark and Emers's second hypothesis for the degraded TLB performance of system references does not apply to caches with small block sizes.

We now attempt to verify Clark and Emer's second hypothesis by observing the relative miss rates of user and system references for larger block sizes (up to 1K bytes). For this experiment, we choose a four-way set associative cache to reduce the overwhelming influence of interference on the miss rate due to the small number of sets. Figure 5.10 shows the miss rates for VMS system-only and user-only workloads for block sizes ranging from 16 to 1024 bytes.

The system-only miss rate varies from 1.20% to 0.54% (by 55%) when the block size is increased from 128 to 1K bytes; the corresponding relative variation in

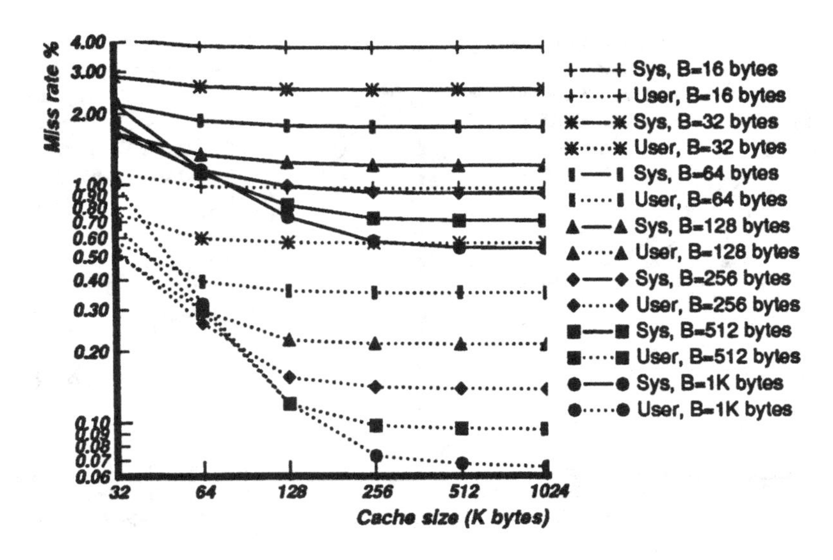

Figure 5.10: Effect of large block size on system miss rate and user miss rate.

user-only miss rate is higher: 67%, from 0.21% to 0.07%. These results show that for system references miss rate is less influenced by large block sizes than user, which weakly supports the hypothesis that system references are scattered over more pages than user for a given amount of data.

It is clear from Figure 5.9 that block-size effects are more significant in caches larger than 32K bytes. This result is not surprising since start-up and non-stationary misses predominate for these caches, and the negative effects due to lower block utilization are also lessened. Larger blocks can cause the program working set to be brought in with fewer misses and the overall number of misses will be reduced. Although the start-up and non-stationary components are always reduced by a large block size in a small cache, the large block size causes increased interference, that can increase the miss rate.

Judging by the positive impact of block size on the system performance of large caches, it may well be that large caches could profit substantially by using smart prefetching techniques [76, 17], or by simply using large block sizes. In the next chapter, we show how the block size that yields the best access time (for given cache and main-memory access times) can be determined.

5.6 Evaluation of Split Caches

Several researchers suggested using split user and system caches to obviate user-system interference (see bibliography in [76]). In multiprogramming environments, a split cache also allows convenient selective flushing of only the user references because system references are shared among the processes and need not be flushed across process switches. (This scheme will be examined in detail in the multiprogramming chapter.) This method somewhat alleviates the penalty incurred in cache flushing on process switches when Process Identifiers (PIDs) are absent. However, Smith [76] argues that the split cache is unlikely to prove useful, chiefly because a large fraction of the misses occur in system space, and the increase in miss rate due to halving the cache for the system space may increase the miss rate more than the gains due to the lack of user-system interference. Our results support this argument.

Unfortunately there is very little literature on the evaluation of split user-system caches to enable a designer to make a suitable choice. In the ensuing discussion we present some of our results on split user-system cache studies. Figure 5.11 show how split caches for system and user perform relative to a unified cache. Combined caches are better than caches split equally, in all cases. While large cache performance is roughly equal for both split and unified caches, the disparity is significant in small caches.

One other method to reduce systematic user-system interaction is to hash the system bit into the address used to index into the cache. This scheme will be beneficial in architectures where the system and user spaces begin at address locations that map into the same cache set increasing the probability of collision. For example, in the VAX architecture, the most significant address bit is the system/user bit. Typically, the system stack starts at the top of the system address space (HEX BFFFFFFF); similarly, the user stack starts at the top of user space (HEX 7FFFFFFF), mapping both user and system top-of-stack to the same cache set. However, this is not beneficial to large caches because of the inherently small user-system interaction.

Interference can also be reduced by not caching some operating system address space portions that have an inherently high miss rate, or those that are not repetitive and used rarely. This decreases the probability of "useful" code and data segments being purged from the cache. To further reduce the inherent system-system interference, commonly executed system routines can be placed in memory locations that do not overlap in the cache. Such routines can be identified from system traces generated by ATUM. This method is expected to be less useful for large caches that already have a small interference component.

This chapter dealt with system references in a uniprogramming environment.

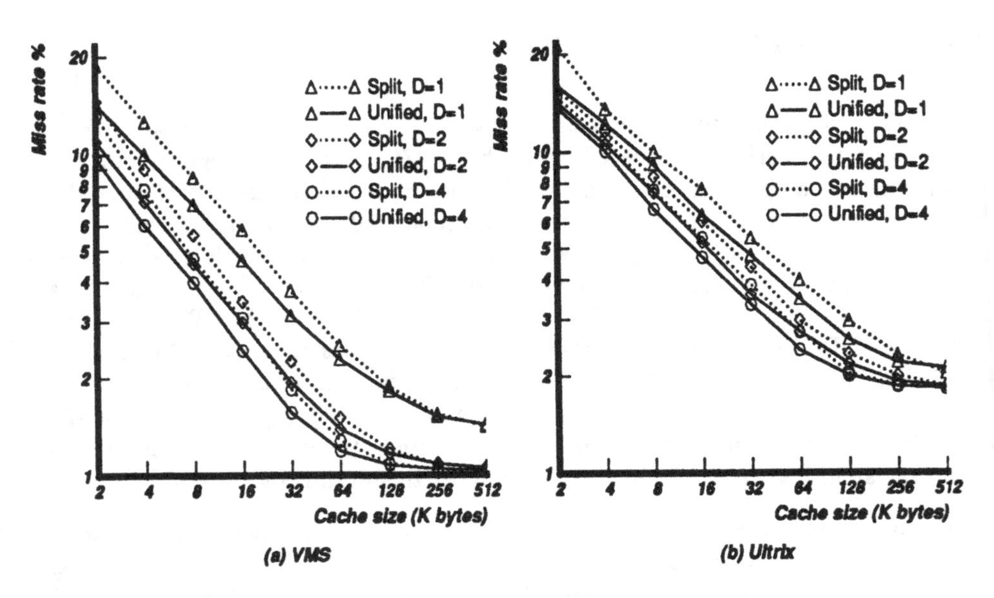

Figure 5.11: Split versus unified cache for system and user references. Block size is 16 bytes.

The sharing of system references by all processes causes some interesting cache behavior for operating system and multiprogramming workloads. We address these issues in the next chapter.

Chapter 6

Impact of Multiprogramming on Cache Performance

This chapter discusses both the performance of virtual caches for multiprogramming workloads, and the validity of the earlier schemes to model multiprogramming effects. After outlining our cache analysis methods for multiprogramming workloads, we compare cache performance data at different levels of multiprogramming to motivate a study of this nature. We evaluate various techniques that have been proposed for improving multitasking in caches, such as cache flushing and PIDs. After initially considering only user references, we then include system references and discuss the impact of system references on cache performance in a multiprogramming environment. We contrast our experimental findings with various synthetic models of multiprogrammed caches used by earlier researchers and examine the validity of assumptions made by earlier studies. We end this chapter by examining various techniques to improve cache performance for multiprogramming.

The effect of process switching can be studied using either physically-addressed or virtually-addressed caches. For a virtual cache, process switching can be taken into account by:

1. Flushing the cache on every context switch. This prevents the data left over in the cache by other processes from being inadvertently used.

2. Assigning a unique process identifier or PID (or ASID, address space identifier [76]) per process and appending the PID to the address tag in the cache. The address-PID pair represent a unique address in a global multiprogramming address space.

In physical caches nothing special is necessary since the the virtual to physical mapping mechanism ensures that the address spaces of the individual processes are disjoint. While we present only virtual cache results here, the behavior of the PID scheme is strongly indicative of the performance of a physical-address cache in the absence of a very large number of address map changes. Both a physical-address cache and a virtual-address cache with PIDs allow multiple processes to share data in the cache.

We explored miss rates for a uniprogramming environment and two multiprogramming environments. The uniprogramming miss rates were determined by simulating a set of caches, each assigned to a unique process space so that the processes would not interfere with each other. Then, the average miss rate is the sum of individual miss rates weighted by the number of references of the process divided by the total number of references; this is the mean miss rate of the processes in the absence of process switching. We call this the uniprogramming miss rate. Next, we collected cache statistics for the traces using the two models of multiprogramming in virtual-address caches described above. The first multiprogramming miss rate assigns a PID per process, and the second assumes purging, or invalidating all cache entries, on every process switch.

6.1 Relative Performance of Multiprogramming Cache Techniques

Figures 6.2(a) and (b) show the warm-start miss rates for user-only traces for multiprogramming levels of three and ten under the VMS operating system. Multiprogramming level of six (MUL6) behaved similar to the above and so we do not show its results to avoid cluttering up the figures. Ultrix results for SAVEC are in Figure 6.1(c). The uniprogramming curves are also shown for comparison. The first observation is that performance of all cache organizations, and all workloads, degrades due to multiprogramming. The degradation becomes substantial for large caches, with the purged cache much more severely affected.

The notable performance degradation in caches encourages us to study multiprogramming caches in greater detail. For example, considering caches with PIDs, the miss rate of a 64K-byte cache degrades by 50% (from 1.69% to 2.53%)

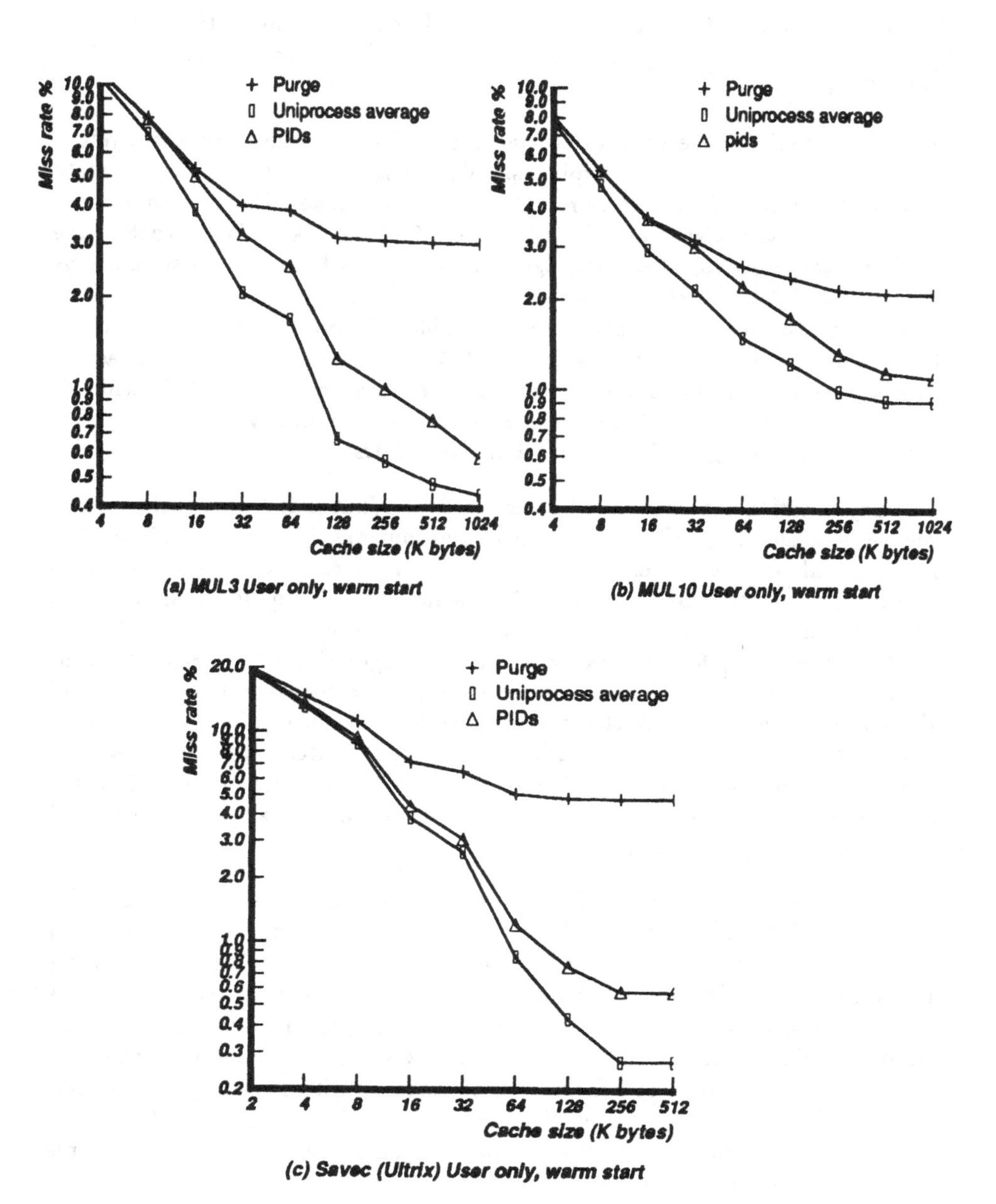

Figure 6.1: Multiprogramming cache performance for user workloads. Set size is 1, and block size is 16 bytes.

in the steady state when multitasking is considered (see Figure 6.1(a)); the miss rate of a large 256K-byte cache deteriorates even more, from 0.57% to 0.99%, or by 75%.

This negative influence of multitasking (in addition to the impact of system references) also explains why typical simulation studies that do not accurately account for multitasking effects report much lower cache miss rates than measurements on actual systems. For the relatively small VAX-11/780 cache (size 8K-byte, set-size two, block-size eight bytes) Emer's trace driven simulations done at DEC [21] showed a miss rate of about 7%, and Smith's results [76] for similar caches predicted a miss rate of roughly 5%, both of which are similar to our uniprogramming user-only miss rate prediction of 7%. Clark's measurements [21] on a real system showed that the miss rate was closer to 10%, which is close to our simulation miss rate of 9% for multiprogramming user-plus-system traces (shown in Figure 6.3(a) for MUL3 with PIDs).

The key question that needs to be answered is: What is the best cache performance possible in a multiprogramming environment? Referring to Figure 6.1, for a virtual-address cache, the best results are for a cache that appends a process identifier to the virtual address. For caches that are smaller than 8K bytes, multiprogramming does not affect performance very much – both the PIDs and purging schemes perform almost as well as uniprogramming. The reason is that in small caches very little data is retained across process switches and most of the misses arise due to interference between the references of the user process itself. Moreover, flushing the cache on a context switch performs as well as PIDs for caches as large as 16K bytes because the lifetime of cache items is short compared to the process switch interval causing the cache to "self purge" even without explicit flushing.

For larger caches, multiprogramming increasingly degrades performance. With purging, caches larger than 64K bytes are not profitable, implying that purging the cache on a process switch makes sense only for small caches. When caches become larger, a significant portion of a process' addresses are retained across context switches, as indicated by the substantial improvement in cache hit rate from assigning PIDs. PIDs become increasingly more valuable as cache sizes become larger; the miss rate for multiprogramming with PIDs approaches that of the uniprogramming case as the cache size begins to exceed 512K bytes. At that size, the cache can simultaneously retain the working sets of multiple processes with relatively little interference.

The disparity in the performance of the PID and the purging schemes decreases at high multiprogramming levels. The reason is that for a high multiprogramming level a larger fraction of the data of a process is purged by the greater expected number of intervening processes.

The non-zero slope of the PID miss rate curve even for large caches shows that for multiprogramming, interference between the references of various processes is a major component of the miss rate, which indicates the potential for further improvement in cache performance by either increasing cache size or set size. The performance benefits achievable by reducing interference in the cache for multiprogramming workloads, and the availability of the technology to build large caches coupled with the speed and complexity disadvantages of set-associative caches over direct-mapped caches, leads us in the quest of alternative schemes to enhance the performance of large direct-mapped caches. We evaluate some schemes in a later section.

6.2 More on Warm Start versus Cold Start

We observed a substantial difference in cold and warm-start miss rates for the multiprogramming workloads. As we discussed earlier, this is because of the larger start-up cost in multitasking workloads. We also observed a significant disparity in the sensitivity of the multitasking cache schemes to cold-start and warm-start simulations (modulo variations in workload characteristics over the initial and latter warm trace portions). These differences are examined here because they yield insight into how multiprogramming caches behave.

Contrast, for example, the warm-start and cold-start miss rates of MUL3 depicted in Figures 6.2(a) and (b) and the data for MUL10 in Figures 6.2(c) and (d). The purging scheme is relatively less sensitive to cold or warm start than either uniprogramming or the PID scheme; the PID scheme is itself less sensitive than uniprogramming. The miss rate for a 512K-byte cache with purging varies from 2.68% for cold start to 3.05% for warm start (a 14% increase), while the PID scheme miss rate varies between 1.03% and 0.78% (a 25% decrease), and the uniprogramming miss rate changes from 0.84% to 0.48% (decreases by 43%) for the same cache.

The underlying reason for these differences stems from the expected "life time" of references in the cache under the various schemes. Recall that our warm start miss rates are calculated by counting the misses only after the start-up period of about 600K references. Therefore, the warm start miss rate is a function of the number of live references in the cache after the initial start-up period. The chief reason for the similarity of the warm start miss rate to the cold-start miss rate for the purging scheme is that the cache is flushed of all references every process switch, shortening reference life times to a maximum of the process switch interval. The small difference in the cold and warm results is attributable to the dissimilar nature of initial and latter portions of the trace.

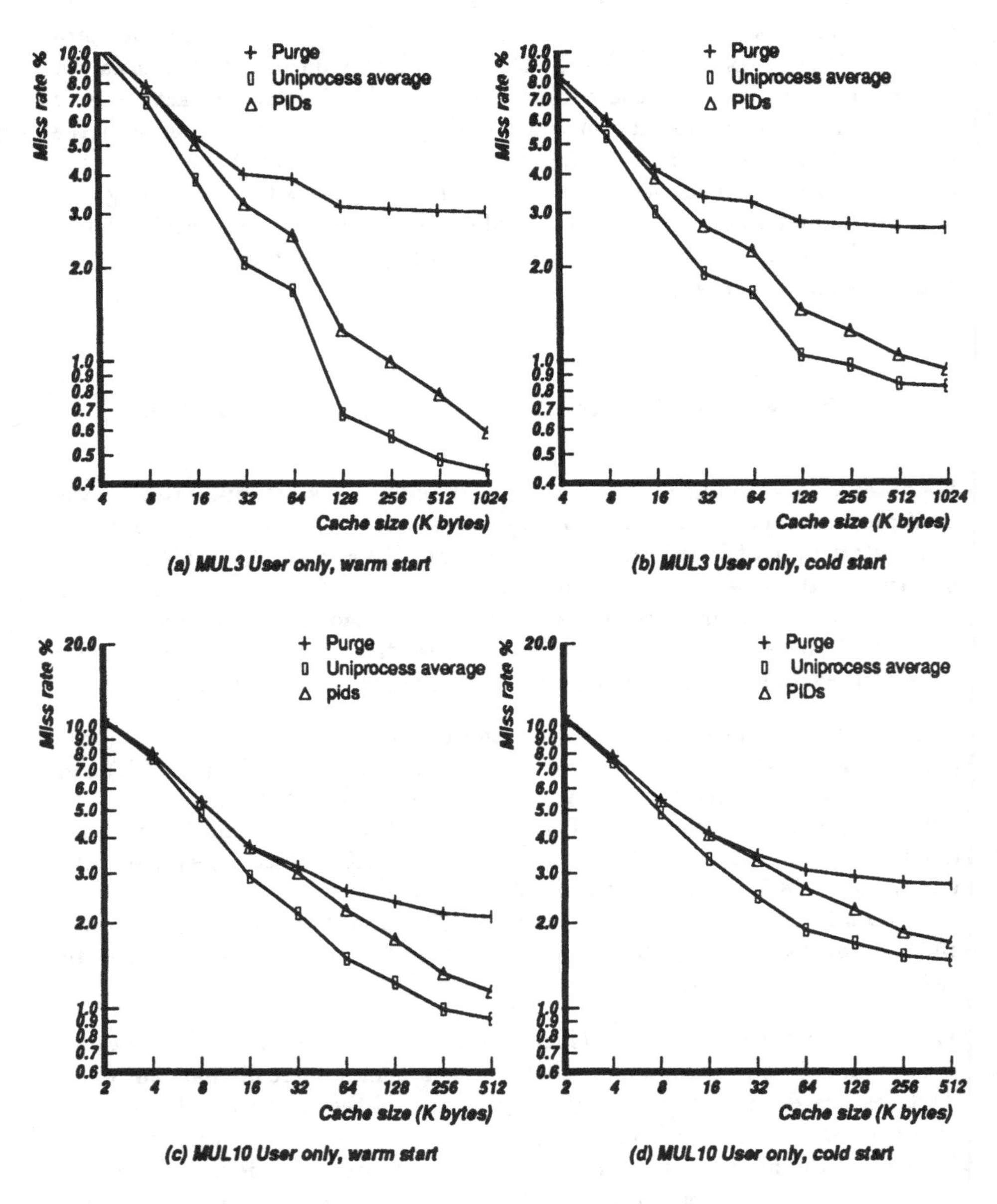

Figure 6.2: Comparison of cold-start and warm-start performance of MUL3 and MUL10. Set size is 1, and block size is 16 bytes.

The uniprogramming scheme is the opposite extreme to the purging case. Lacking interference from other processes, or explicit purging, reference life times are the longest achievable, and limited only by interference from the references of the same process. Therefore, the warm start miss rates for uniprogramming are expected to be considerable lower than cold start barring significant workloads variations in the latter portions of the trace.

Caches with PIDs fall in between: the life times of references are not as long as uniprogramming because of interference from other processes, nor are they as short as in purging.

As an example, let us compare the average life times of the references of a given process in the MUL3 trace in a 64K-byte direct-mapped cache, with a block size of 16 bytes. The life time of the references in the uniprogramming case is the highest at 23,805. In other words, there are 23,805 references to the cache from the time an average reference is fetched into the cache to the time it is purged. For multiprogramming with PIDs, this number falls to 15,865, and is further reduced to 6,209 for the purging scheme.

Our experiments showed that higher multiprogramming levels had little impact on the relative cold-start versus warm start performance. The reason is that at the higher multiprogramming level there are two conflicting forces, which somewhat balance: the increased interference component at higher multiprogramming levels tends to decrease the difference between cold and warm start miss rates; however, a higher multiprogramming level also has a larger start-up cost, which is obviated in warm-start simulations. Therefore, the net difference in the cold-start and warm-start miss rates of large caches, is not expected to be a strong function of the multiprogramming level.

Using life-time arguments, large cache performance is much more sensitive to differences in the warm-start and cold-start models. Differences in the cold-start and warm-start miss rates of small caches are usually attributable to behavior changes in the workload. For example, the MUL3 trace shows a cold-start miss rate of 8.41% for a 4K-byte cache with PIDs, which is less than the warm-start miss rate of 10.86%, implying a variation in workload characteristics; while, for the same trace, the corresponding miss rate of a 512K-byte cache drops from 1.03% in cold start to 0.78% in warm start indicating the retention of a large fraction of the working set in large caches. For the same process in MUL3 and the same block size mentioned in the earlier example, the life time of an average reference under uniprogramming in a 16K-byte cache is just 6822 – less than a third of the life time in the 64K-byte cache.

6.3 Impact of Shared System Code on Multitasking Cache Performance

We now include the effects of system references. Since system references are common to all the processes, they are assigned a separate unique PID. We first perform the same three experiments as with the user-only traces, i.e., uniprogramming, purge all cache entries on a process switch, and PIDs. An interrupt into system space is not considered a process switch for the purpose of purging; only a user-level context switch is. Purging on all interrupts would only degrade the performance of this scheme further. In addition, to take advantage of shared system references, we also simulate only purging all non-shared user references from the cache on a process switch. Split user-system caches yield an efficient hardware implementation of this scheme.

Figure 6.3 summarizes warm-start miss rate statistics for MUL3, MUL10, and SAVEC. Purging only user references has a distinct advantage over purging the whole cache. In fact, it approximates the miss rate of the PID scheme reasonably well for cache sizes up to 32K bytes, and the relative advantage increases with the multiprogramming level because of the increased opportunity for sharing system code. This scheme is important because in the absence of process identifiers, selectively purging a large cache of only user references is substantially superior to purging the entire cache of all its contents. The performance of the split-cache implementation of this scheme is similar to the performance of the unified cache for caches greater than 32K bytes (for example, see Figure 6.3(a)).

In the presence of system references the performance of the PID scheme is the cause of some surprises. Warm-start performance is very close to the uniprogramming case and actually surpasses it for cache sizes greater than 512K bytes for MUL3 (and 256K bytes for MUL10 and SAVEC)! The relative improvement is greater for higher multiprogramming levels. The reason for this seemingly anomalous behavior is quite simple. Since system references are shared, the cost of fetching system references is amortized over a larger number of processes, hence bringing the overall miss rate down. This effect is greatest for large caches where the miss rate is dominated by the cost of first-time fetches of references into the cache. The point where PID miss rates cross over uniprogramming miss rates occurs for smaller cache sizes in cold-start simulations where the relative impact of first-time fetches is greater. The PID scheme surpasses the uniprogramming case in performance for caches larger than 256K in MUL3, and 128K in MUL10 and SAVEC.

The improvement in performance of the PID scheme for all cache sizes due to system references is evident from Figure 6.4, which shows the relative change in

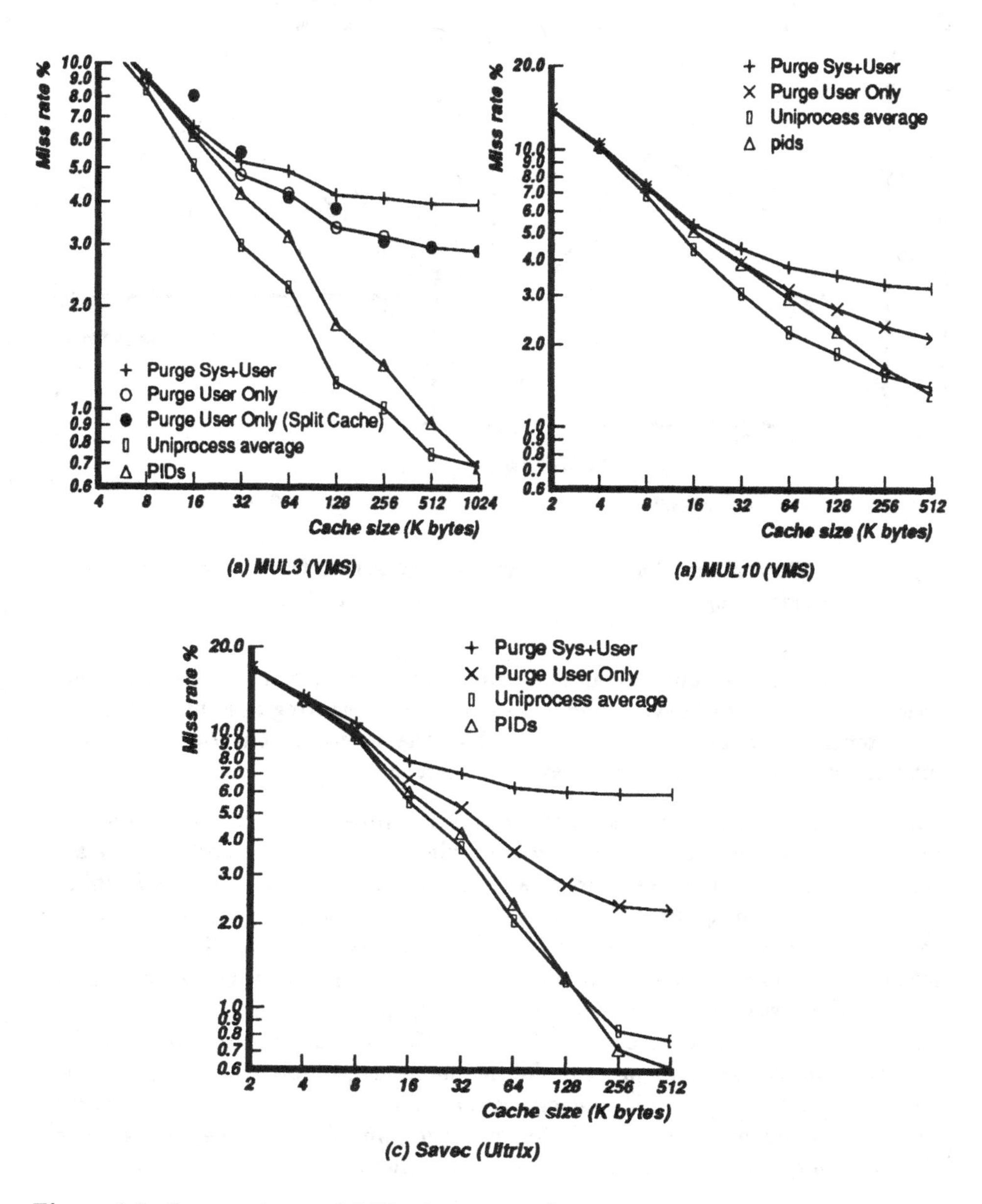

Figure 6.3: On purging and PIDs for user and system workloads. Set size is 1, block size is 16 bytes, and miss rates are warm start.

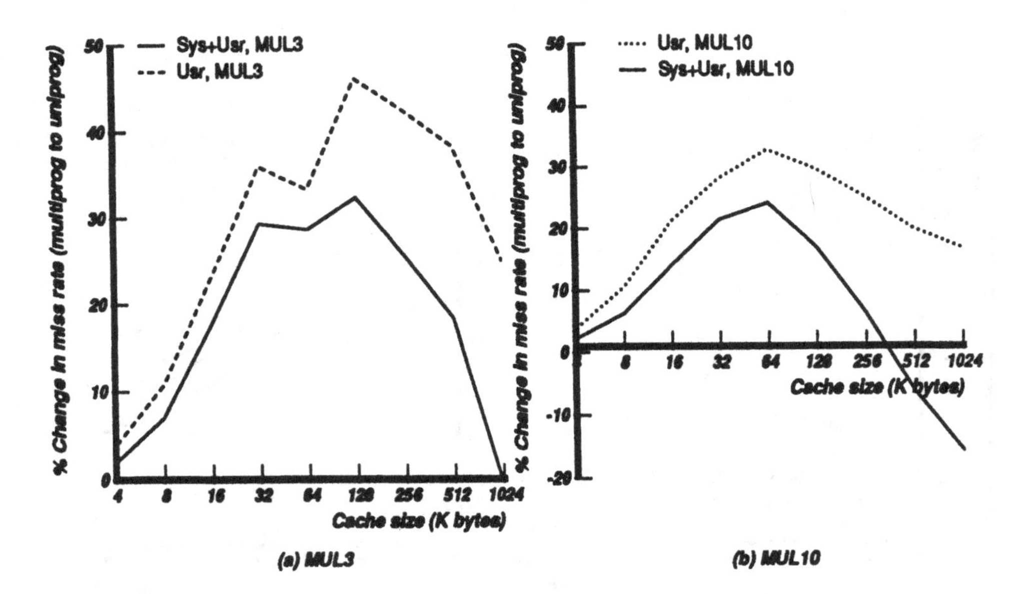

Figure 6.4: Percentage change in warm-start miss rate from uniprogramming to multiprogramming. Set size is 1 and block size is 16 bytes.

performance between uniprogramming and multiprogramming for user-only and user plus system workloads. The solid curves, representing system workloads, consistently show better performance than the user-only curves despite the inherently poorer performance of system references.

Another explanation for this performance improvement is to focus on the uniprogramming model. Our uniprogramming miss rates are obtained by assigning each process its own cache, which achieves the same effect as flushing the cache after an application terminates. System references fetched into the cache by a process are not available to the next process. In a different model, when an application runs to completion, a newly initiated program can utilize parts of the system references left behind by the previous one to reduce its system start-up cost, of course, using PIDs or selective flushing to invalidate the references of the previous process. With this model, uniprogramming also exploits the relative benefits of sharing system references, and we will not observe the same anomalous improvement for multiprogramming. The key inference is that allowing sharing is advantageous to any scheme.

Figure 6.4 also shows that the impact of multiprogramming is most severe for caches in the size range of 32 to 256K bytes. For larger caches, sharing system references (and the lower interference level) compensates for multiprogramming interference and the multiprogramming degradation is less severe.

6.4 Process Switch Statistics and Their Effects on Cache Modeling

The process switch intervals, the process scheduling order, and the multiprogramming load impact cache performance strongly. The longer the process switch interval the greater the potential for a reference to get reused by a process before being purged by an intervening process. The sooner a process resumes execution after being switched out the more likely it is to find a sizable part of its working set still in the cache. The multiprogramming load determines the total multiprocess working set.

Figure 6.5 shows the distribution of execution time quanta between process switches for MUL3, MUL6, and MUL10. For all the three workloads the interval varies from less than ten to over fifty thousand references. Interestingly, the process-switch interval lacks a significant load dependence. The average process switch intervals for MUL3, MUL6, and MUL10 are 19K, 17K, and 16K references respectively. Multiprogramming was conjectured to degrade cache performance by reducing the average time quantum between process switches, thereby causing greater interference between the data of different processes. The similar distribution of the process switch intervals at three levels of multiprogramming shows that this may not be a significant factor in performance degradation.

Next, we investigated the scheduling order. We computed the probability of scheduling the nth task in the LRU stack of tasks. The probability distribution of the stack distance is plotted in Figure 6.6 for MUL3, MUL10 and SAVEC. The figure shows, for example, that the MUL10 trace has roughly nine to twelve intervening processes between invocations of a given process.

One of the simplest models, used by many studies to predict the multiprogramming performance of a physical cache (or an optimal virtual cache) was to flush the cache on a context switch, or on every interrupt [45, 84, 26, 33]. Assuming that the PID scheme and physical caches perform similarly, the wide disparity in the PIDs and purging curves in Figure 6.1 shows that the flushing model becomes extremely inaccurate as the cache gets larger. Furthermore, lacking accurate context switch information, the cache was flushed at some constant period (e.g., in [45]), while in practice the context switch interval is not constant, as Figure 6.5 indicates. Flushing the cache at constant intervals results in worst case miss rates as shown by Easton and Fagin [25]. We expect that the fraction of residual valid data a process finds in the cache when it returns (after being switched out) is an increasing function of the cache size, and a decreasing function of the number of intervening processes and the time it is switched out.

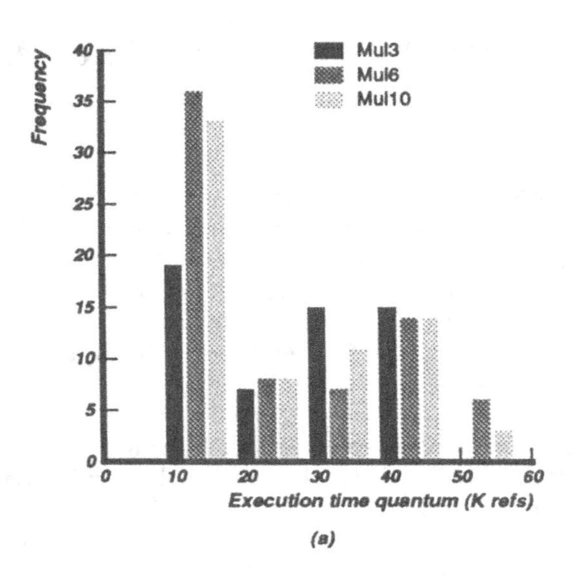

Figure 6.5: Distribution of execution time quanta.

A better technique that some studies (e.g., [76]) used to predict multiprogrammed performance was to interleave multiple single process traces in a round-robin fashion with constant duration time slicing to form one long multiprogram trace. This is still an inaccurate model because the time slice durations are not constant as Figure 6.5 shows. Studies of Easton and Fagin [26], and Haikala [33], among others, have shown that multiprogramming performance depends heavily on the distribution of the number of references between process switches. The approximate round-robin scheduling order evidenced from Figure 6.6 largely validates the round-robin scheduling assumption. If multiprogramming traces are unavailable, a reasonable method of obtaining miss rate statistics would be to interleave traces and choose the process switch intervals from some distribution, for example, from the distribution shown if Figure 6.5 (with the caveat that the average process switch interval will probably increase with processor performance).

6.5 Associativity

The increased interference generated by multiprogramming increases the miss rate. Increasing the cache associativity directly addresses this. Figures 6.7(a) and (b) show the relative performance of set-associative caches for uniprogramming and multiprogramming levels of three and ten under VMS.

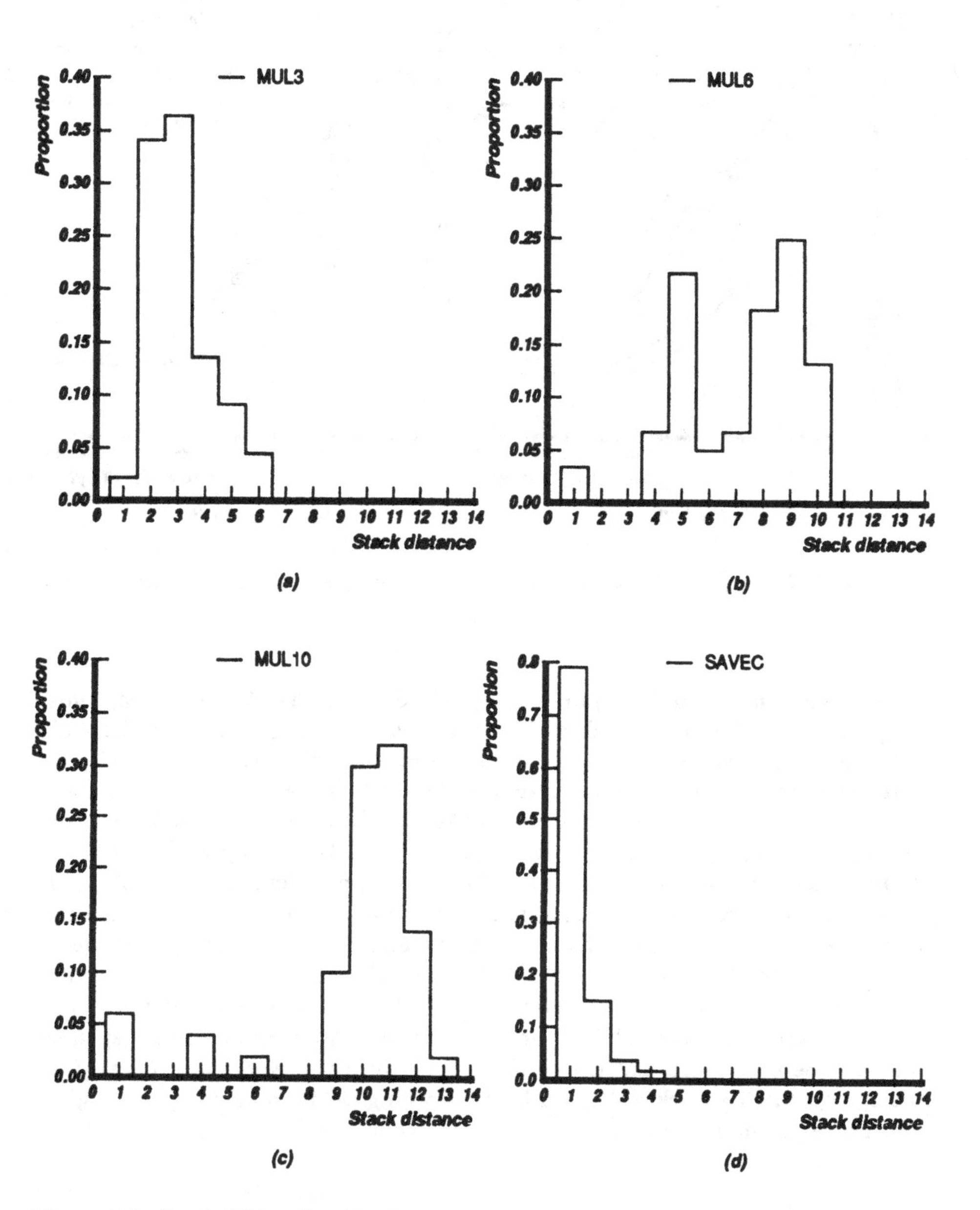

Figure 6.6: Probability distribution of the LRU stack distance for task switching for MUL3, MUL6, MUL10, and SAVEC.

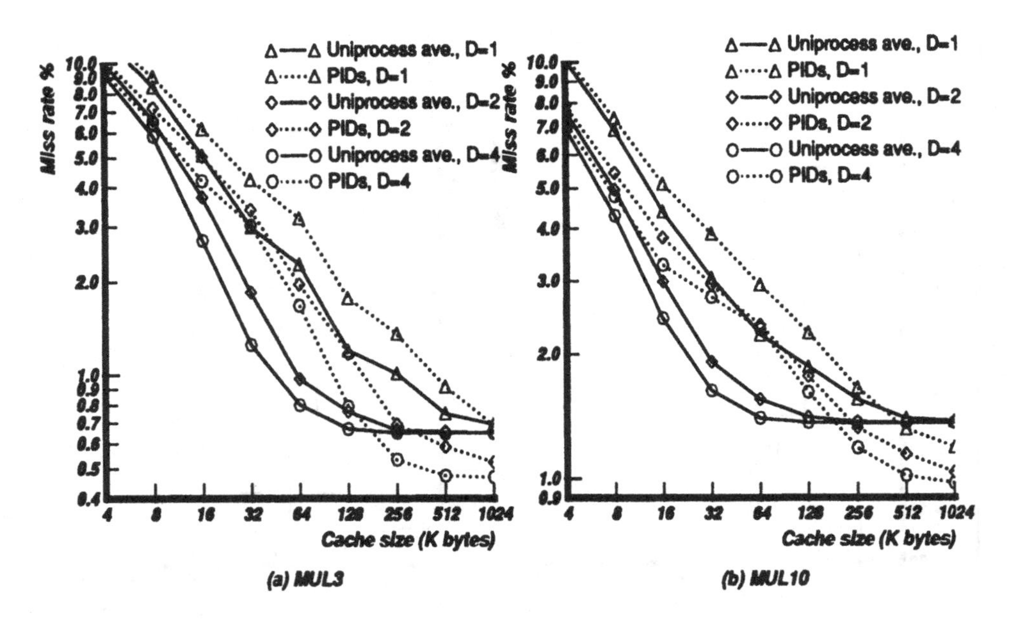

Figure 6.7: On associativity. Block size is 16 bytes and miss rates are warm start.

Associativity impacts uniprogramming workloads more than the multiprogramming workloads for small caches. Quantitatively, for a 32K-byte cache and MUL3-uniprogramming, the miss rate drops by 40% when the associativity is increased from one to two, and further by 30% when the associativity is doubled. Corresponding fractional decreases for MUL10 are 40% and 15%. For multiprogramming, however, the miss rate for MUL3 drops by 20% and 10%, by increasing associativity from one to two, and two to four; and by 25% and 7% for MUL10. A possible reason is that in small caches, when the working set of the workload does not fit in the cache and the interference component of misses is very high, associativity is not profitable, nor is replacement strategy; size is the only cache parameter that counts. This was demonstrated by a number of earlier studies [80, 2]. The interference component of misses depends both on the cache size and the working-set size of the workload. Clearly, a multiprogramming workload has a larger working set than each of its component processes in a uniprogramming environment, thus decreasing the impact of associativity.

An opposite trend is observed for large caches. Associativity impacts multiprogramming workloads more strongly in comparison with uniprogramming. For example in MUL3, for a 256K-byte cache with uniprogramming, the fractional decline in the miss rate in doubling the set size from one to two is 30%, and is 15% when the associativity is further doubled. The decrease is greater for multiprogramming: 50% and 30% for set size increase from one to two, and two to four. A large cache can comfortably sustain the entire working set of a single process in our uniprogramming workloads. The little interference present in a direct-mapped cache is obviated by a two-way set-associativity cache; increasing associativity further, or using larger caches, is to no avail. However, for multiprogramming, while the large cache is bigger than the working set, the interference component is still substantial. Therefore, increasing the associativity, or enlarging the cache, both of which reduce interference, can improve performance significantly.

An interesting rule of thumb for large multiprogramming caches is that the performance gained by increasing associativity from one to two is roughly the same as doubling the cache size. The choice of either extension will depend on access time and complexity considerations.

6.6 Block Size

Figures 6.8 and 6.9 compare the relative merits of larger block sizes for multiprogramming. In multiprogramming, a large proportion of the misses occur when processes get a part of their working sets back into the cache after having it purged by intervening processes. Hence block size has a strong impact on multiprogramming performance. It is interesting to see that the marginal utility of increasing block size is approximately constant in a large cache, e.g., in a 512K-byte cache, for block sizes up to 128 bytes, while for smaller cache, e.g. 64K-bytes, the limit is reached at a block size of 64 bytes. Larger block sizes in small caches tends to increase interference because the number of cache sets decreases in proportion to the block size.

For multiprogramming workloads, considering caches smaller than 1M bytes, less than one percent miss rates are achievable only by block sizes greater than or equal to 16 bytes. It is possible that for high multiprogramming levels smaller block sizes can never yield less than one percent miss rates because the miss rate curves of MUL10 tail off.

If the block size can be increased over a wide range in large caches without adversely impacting performance, large blocks have another important advantage. Often, the latency in main memory accesses is largely due to either bus contention or in the bus architecture specification itself. The performance penalty of this fixed cost on every access can be reduced by transferring large blocks. However, there is also a variable cost which increases with block size. The following experiment aims to determine the block size that gives the best mean

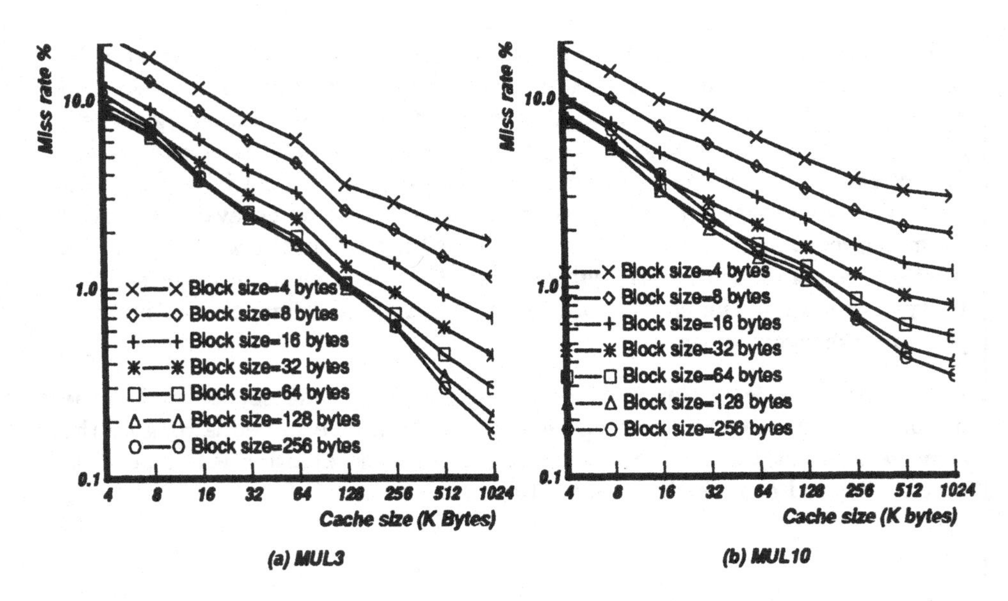

Figure 6.8: Effect of block size on cache miss rate. Miss rates are warm start and caches are direct-mapped.

memory access time ($T = T_c + mTm$).

The memory system parameters chosen for this analysis are similar to those in the MIPS-X system design [71]. We assume the cache access time (T_c) is one cycle, and use two simple models for the mean miss service time (T_m). Both models have a fixed overhead of 12 cycles associated with each main memory transfer, and an additional two cycles for each word in the block (i.e., two extra cycles for every four bytes). The first model assumes that the processor waits until the entire block is fetched from memory. The second model assumes *fetch bypass*, where the word requested by the processor is fetched first to enable the processor to resume execution earlier; however, the processor stalls if it makes another memory request before the previous miss has been completely serviced by the cache. Therefore, on average, the processor advances three cycles before being stalled by another memory request. Therefore, for the first model, $T_m = 12 + 0.5B$, and for the second, $T_m = 9 + 0.5B$, where B denotes block size. For example, the mean miss service time with a block size of 16 bytes is 20 cycles without fetch bypass and 17 cycles with fetch bypass. Figure 6.9 shows the average memory access times for various block sizes for MUL3 and MUL10. For most cache sizes and both fetch models we see that 16 byte blocks yield the best access times.

The block size also impacts the write traffic to main memory in a write-back

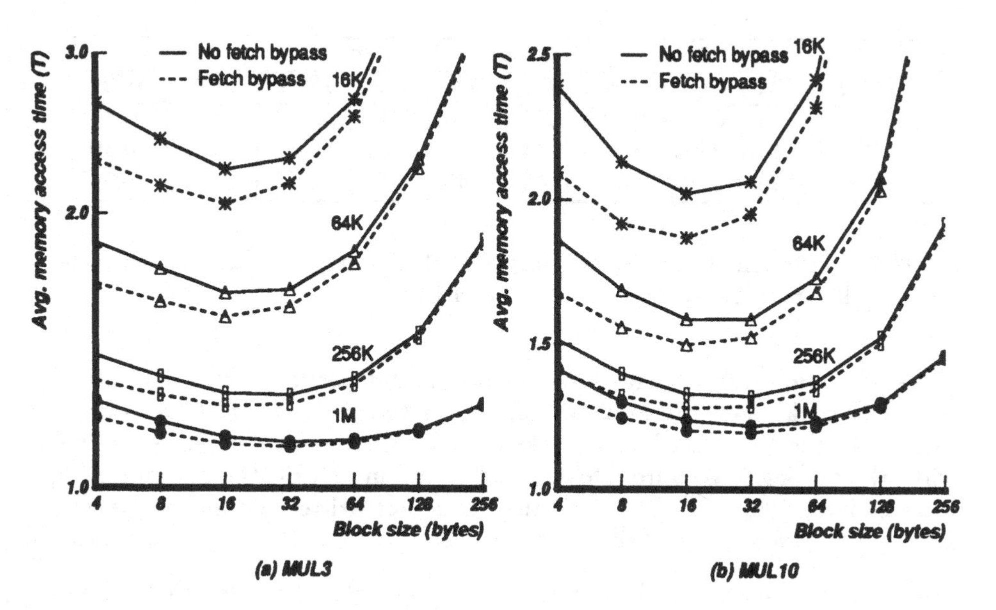

Figure 6.9: Effect of block size on average memory access time. Cache sizes are in bytes.

cache. The write traffic is the fraction of misses that result in writes to main memory times the block size. A miss results in a write to main memory if the block to be purged from the cache is dirty. To enable comparison, we will adopt the metric used by Smith [75], i.e., the fraction of data blocks purged that are dirty, as an indication of the write traffic (assuming the code is re-entrant). Measuring the fraction of data blocks purged that are dirty is problematic in large caches due to the diminished write back activity. However, we can estimate the fraction of data blocks that will be dirty when purged by simply noting the fraction of the data blocks in the cache that are dirty at the end of a simulation run. The estimate will be exact if the probability of purging a cache block is uniform for the entire cache.

Our first observation is that roughly half the data blocks purged are dirty, which is similar to Smith's measurements [75]. Our experiments indicate that the relationship between block size and the fraction of data blocks purged does not show a consistent trend for different benchmarks. For MUL10, the fraction of data lines purged dirty in a 256K-byte cache increases from 0.41 to 0.46 (a 12% increase) when the block size increases from 4 to 256 bytes, for SAVEC it increases from 0.39 to 0.45 (a 15% increase), while for MUL3 it *decreases* from 0.58 to 0.47 (a 19% decline). The behavior in MUL3 is unusual because the opportunity for a block to get written into is greater when block size is increased.

Trace	Cache Size (Bytes)								
	2K	4K	8K	16K	32K	64K	128K	256K	512K
MUL10	0.35	0.35	0.37	0.34	0.36	0.44	0.44	0.45	0.43
SAVEC	0.41	0.42	0.42	0.43	0.41	0.30	0.31	0.30	0.30
MUL3	0.46	0.47	0.49	0.46	0.46	0.47	0.52	0.53	0.54

Table 6.1: Fraction of data blocks purged that are dirty as a function of cache size, for the trace MUL3 and a block size of 16 bytes.

The explanation is that there is another workload dependent factor that affects the write back rate: the locality property of the read and write references. In MUL10 the fraction of data blocks that are written into increases by 15% when the block size goes from four to 256 bytes, in SAVEC the corresponding increase is by 10%, while in MUL3 the fraction of written blocks *decreases* by 23%, which lowers the probability that a data block purged was written into.

The fraction of dirty data blocks purged increases slightly as the cache size is raised from about 2K bytes to 8K bytes, and does not vary significantly or show any consistent increasing trend in caches larger than 64K bytes. For example, see Table 6.1 for data relevant to a block size of 16 bytes. (The discontinuity in the fraction of data blocks purged dirty at a 64K byte cache is a result of the approximate measurement scheme used for large caches.)

There are two reasons why the fractions are so similar. First, the fraction of data blocks that are first read and then written into are a small fraction of all the data blocks. In MUL3, for instance, this fraction is 0.16 for a block size of 16 bytes. Since only the blocks that fall into this category cause the write back activity to vary with cache size, the sensitivity of the write back activity to cache size is lessened. Second, in a block that is read and subsequently written, the write happens in a short period of time after the read. In the MUL3 trace, roughly half of the updated data blocks are written into within 1K references after the read. Thus, one can expect slight increases in the write activity with cache size only when caches are so small that the life times are comparable to the interval between read and write times.

6.7 Improving the Multiprogramming Performance of Caches

The straightforward ways of improving cache performance are increasing cache size or associativity or block size. Unfortunately, cost, complexity, traffic, and access time constraints can limit the arbitrary increase of one or more of the above parameters. This section will explore some other simple techniques to improve cache performance. The hashing scheme applies to virtual address caches, while the hash-rehash method can be used with either a physical or virtual address cache.

6.7.1 Hashing

One factor that might be a problem in virtual-addressed caches is that most processes tend to use specific regions of the virtual address space more than others. These systematically map to the same cache sets and interfere with each other. For example, addresses in the top of user-stack area and in the user-code area are heavily used in the VAX architecture. We have investigated some techniques to reduce the expected number of collisions caused due to these systematic effects without increasing the associativity. One method is to have the system assign different starting addresses to the code and stack top of different processes so as to have them map into orthogonal cache areas. For example, for a 64K direct-mapped cache, the processes can have starting addresses randomly chosen between zero and 64K.

A more practical technique is to index the cache with a hash of the PID (and maybe the system bit) and the address bits. Hashing is akin to increasing associativity in the sense that associativity reduces interference by providing an alternate location for a colliding reference, while hashing tries to achieve the same goal by making the probability that two references will map to the same location uniform over the entire cache.

Complete randomization of each address into the cache sets is not easy, nor is it desirable. The spatial correlation of program blocks in a given time interval has the advantage that the indexing mechanism used in selecting a set ensures a lesser chance of collision between spatially adjacent blocks; randomizing the selection of a set will only increase collisions. Smith's results [73] also indicate that the miss rate of caches with random mapping is generally higher than for bit selection mapping.

Figure 6.10(a) depicts the miss rates for a cache in a multiprogrammed environment using process identifiers with and without hashing. As expected, the effect of hashing increases with increasing cache size. The opportunity for cache regions to be relatively unused is greater in large caches which hashing tries to reduce. While the improvement is not substantial, the merit of this scheme is evident if we consider the improvement as a fraction of that achievable by doubling associativity, but at a much reduced cost. The miss rate of a 512K-byte direct-mapped cache decreases by 12% (from 1.29% to 1.14%) with

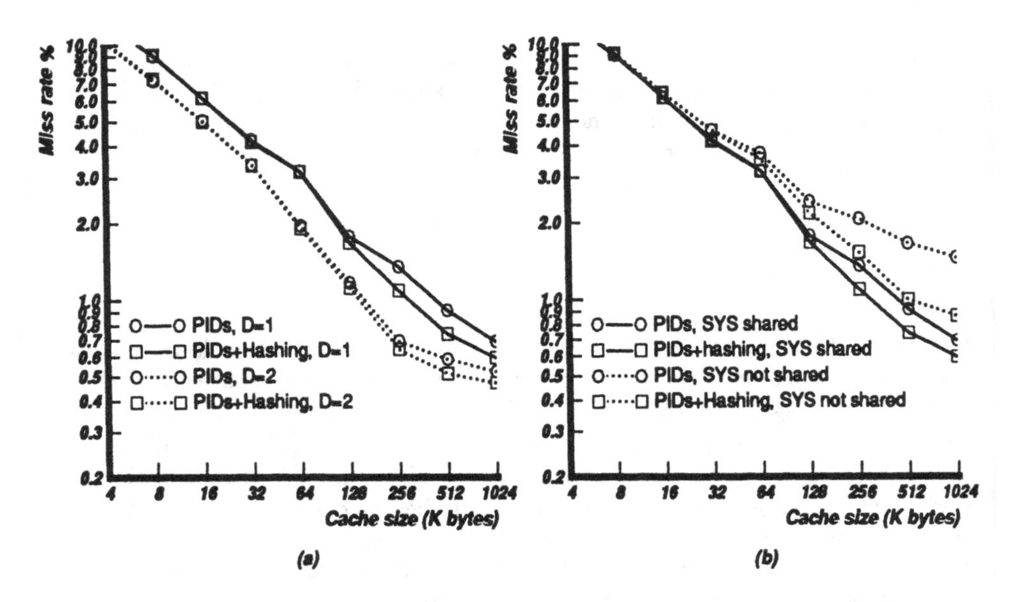

Figure 6.10: Effect of hashing. Trace is MUL3, block size is 16 bytes and D is set size. (a) Hashing (b) Hashing with system not shared (D=1).

hashing. The reduction in the miss rate is over half of 19% that is achievable by doubling set size.

Hashing has a negligible impact (less than 6% miss rate reduction for a 512K-byte two-way associative cache in Figure 6.10(a)) on set-associative caches for obvious reasons. Furthermore, the advantage of hashing is somewhat blurred by including shared system references because hashing does not affect system references. As an illustration, consider the miss rate curves in Figure 6.10(b). The solid curves depict the influence of hashing on the miss rate of a cache with PIDs; the dotted lines demonstrate how hashing would influence the miss rate in the hypothetical case where the system references are not shared. The effect of hashing is more pronounced for non-shared system (25% improvement over PIDs in a 512K-byte direct-mapped cache) and less evident otherwise (12% improvement).

6.7.2 A Hash-Rehash Cache

Another way to get almost all the benefits of associativity, albeit at the cost of more complex cache control, is to use a "hash-rehash" cache. This method is not new – it is a much-simplified version of existing methods used in the design of translation lookaside buffers (e.g., see [89]). In its simplified form, the hash-rehash technique reduces the miss rate of a direct-mapped cache to that of a two-way set-associative cache, while allowing common-case accesses (cache hits) at the speed of a conventional direct-mapped cache.

The hash-rehash cache operates as follows. First, as in a conventional cache, the address indexes into a cache set S1, and data is available to the processor if it is present in that set. This case is called a *first time hit*. On a miss, the address again indexes into the cache using a different hashing function (typically, inverting one of the address bits that are used to index into the cache). If the data is present in this alternate location S2, a *second time hit* occurs, and the data is transmitted to the processor. Only if the second access is also unsuccessful, does the data need to be fetched from main memory. After the data is sent to the processor, either from S2 or from main memory, the data in locations S1 and S2 are swapped to allow the most recently used data to be accessed first. If another memory access does not closely follow, the swapping can be done without making the processor wait.

To understand the advantages of a hash-rehash cache, we must look beyond the first-level miss rate. Instead, we propose a simple model of the memory system that allows us to assign costs for a first-level miss satisfied by a rehash hit and a miss satisfied by a main memory reference. The processor gets the data in one cycle on a first-time cache access hit. An additional cycle is required if the data is present in S2 and two more cycles are required to swap the data in S1 and S2. If the processor is allowed to proceed during the swapping operation half the time, the average number of extra cycles the processor has to wait for the second time access is two cycles. A main memory access takes 20 processor cycles to fetch 16 bytes (assuming no fetch bypass). As an example, for the MUL3 trace, in a 256K-byte cache, the probability of a first-time miss is 0.71% and that of a second-time miss is 73% yielding a net miss rate of 0.52%. The average access time is given by, $T = 1 + 0.0071 * 2 + 0.0071 * 0.73 * 20$, or 1.118 cycles.

Figure 6.11 compares the miss rates of the hashing scheme and the hash-rehash cache with a direct-mapped cache and a two-way set-associative cache. Table 6.2 also compares the performance in terms of average memory access time. The average access time of the hashing scheme is better than a direct-mapped cache, though not as good as a two-way set-associative cache. A hash-rehash cache and a cache with set-size two have similar miss rates, but its average access time is greater. A set-associative cache, however, has the additional drawbacks that it is more complex, and may require stretching the basic clock cycle to accommodate the extra associative compare and multiplex. The hash-rehash cache looks more attractive when the traffic (proportional to the miss rate) generated by the respective schemes is considered. For the 256K-byte

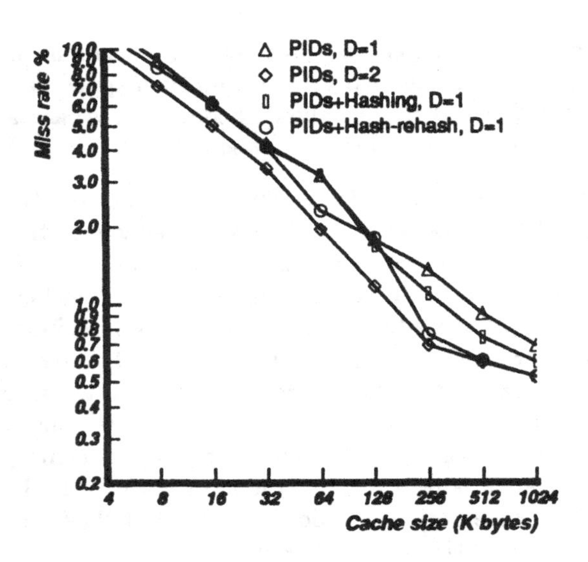

Figure 6.11: Miss rates of hashing schemes. All statistics assume warm-start. Trace is MUL3, block size is 16 bytes and D is set size.

cache, the hash-rehash scheme generates 44% less traffic than a direct-mapped cache.

6.7.3 Split Caches

Multiprogramming deteriorates cache performance by increasing the interference component of misses. Code and data interaction is another source of interference, which if eliminated might prove beneficial in reducing the miss rate.

Cache size (bytes)	Set size = 1		Set size = 2		Hashing		Hash-rehash	
	m	T	m	T	m	T	m	T
64K	3.19	1.637	1.96	1.392	3.17	1.634	2.31	1.539
256K	1.36	1.272	0.69	1.139	1.10	1.219	0.76	1.181
1M	0.69	1.138	0.52	1.105	0.59	1.119	0.52	1.118

Table 6.2: Performance of a direct-mapped hashing and hash-rehash cache for MUL3. Block size is 16 bytes. m denotes cache miss rate, and T denotes average memory access time in cycles.

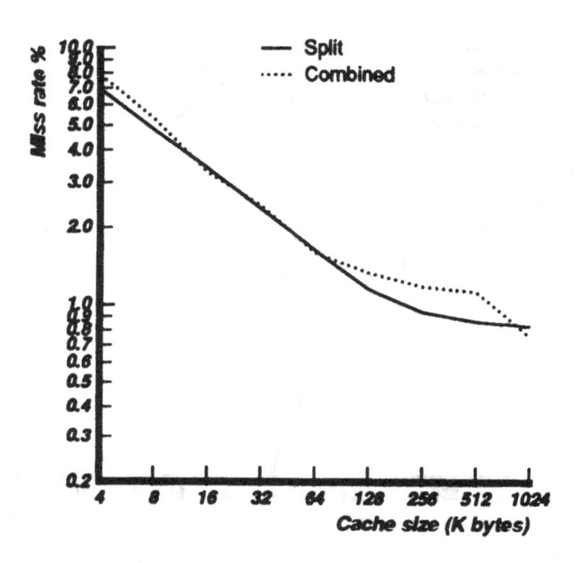

Figure 6.12: Split instruction and data caches for uniprogramming. Set size is one and block size is 16 bytes.

Split caches are a way of achieving this. A study of split caches is also interesting because a number of current systems use split caches to obtain higher cache bandwidth and one would like to know their multiprogramming performance. Also, we would like to analyze the impact of hashing on split cache performance. All caches considered in this section are direct mapped with block size 16 bytes.

For reference, we plot the effect of cache splitting between instructions and data for uniprogramming in Figure 6.12. The performance is similar except when the cache is between 128K and 512K bytes, where a split cache is decidedly superior. The increased miss rate can be attributed to collisions between instructions and data that are nonexistent in split caches and are resolved by a unified cache larger than 512K bytes.

Figure 6.13(a) depicts the miss rate of a direct-mapped split cache for instructions and data. We observe that split caches perform as well as unified caches for most cases. These are similar to the results of Haikala and Kutvonen [34] for uniprogramming workloads. Figure 6.13(b) shows the corresponding miss rates assuming that hashing (as described earlier) is used. It can be seen that hashing influences both split and unified caches positively.

Figure 6.14(a) depicts the miss rate of a two-way set-associative split cache for instructions and data, and Figure 6.14(b) shows the corresponding miss rates

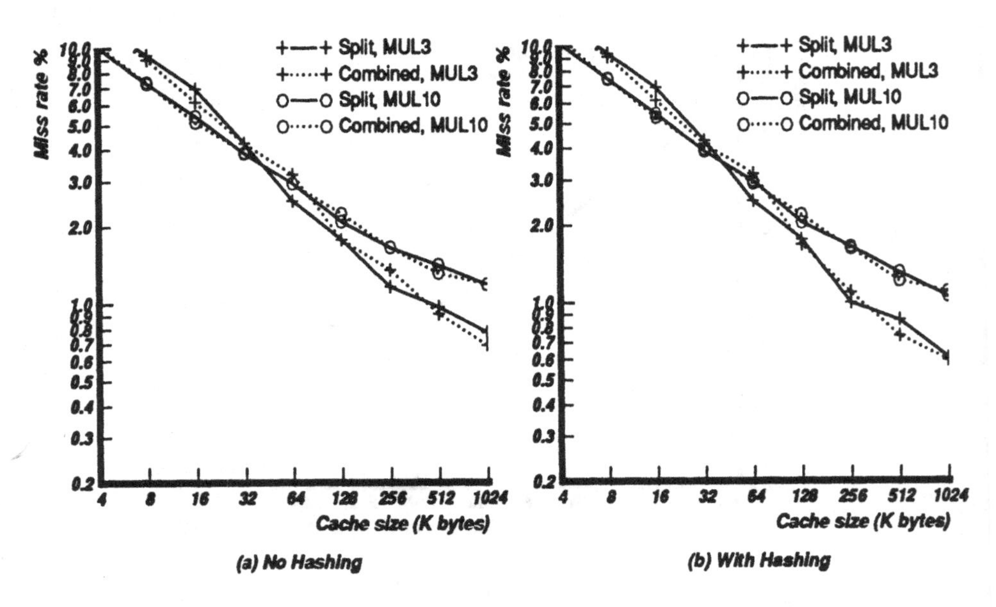

Figure 6.13: Split instruction and data caches for multiprogramming. Miss rates are warm start. Set size is one and block size is 16 bytes.

with hashing. As for direct-mapped caches, the results for split and unified caches are very similar.

This chapter showed that multiprogramming deteriorates cache performance. The impact is less severe in large physical caches and caches with process identifiers, when system references are shared across context switches. Hashing or rehashing techniques can improve the performance of large caches; unified and split caches for instructions and data perform equally well.

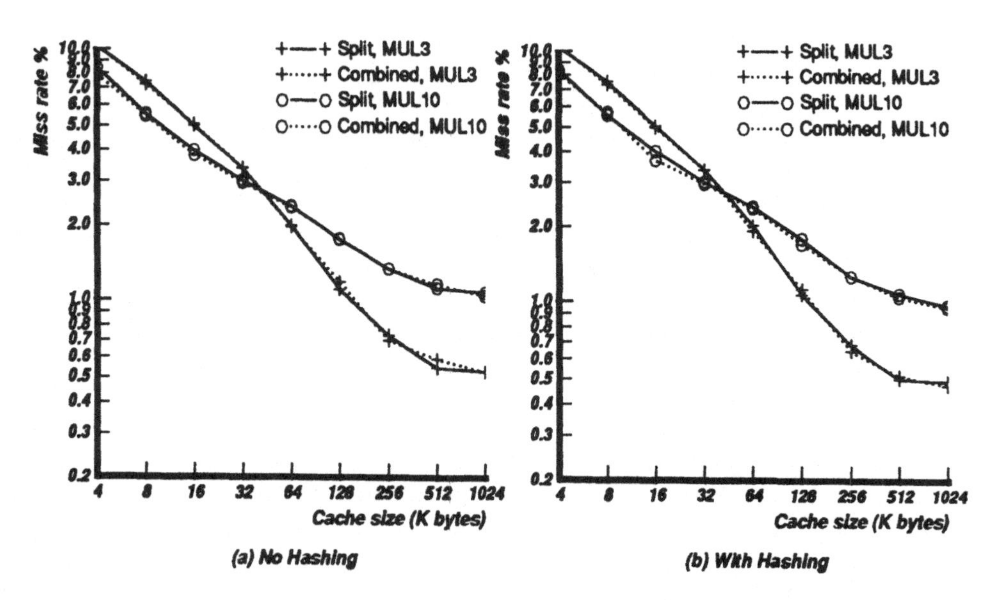

Figure 6.14: Split instruction and data caches for multiprogramming. Miss rates are warm start. Set size is two and block size is 16 bytes.

Chapter 7

Multiprocessor Cache Analysis

In recent times multiprocessing has become a popular means of achieving performance levels that can far exceed those of single processors. The design of high-performance multiprocessors necessitates a careful analysis of the memory system performance of parallel programs. The common theme of this section is the increased understanding of the dynamics of large writeback caches in multiple processors with shared memory. The multiprocessor extension of ATUM for gathering multiprocessor traces and its implementation on a VAX 8350 multiprocessor is first described. Because the resulting parallel traces are dissimilar to the traces used in our single processor studies, and since we would like isolate the effects of multiprocessing on cache performance from the effects of multiprogramming, we will first repeat some single processor experiments with the new traces, and compare the effect of cache interference between multiple processes in both physical-addressed and virtual-addressed caches. Such a study is possible with the extended ATUM scheme because a complete virtual to physical address map is contained in the traces. The performance degradation due to cache interference between multiple processors is then analyzed. The improvement in cache performance if process migration is disallowed is evaluated. We also study semaphore usage and its effect on cache performance.

7.1 Tracing Multiprocessors

The analysis and design of high-performance computers has benefited greatly from the availability of realistic address traces, such as those obtained through ATUM, to drive simulation models. Typical examples of the use of address traces include the analysis of instruction sets, memory hierarchies, branch strategies, pipeline organization, and uniprocessor caches. Unfortunately, due to the difficulty of data collection on multiprocessors, and in fact due to the unavailability of instrumentable multiprocessors, these address traces were limited to single processors. Lacking multiprocessor trace data, researchers had to limit themselves to using analytical models or had to build hardware to test ideas and evaluate design choices. Even in the single processor case, the availability of only small samples of address traces made it hard to estimate long term or steady-state performance, for example in the study of large caches.

We extended the single processor ATUM tracing facility to allow the capture of large address traces of multiprocessors. In ATUM, the microcode of a machine is modified to record the addresses of the memory references as a side effect of normal execution. The addresses were recorded in a reserved portion of main memory, and periodically transferred to disk. Although limited to single processors, this version of ATUM did capture complete operating system traces of multitasking workloads.

The extended tracing method, called ATUM-2, uses the same basic method of tracing, but can work in a multiprocessor environment [72]. ATUM-2 has definite advantages over other tracing schemes: it captured operating system and multiprogramming behavior, it did not slow the machine down drastically (the slowdown is roughly a factor of 20) and it recorded addresses at their full granularity, and not at the block or page level. Not unimportant was the fact that the machine that ATUM-2 was implemented for – a VAX 8350 – supported several multiprocessing operating systems and there were several large parallel applications available. One of the limitations in our traces, however, is that ATUM-2 supports only a maximum of 4 CPUs.

The address tracing has been implemented on a VAX 8350. Appendix E describes the ATUM-2 tracing facility in more detail. The ATUM-2 microcode patches modify the normal microcode so that the addresses touched by the processors are stashed away in a reserved portion of memory. Access to the trace memory is via a pointer that is itself stored in a known location in the beginning portion of the trace memory. The operating system has no knowledge of this trace memory and so all accesses to this memory have to be via physical addresses. The microcode also writes out all of the instruction opcodes and specifiers (not just their addresses) used by the processor. This helps in later analysis, and in expanding complex VAX instruction memory references from the limited amount of information recorded by the microcode.

The user controls through tracing a high-level (Pascal, C) program that executes the reserved VAX extended function call (XFC) instruction [91] with an argument in a register. The XFC instruction is patched so that the microcode of the processor executes a set of actions that can change tracing state depending on the input parameter in a given register. As in ATUM, the possible tracing state changes include starting tracing, stopping tracing, or transferring data out of the trace memory to a file. When tracing is on, the machine slows down by about a factor of 20 in ATUM-2.

ATUM-2 records the addresses of memory references of multiple CPUs. In addition, ATUM-2 records some other useful information. For example, the virtual-to-physical address translation is recorded in a translation lookaside buffer (TLB) miss. The availability of the translation allows a postprocessor to later generate a physical address trace from the virtual trace. The physical address traces are valuable in that they can provide accurate estimates of physical cache performance. Perhaps a more important benefit of having the knowledge of physical addresses is that they provide the key piece of information necessary to detect when two processes share data. There is often no way of knowing from the virtual address trace alone when sharing happens.

7.2 Characteristics of Traces

A number of large traces of several parallel applications running under various operating systems were gathered via the ATUM-2 microcode trace facility. These traces were post-processed to recreate the actual sequence of virtual addresses issued by each VAX instruction with some small number of systematically missing references (such as the manipulation of the backward link in queue instructions). An almost-complete copy of the actual instruction stream is contained in each trace.

In the multiprocessor ATUM-2 traces, each trace record is five bytes long: a type byte followed by a four-byte entry. The type byte denotes the processor number and the type of the following entry, such as an instruction address, data read or write with the length of the data field accessed, a process identifier etc.

The types include RB (read byte), RW (read word), RL (read long), RQ (read quad), RO (read octa); WB..WO are corresponding write types; MB..MO are reads followed by writes; IMB..IMO are interlocked reads followed by writes.

CPU #	Entry Type	Virtual Address	Comment
1	IFETCH	0000021F	Instr. fetch, CPU 1
1	IFETCH	00000222	
0	IFETCH	8000A0C8	Instr. fetch, CPU 0
1	IFETCH	00000225	
0	IFETCH	8000A0CF	
0	IFETCH	8000A0D0	
1	WL	000012FF	Write longword
1	SCBOFF	007BB6C0	Timer interrupt
1	WPTE	B4003DDF	Page table entry
1	TBMISS	801C31FC	TB miss
0	WL	8047D3F4	Write longword
0	IFETCH	8000A0D2	
0	ML	80002B40	Modify longword
0	IFETCH	8000A0DB	
1	IFETCH	801C3978	First instr. of timer

Table 7.1: Excerpt of raw ATUM-2 trace.

Other relevant types are PCBB (process control block base, used as process-ID); RPTE, WPTE, TBMISS for address translation information; IFETCH for instruction fetch and IBYTE for instruction stream recording.

Each trace consists of a number of interleaved reference streams from up to four CPUs. Each instruction fetch reference gives the byte address of the instruction opcode, and each data reference gives the byte address of the lowest-numbered byte of data, plus the data length (1, 2, 4, 8, or 16 bytes). The addresses are typically not aligned on memory-word boundaries, as you can see in the excerpt of a raw ATUM-2 trace, Table 7.1.

We traced several operating systems: VMS, Ultrix[1] and MACH [10]. The traces were done on experimental VAX 8350 configurations that included 1, 2, 3, and 4 CPUs. Table D.4 in Appendix D summarizes the 10 traces analyzed in various parts of this multiprocessor cache analysis.

ABAQUS is a parallel finite-element analysis program hand-decomposed to run multiple processes, one per CPU, operating on a large shared matrix structure. CAYENNE is a parallel version of SPICE. JUN9 is a batch multiprogramming workload, with no shared data beside the operating system. SITES1 is a very stylized trace of a network loopback exerciser. DHRY is a trace of the C Dhrystone benchmark, with a substantial amount of background network traffic.

[1] VMS and Ultrix are trademarks of Digital Equipment Corporation.

16-byte blocks
Direct mapped
Physically addressed unless otherwise stated
Writeback
4KByte ... 1024KByte total size

Table 7.2: Cache configuration.

MAKEX is a trace of two X-windows network processes plus two batch jobs, a disk copy and a make. THOR is a parallel logic simulator written by Larry Soule at Stanford. PERO is a parallel routing program for VLSI layout written by Jonathan Rose at Stanford. POPS and POPS5 are traces of a parallel rule-based system [32].

7.3 Analysis

The multiprocessor traces yield useful insights on several aspects of multiprocessor architecture. We discuss the behavior of large caches analyzed with traces of large applications captured using ATUM-2. It is clear that large caches are necessary to minimize the bus traffic in multiprocessor organizations that use a single bus as the communication path between the processors and main memory. We analyze large caches both from the point of view of a single processor and from the view of a multiprocessor. The single processor viewpoint gives the minimum amount of bus traffic that will be generated by each processor/cache, and the multiprocessor analysis yields the additional traffic that must be generated due to inter-CPU interference. Handling of locks to improve cache performance in a multiprocessor environment is also addressed.

Additionally, we contrast the performance of large physical and virtual address caches. Virtual caches have better access times by obviating the address translation. We observed that virtual addressing reduces the interference in caches when the multiprogramming level is low; however, virtual caches are more susceptible to increased interference at high multiprogramming levels.

Except as noted in individual sections, the simulations reported below all use the cache configurations given in Table 7.2. We have looked at other cache configurations, such as different block/sub-block sizes and different associativity. For other configurations, the absolute miss rates change but not the relative behavior.

7.3.1 General Methodology

Our overall simulation methodology is as follows. All our results (excluding virtual cache performance) need physical address traces. For these results, the virtual address traces were post-processed to convert all references to physical addresses; an almost-complete mapping is contained in each trace from the TLB-miss entries. Further postprocessing for particular experiments is described in the respective experiment sections.

We used these traces to simulate individual caches for each CPU, with misses on a single shared-memory bus. We assumed a simple writeback cache coherence protocol using block ownership:

1. Any number of caches may contain read-only of a block.
2. At most one cache may contain a write-owned (dirty) copy of a block, with no read-only copies in other caches.
3. A read miss causes a (16-byte) block read on the shared memory bus. Such a read does not affect caches holding read-only copies of the block, but triggers a writeback from a cache holding the block write-owned (that cache retains a read-only copy).
4. A write miss causes a block ownership read on the shared memory bus. An ownership read triggers an invalidate in caches holding read-only copies of the block. An ownership read triggers a writeback and invalidate in a cache holding a write-owned copy of the block.
5. Bus traffic consists entirely of reads, ownership reads, and writebacks.

This protocol does no cache-to-cache transfers, but instead moves a block from one cache to memory, then from memory to the other cache. A more sophisticated protocol could be used, but cannot be justified unless analysis of a simple protocol shows performance bottlenecks. For some other methods of maintaining cache coherence and their performance analysis see for example [31, 88, 3].

All simulations start with empty (cold) caches, and leave dirty blocks in caches at the end. The effects of these simplifications roughly cancel, and our traces are long enough to make the distortion small for cache sizes up to 256KB. All simulations just truncate addresses to a multiple of the block size. A more careful simulation of converting each unaligned reference to multiple cache-block references and converting sequential instruction fetches to the minimal number of cache references (as standard instruction prefetching hardware does) gives almost-identical results.

As a baseline, each trace was simulated against caches sizes of 4KB, 16KB, 64KB, 256KB, and 1024KB. For each simulation, the amount of memory-bus traffic in a multi-CPU environment was counted. Figure 7.1 shows the resulting bandwidth demands for four traces at the five cache sizes. The Y-axis is in units of megabytes of bus bandwidth per million references, reflecting our focus on shared memory as a performance bottleneck. Dividing by the 16-byte block size gives the miss rate:[2]

$$0.16\ MB/Mref = 1\%\ cache\ miss\ rate$$

A number of computer architectures generate about a million cache references per million instructions, including the VAX architecture if the VAX-11/780 is taken to be a "1 MIPS" machine. Thus, in terms of memory-bus bandwidth,

$$1\ MB/Mref = 1\ MB/sec\ per\ MIPS$$

The above two relationships can be used to convert our results to other contexts.

7.3.2 Multiprocess Interference in Large Virtual and Physical Caches

What happens to cache blocks used by process X when processes Y, Z, etc. are running? The model is that a set of processes are available to run, one at a time. Each process runs for some execution interval, then a context switch to another process occurs. Eventually, each process runs for many intervals. One would expect blocks used by process X to be replaced eventually by blocks from the other processes. How quickly does this occur, and how is it related to the size of the cache?

Methodology: Four ATUM multi-CPU traces contain a significant amount of switching between processes: Abaqus, Cayenne, Jun9, and Makex (see Table D.4 for trace details). Each of these was simulated twice for various cache sizes. The first simulation is of the full trace with each execution interval run in the recorded order, but one at a time on a single CPU to remove inter-CPU interference (inter-CPU interference is discussed in the next section). The second simulation artificially runs all references from process 1, then all references from process 2, etc., again one at a time on a single CPU. The cache is not

[2] This miss rate is approximate because writebacks are also included in the traffic numbers. The writeback rate (writebacks/total misses) ranges between 10% and 25%.

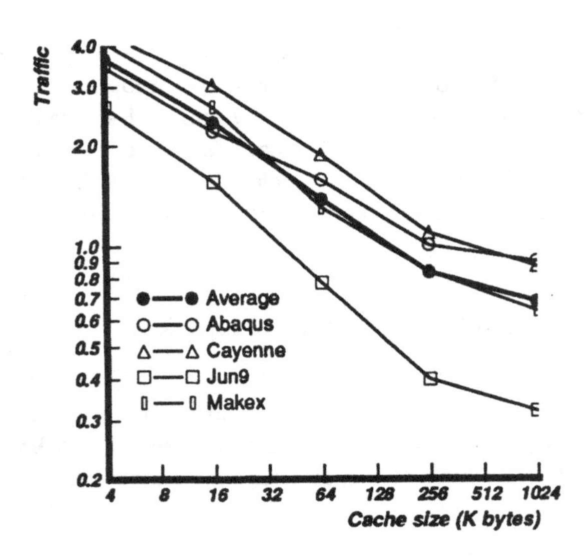

Figure 7.1: Baseline traffic rates in physical-addressed caches. Block is 16 bytes and caches are direct-mapped.

cleared between process switches, allowing later processes to take advantage of the system blocks left behind in the cache by the earlier processes. A different model, such as that used in our single processor cache studies in the previous chapters, might disallow later processes from using the system blocks used by earlier processes, but does not significantly change our results.

The first simulation has interference between processes: execution intervals for process X are interspersed with other processes. The total miss rate includes intrinsic misses for each process, plus traffic caused by inter-process interference.

The second simulation has no interference between processes: the number of blocks in the cache used by the current process monotonically increases. Only the intrinsic cache-miss rate of the current process is seen. The difference in traffic rates between the two simulations is due to inter-process interference.

We first focus on physical caches and then compare these results with those for virtual caches. For brevity, we will henceforth present average results for the four traces.

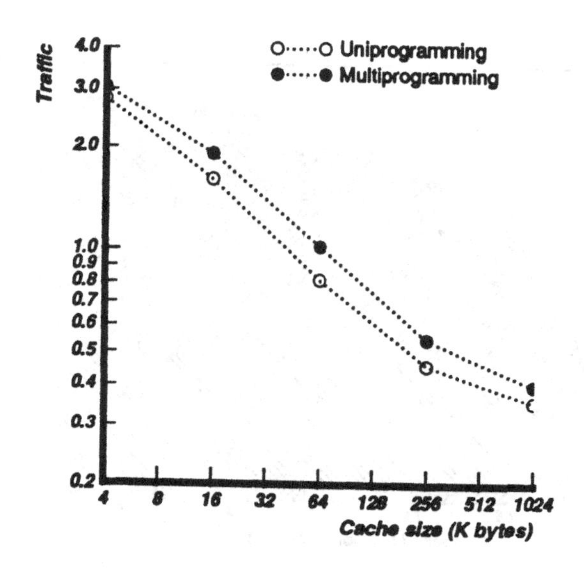

Figure 7.2: Inter-process interference in physical caches.

Physical-Address Caches

Figure 7.2 shows the average differences for four traces. The solid circles denote the first simulation with inter-process interference, and open circles the second simulation, with no interference. In small caches (4KB-16KB), inter-process interference is relatively low. For caches 64KB...256KB, interference grows to be about 20% of all memory traffic, then declines again for caches of 1MB (and presumably larger).

Figures 7.3 and 7.4 show the cache occupancy versus time for the two Cayenne simulations with a 256KB cache. In both figures, the vertical axis shows how much of the cache is used by each process, and the horizontal axis shows total number of memory references simulated. Each cache block is either empty, assigned to a single process 1..8, or "shared." A cache block is assigned to a single process if all references to it have been only from that process. A cache block is assigned "shared" if references to it have occurred in two or more processes. The graphs show all blocks belonging to process 1 at the bottom, then processes 2, 3, etc., and finally the shared blocks are denoted by the cross-hatched section at the top of the graph.

At 256KB, the traces show over 20% savings in memory traffic (misses and writebacks) if there is no inter-process interference. Thus, substantially reducing inter-process interference could allow the useful addition of a 5th processor

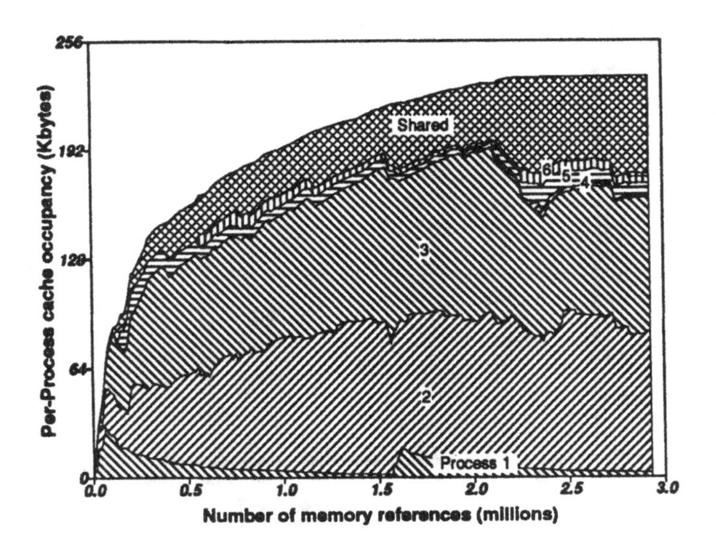

Figure 7.3: Cache occupancy vs. time, no sorting. Process 1 blocks are shown as the hashed region at the bottom, then processes 2, 3, etc., and shared blocks as the cross-hatched section at the top of the graph. Cache size is 256KB.

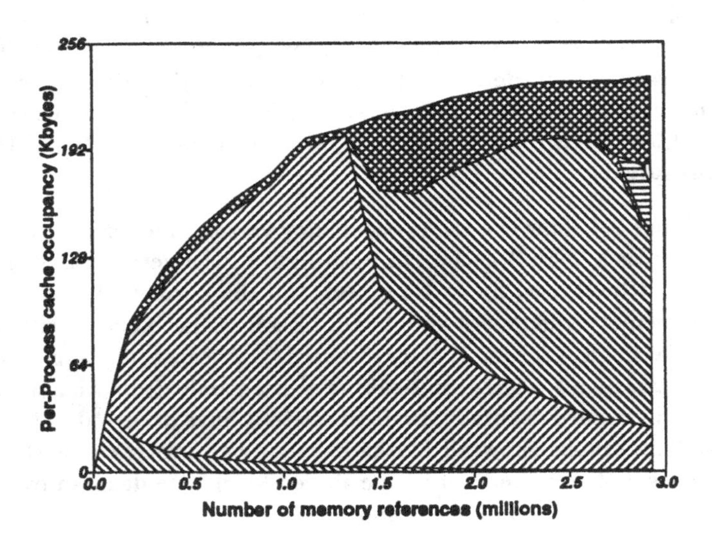

Figure 7.4: Cache occupancy vs. time, processes sorted. Cache size is 256KB.

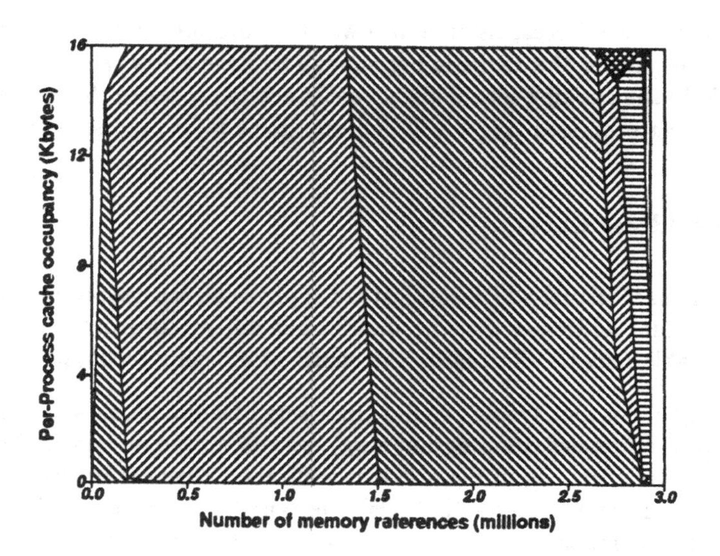

Figure 7.5: Cache occupancy vs. time, processes sorted. Cache size is 16KB.

to a memory-bandwidth-limited 4-processor configuration. Taking a closer look at inter-process interference in Figures 7.3 and 7.4, we see that a process in Cayenne uses about a fourth of the cache for its data in a multiprogramming situation, while over two-thirds of the cache in a uniprogramming case. In other words, multiprogramming-induced interference has the effect of reducing the net cache size seen by a given process.

The rate of decline in cache occupancy by process X while the following processes are running shows the long-term effect of the interference. At 256KB, the Cayenne trace shows approximate exponential decay of the number of cache blocks private to a given process, with a half-life of about 150K instructions. This data indicates that if the Cayenne process were to continue execution on the same CPU after being switched out for a period corresponding to the execution of about 150K instruction, it will still find half its data in the cache. (The Jun9 trace shows a 256KB cache never filling up, and an exponential decay half-life of about 100K instructions.)

Small caches behave differently. At 16KB, the same Cayenne trace has very sharp decay, as shown in Figure 7.5. Thus, we have some preliminary evidence to support the intuitive feel that for small caches almost nothing useful is left upon return from a context switch, while for large caches just the opposite is true.

Conclusions: Inter-process interference will be a significant source of memory-bus traffic whenever the cache is big enough to have a low miss rate, but too small to hold the working sets of all currently-active processes. Software designs that run fewer processes longer will help minimize inter-process interference.

Virtual-Address Caches

What happens if virtual addresses, instead of physical, are used to index caches? Because virtual addresses may be distributed differently from physical ones, memory traffic may be affected by the choice of indexing technique.

Methodology: For four traces, we did three sets of simulations with virtual addresses. In the first set (uniprogramming), we ran all the references for process 1, then process 2, etc., as in the previous section on physical addressing. In the second (multiprogramming with PIDs), we ran the processes in their natural order, using virtual address plus process identifier (PID) to form the cache tags. Introducing the PID lets virtual address A in process 1 be distinguished from virtual address A in process 2. The third set of simulations (multiprogramming with PIDs and hash) is like the second, except the tags are a hash of the virtual address and the PID. This tends to place address A from process 1 and address A from process 2 into different cache blocks, even for a direct-mapped cache.

Caveat on synonyms in virtual address caches: We assume that when an object is shared, it is assigned the *same virtual address* in all the processes. This happens to be the case in our current traces. When process migration takes place, synonyms in the cache can be obviated if a shared object flushes the copy left there by a previous process. A direct-mapped virtual cache ensures this but a virtual set-associative cache does not. Additionally, hashing can place the same shared block of two processes in different rows. Thus our hashing results are not completely accurate.

Figure 7.6 shows cache traffic for uniprogrammed and multiprogrammed virtual caches (with and without hashing), and Figure 7.7 compares physical and virtual cache performance. In large, direct-mapped, virtual caches, the disparity between uniprogramming and multiprogramming traffic increased tremendously with cache size. Consequently, large virtual caches seem to perform poorly compared to physical caches. However, the results for 4-way set-associative virtual and physical caches were similar (results not shown here).

Our hypothesis for the poor performance of the direct-mapped virtual cache is that in multi-CPU traces, several parallel processes of a given application have similar basic code and memory reference patterns. So, the references of the various processes of a parallel application in a multi-CPU environment will collide

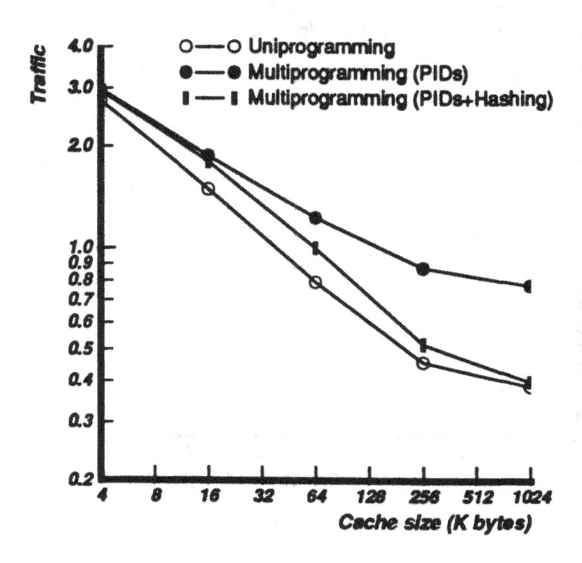

Figure 7.6: Inter-process interference in virtual caches.

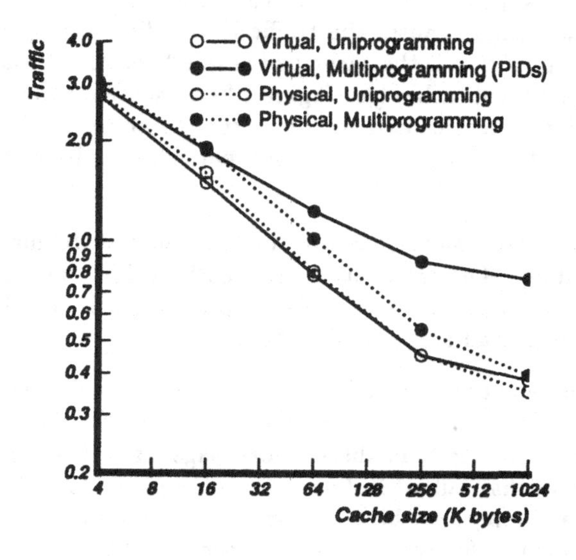

Figure 7.7: Virtual vs. physical addressing.

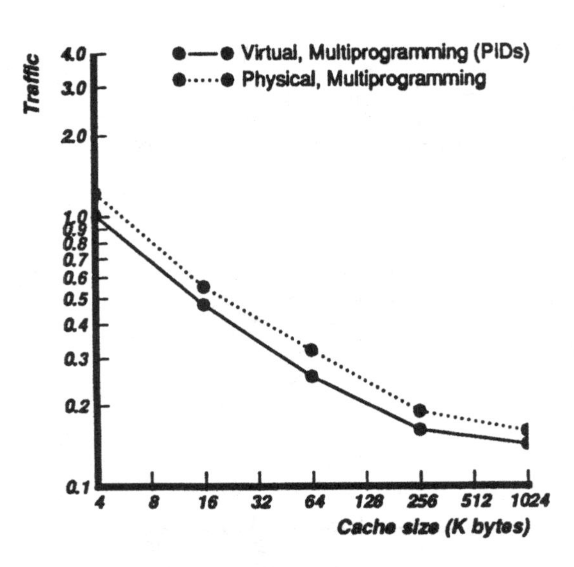

Figure 7.8: Virtual vs. physical addressing in caches for workloads with few context swaps.

severely in a direct-mapped virtual address cache, if process migration takes place. Observe that hashing causes the traffic in the direct-mapped cache to drop significantly implying that the cache had severe "hot-spots" that hashing reduced. Similarly, physical caches (see Figure 7.2) do not show these hot-spots because of the hashing effect caused by the virtual to physical address translation. Therefore, virtual caches with hashing performs similarly to physical caches.

We also experimented with workloads with little context switching and negligible process migration. The traces used are POPS, THOR, and PERO (see Table D.4 for details). The performance of multiprogrammed virtual and physical caches for this workload are plotted in Figure 7.8.

For these traces, physical caches do slightly *worse* than virtual. The reason for this difference is subtle. Consider caches where the product of the number of sets and block size is greater than the memory page size. Then, in a virtual cache, program blocks that fall into adjacent memory pages cannot occupy the same cache block (assuming that bit selection is the method of indexing used), while there is a potential for collision in a physical cache. Thus, a physical cache tends to perform better than a virtual address cache in a high context-switching environment, while a virtual address cache is likely to be superior for low multiprogramming levels.

7.3.3 Analysis of Interference Between Multiple Processors

What happens to cache blocks used by CPU X when CPUs Y, Z, etc. are also running? The model is that each CPU has its own private cache, and that some form of bus watching [31] invalidates a block in a cache when some other processor writes to that block. One would expect blocks used by CPU X that contain shared data to be displaced eventually by references from the other CPUs, while blocks that contain read-only data/instructions and blocks that contain only private data never to be displaced. How much interference is there, and how is it related to the size of the cache?

Traditionally, single-process small-cache simulations have ignored this effect. This approximation becomes less realistic as multiprocessor shared-data configurations become more common. The analysis here suggests better approximations for large caches.

Methodology: Four of the ATUM multi-CPU traces contain a significant amount of multiprocessor interference: Abaqus, Cayenne, Jun9, and Makex. Each of these was simulated twice for various cache sizes. The first simulation is of the full trace in the recorded execution order. The second simulation artificially runs all references from CPU 0, then all references from CPU 1, etc.

The first simulation has normal amounts of interference: intrinsic misses plus extrinsic misses caused by the other CPUs. The second simulation has no interference between CPUs. The difference in number of cache misses between the two runs shows the effect of multi-CPU interference. Figure 7.9 shows the differences for four traces. The solid circles are the first simulation with inter-CPU interference, and the open circles are the second simulation with no interference.

Conclusions: The inter-CPU interference appears to grow without bound as the cache size increases. At 256KB, the average memory bandwidth savings (misses plus writebacks) is 17% if there is no inter-CPU interference. At 1MB, the average savings is 26%. As the cache size increases, the intrinsic cache-miss rates become very low, while the inter-CPU interference traffic remains essentially constant (the same number of accesses to shared variables occur per unit time). Thus, the inter-CPU interference becomes a substantial proportion of all the memory traffic.

Analysis of Multiprocessor Interference with Process Affinity

What happens to cache miss rates when each process is redispatched only on the CPU it previously ran on? The model is that each CPU has its own private

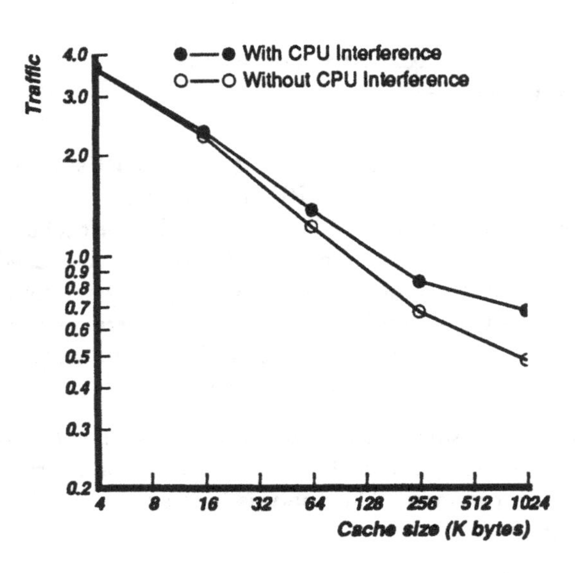

Figure 7.9: Impact of inter-CPU interference in direct-mapped caches. Solid circles are with inter-CPU interference and open circles are without.

cache, and that an operating system dispatching algorithm may dispatch a process on any available CPU, or may deliberately bias the choice so that with high probability a given process runs on the same CPU each time it runs.

One would expect that migrating a process from one CPU to another would result a number of misses in the second CPU's cache to (re)load blocks that had previously been in use in the other cache, plus a number of forced invalidates and writebacks in the first CPU's cache as writes occur to blocks that were left there. How much interference is there from process migration, and how is it related to the size of the cache? How much performance could be gained by implementing a form of process affinity?

Methodology: Four of the ATUM multi-CPU traces contain a significant amount of multiprocessor dispatching: Abaqus, Cayenne, Jun9, and Makex. Just the user-mode references from each of these was simulated twice for various cache sizes. The first simulation is of the full trace in the recorded execution order. To approximate the effect of process affinity, the second simulation artificially runs all references from process N on CPU = (N mod K), where K = number of CPUs. System-mode references were excluded because our current asymmetrical multiprocessing traces execute a large fraction of the operating system code on CPU 0. Artificially redistributing these system references across multiple CPUs would actually increase miss traffic, and is not a valid approxi-

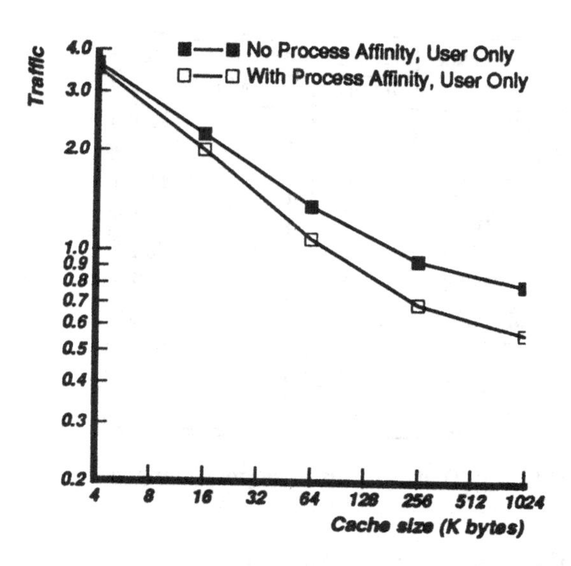

Figure 7.10: Impact of process migration. Solid squares are with process migration effects and open squares are without.

mation of true process affinity.

The first simulation has normal amounts of migration interference: intrinsic misses plus extrinsic misses caused by the migration. The second simulation has no migration, and hence no migration-induced memory traffic. The difference in traffic between the two runs shows the effect of process affinity. Figure 7.10 shows the differences for four traces. The solid circles are the first simulation with no affinity, and the open circles are the second simulation with affinity.

Conclusions: Process migration causes increasing amounts of inter-CPU interference as caches get larger. Process migration means that N processes contend for space in each CPU's cache, instead on N/K processes, where K is number of CPUs. Thus, migration increases the inter-process interference. Process migration also means that a large number of read-only blocks end up with multiple copies in multiple caches (not shown here), effectively reducing the total system cache size. Therefore, if bus traffic is to be minimized, operating systems should implement process affinity.

Trace	Accesses on same CPU	
	Average	Maximum
ABAQUS	2.48	113
CAYENNE	3.45	550
THOR	2.81	416
DHRY	6.61	194
PERO	9.83	254
JUN9	3.31	102
MAKEX	6.88	138
POPS1	2.61	691
POPS5	2.19	264
SITES1	80.29	204

Table 7.3: Distribution of segment lengths.

7.3.4 Blocks Containing Semaphores

Should writeback cache algorithms differ for semaphores? The model is that each CPU has its own private writeback cache, and that cross-CPU semaphores are accessed via atomic read-modify-write instructions.

A cache design might treat these semaphore accesses differently if their access behavior is sufficiently different from normal data accesses. In particular, *if* these semaphores are hardly ever accessed twice in a row on the same CPU, and the normal cache is a writeback cache, almost every semaphore access will miss and will cause both a block read and a block writeback. This might use a lot of bus bandwidth to change just one bit, especially for large cache blocks. In such a case, it might be more efficient not to cache semaphores at all, and always access them directly from memory.

Methodology: Ten of the ATUM multi-CPU traces contain a significant amount of multiprocessor dispatching: Abaqus, Cayenne, THOR, Dhry, PERO, Jun9, Makex, Pops1, Pops5, and Sites1. For each trace, every cache block touched by an interlocked access (stemming from a VAX interlocked instruction such as branch on bit set and set interlocked, BBSSI) is marked, and a subset trace created containing only references from instructions that access those blocks.

All accesses to a given interlocked-access cache block are then examined in order, and broken into segments of accesses all by the same CPU. The distribution of the segment lengths is given in Table 7.3.

For a given semaphore, most of the traces show at least a pair of accesses (typically BBSSI/BBCCI) executed together on one CPU, without interleaved accesses from other CPUs. This case typifies a low level of contention for shared resources. There are still a number of single accesses, and these are often concentrated on a small number of semaphores. A little effort cutting down the frequency of semaphore access for just a few key semaphores can pay off in longer sequences of accesses on the same CPU. For example, in the Jun9 trace, a single operating-system semaphore accounts for most of the length-one sequences, with alternating accesses between CPU 0 and CPU 1. Removing this semaphore from consideration raises the average run length from 3.31 to 9.75.

Similarly, in the Abaqus trace, a single user semaphore accounts for the vast majority of length-one sequences. Doing, say, twice as much work between accesses to this software lock would cut down on thrashing the associated cache block. In a trace of 520K instructions, that one cache block is invalidated in another CPU's cache about 2500 times, or 1/3 to 1/2 of ALL invalidates for cache sizes from 4KB to 1MB.

The Sites1 trace is from a single CPU, so there is NO contention for cache blocks containing semaphores. In this trace, the average simply reflects the total number of semaphore accesses divided by the total number of semaphores (7). A longer trace would have given a higher average.

Conclusions: For many cache designs, it is probably not worthwhile to special-case semaphore access, at least for small numbers of CPUs. All traces show an average of at least two consecutive accesses by a given CPU before some other CPU forces the block to be invalidated. Semaphore accesses can, however, be a major cause of cache-miss bus traffic, so it is worthwhile to examine software locking designs and minimize actual semaphore use. It can also be important not to put two unrelated semaphores into the same cache block, and in fact not to put ANY unrelated information in the same cache block with a semaphore.

If a large number of CPUs are busy-waiting on the same semaphore, the form of the busy-wait loop becomes important. If the waiting is done with a read-modify-write instruction (such as BBSSI, or the IBM 370 test and set), then almost every semaphore access will cause a dirty block to transfer from on CPU's cache to another, even though the semaphore value is not in fact changing (stays locked). In this case, it is better to precede the read-modify-write instruction with a read-only loop to wait for an unlocked semaphore value (e.g., a test-and-test&set sequence).

Chapter 8

Conclusions and Suggestions for Future Work

8.1 Concluding Remarks

We began this research with several goals: The main aim was to accurately characterize cache performance with particular attention to large caches in realistic environments. This required more accurate and efficient cache analysis techniques than were available earlier, and also reliable trace data to derive accurate cache performance statistics.

We proposed a new data collection scheme called ATUM that captures distortion free traces of multitasking operating system workloads. An extended ATUM facility also captures multiprocessor address traces. Advances have also been made in cache evaluation techniques. We developed an analytical cache model, a new appropach to cold-start and warm-start anaysis, a trace sampling and trace stitching technique, and a trace compaction strategy. We used these techniques to investigate the effects of system references, multiprogramming, and multiprocessing on the performance of large caches.

The traces obtained using ATUM proved invaluable in all our cache studies. By making a few changes to the microcode of a machine, we were able to write out to main memory all the memory addresses used by the processor.

Because ATUM captured high-fidelity multiprocessor traces that included operating system, interrupt, and multiprogramming activity, we were able to accurately characterize the performance of large caches for realistic workloads. The ATUM traces also helped validate our trace sampling methodology and the analytical cache model.

The trace sampling method, the analytical cache model, and the trace compaction scheme tackled the problem of efficient and accurate analysis of large caches. The analytical cache model combines measurement and analysis to yield quick estimates of cache performance for a wide range of cache parameters. The basic model is very simple; it uses three measured parameters: the average working set for a time window T, the total working set of the trace, and the collision rate c, to predict cache miss rates for a constant block size. With an additional measurement to characterize run lengths, block size variations can also be included. In addition to its predictive capability, the model enhances our understanding of cache behavior and program-cache interactions.

Many of the concepts and ideas derived for the mathematical analysis of caches also formed the basis of our trace sampling and trace compaction methodologies. The trace sampling technique, with a thorough understanding of cold-start and warm-start cache behavior, significantly speeds up cache simulations. We proposed that the start-up period be defined as the period between an initially empty cache to when either the cache fills up or the workload working set is resident in the cache – whichever happens first. In addition to speeding up cache performance studies, the cold-start and warm-start analyses should help in designing steady-state simulation experiments without the introduction of error due to short trace lengths. We also investigated conditions under which several short trace samples of a given workload can be catenated to yield a longer trace to obtain accurate steady state results.

The trace samples can be further compacted for efficient simulation and trace storage with a small loss in the accuracy of cache performance prediction. Our method extends previous compaction techniques to exploit spatial locality in addition to using temporal locality to achieve trace compactions of over an order of magnitude.

Our performance experiments using ATUM trace samples enhanced our understanding of the effects of system references and multitasking on cache performance. In particular, our analyses of large caches have produced new insights into their behavior not evident from extrapolating the characteristics of small caches. The disparity in our uniprogramming results for user workloads and the results for multiprogramming user-plus-system environments indicate the importance of considering multiprogramming effects and the influence of system references for realistic cache performance statistics. Because this divergence only increases as cache sizes increase, the inclusion of these two factors is even more critical for large caches.

We demonstrated that multiprogramming is deleterious to cache performance because the references of different processes interfered with each other. Put another way, the degradation is caused by a larger working set for the multiprogramming workload. To enhance multiprogramming cache performance, process identifiers or PIDs are essential in large virtual-address caches; purging the cache performs abysmally. Predictably, small caches are indifferent to any of the above schemes.

Earlier techniques for modeling multiprogramming activity in the cache were shown to be inaccurate for large caches. Purging caches to take into account context switching in virtual-address caches is reasonable only for small caches; round-robin interleaving, with constant duration time slices, is also inadequate because, in practice, the time duration between process switches varies widely, although the scheduling is more or less cyclic.

Large strides have also been made in our understanding of the influence of system references. System references degrade cache performance considerably for single-user traces due to larger working sets and less repetitiveness than user. Interestingly, system references actually enhance performance when multitasking is taken into account because system references constitute shared memory, thereby amortizing the cost of initially fetching system code and data into the cache between the various processes.

We took a second look at associativity. Our results show that associativity has negligible impact on large caches in a uniprogrammed environment. In a multiprogrammed environment, associativity shows promise; although, associativity has a decreasing impact as cache sizes increase. Furthermore, the marginal utility of increasing associativity is shown to decrease rapidly. In large caches, two-way set-associativity picks up almost all the benefits of full associativity.

Our analysis of multiprocessors with very large caches and several processors showed that, in addition to inter-process interference, inter-processor interference will come to be a dominant source of memory traffic. In such systems reducing the main memory traffic assumes greater importance than just reducing the miss rate. The burden will fall on software, not hardware, designs to minimize this interference. Software design techniques available include process and interrupt-handler affinity, increased times between context switches, increased time between shared-variable writes, and rigorous minimization of unneeded sharing.

Future research in this area will need yet longer traces of yet more processors coupled together. An important conclusion of this research is that consideration should be given to adding simple hardware instrumentation to future CPU designs, to allow more direct measurement of the causes of memory bus or network traffic.

8.2 Suggestions for Future Work

The research presented in this book provides a basis for several further investigations. The ATUM tracing technique can be modified to capture longer trace samples that can help validate our trace sampling and trace stitching procedures. Longer samples can be obtained either by recording trace information at a coarser granularity, or by simply allocating more trace memory. The latter becomes trivial with the availability of denser memory boards. It is also possible to gather time sharing information using remote terminal emulators. This data is useful to study cache performance in a highly interrupted environment.

More importantly, our tracing methods must be extended to yield multiprocessor traces of a much larger number of processors. With this data, we can study memory referencing patterns in large-scale multiprocessors. Accurate evaluation of cache performance in large multiprocessors and the scalability of cache consistency algorithms will also become possible with this data. If the traces contain detailed information on when and how locks were used, future multirocessor cache research can also analyze the effect of synchronization variables on cache performance.

Our work on analytical cache models can be extended to include other caching strategies; for example, prefetching, and more accurate sub-block size characterization. The model can also be generalized to multi-level caches. The multiprogramming cache model can be further tuned to accept context switch intervals from some given distribution. The model can also be extended to include multiprocessor interference.

The model can be used as a basis for further research. The model, or its simplified version, can be incorporated into an optimizing compiler for optimizing cache performance, or to evaluate the tradeoffs in making other kinds of optimizations that might be deleterious to cache performance. For this purpose, the model can be modified to accept even simpler and easy-to-obtain parameters.

Cache performance is significantly different for vector-intensive workloads. Some of the important issues to be looked at include the block size, sub-block size, prefetch strategy, separate caches for vectors, and non-cachable vectors.

Other areas of research include accurate characterization of large caches in time-sharing environments, and where cache traffic includes I/O. With the increasing speed differential between processors and cache memory, multi-level caches are becoming important. Such an environment brings up interesting issues regarding relative sizes and organizations of the caches in various levels of the hierarchy.

As we build progressively larger multiprocessing systems, the network performance of caches and cache consistency algorithms assumes a critically important role. The efficiency of simulation techniques will need to increase, and perhaps, pure simulation methods will have to be replaced by hybrid simulation-analytical techniques. Scalability studies and evaluations of caches in such systems will be feasible once we develop better tracing techniques and evaluation methods, and obtain parallel traces of large numbers of processors and realistic applications.

Appendix A

Sensitivity of the Miss Rate on Time Granule τ

The choice of τ in the cache model has been rather ad hoc; we now examine the sensitivity of the miss rate for uniprogramming to this choice. We will concentrate only on the intrinsic interference component because the sum of the start-up and non-stationary components of the of the miss rate for the entire trace is simply the ratio of the total number of unique references to the total length of the trace and hence does not depend on the choice of the time granule τ. The choice of τ directly affects the parameter u, which is the average number of unique references in a time granule.

The following equation gives the intrinsic miss rate component for direct mapped caches:

$$m(C,t)_{intrinsic} = \frac{c\,[u(B) - S\,P(1)]}{\tau}$$

Replacing the collision rate and $P(1)$ by their respective formulae and gathering the factors that are independent of u into the constant K shows the complete dependence of the intrinsic miss rate component on u:

$$m(C,t)_{intrinsic} = K\,\frac{u(B)}{u(1)}\,\frac{1-\left(1-\frac{1}{S}\right)^{u(B)}}{1-\left(1-\frac{1}{S_0}\right)^{u(1)}}$$

If τ is chosen to be at least as large as the start-up portion of the trace, then variations in τ will not affect the miss rate significantly because u changes very gradually after the start-up region, and the ratio of $u(B)$ and $u(1)$ will be relatively stable.

Since the discussion hinges on the definition of a ***start-up*** period, we will digress a little to analyze some of the common notions of start-up time. Recall that for the purpose of our model the start-up period in a trace is the time (or number of references) required to bring the initial working set of the program into the cache for the first time. This definition is solely a function of the program and independent of the cache organization. Because the initial working set of a program is hard to quantize precisely, estimating the start-up period in a trace is non-trivial.

The ***cold-start*** period is a related term that we used earlier to assess the impact of starting with an empty cache on cache simulation results. This definition is inappropriate in this case because (1) it depends on cache size, (2) in small caches start-up misses can occur even after the cache has been heavily filled, and (3) in large caches, non-stationary misses can occur long before the cache is filled. Section 4.2 gives a detailed discussion of cold-start and warm-start analyses.

A pertinent definition for the start-up period that is not a function of cache size, but solely dependent on the address trace in question is based on the working set model [23] of program behavior. The number of unique blocks used by a process in a time granule increases rapidly as the time granule is increased from zero to some value and increases only gradually thereafter causing working set curves to have a bilinear nature [82]. We will define the ***start-up portion*** to be the region of the working set curve before its knee point. The latter part will then represent the non-stationary region. Figure A.1 shows $u(1)$ as a function of time granule size τ for the benchmark Interconnect Verify. The knee occurs between ten and fifteen thousand references. The dotted line, which is the derivative of the working set curve, is the number of additional blocks accessed for a given increase in granule size. After about 10,000 references the increase in u is small and steady.

There is one caveat, however, in this discussion. For phased programs the working set curve will show slightly different behavior, although the nature of the curve in any one phase is still expected to be the same provided the phases are long enough for the working set model to apply. As before, the start-up period is measured from the working set of the initial phase, and the rest of the first-time misses are swept into the non-stationary category. Traces showing multiple short phases (e.g., for inter-active workloads) may theoretically exhibit very long start-up times; but for such behavior a large portion of the misses

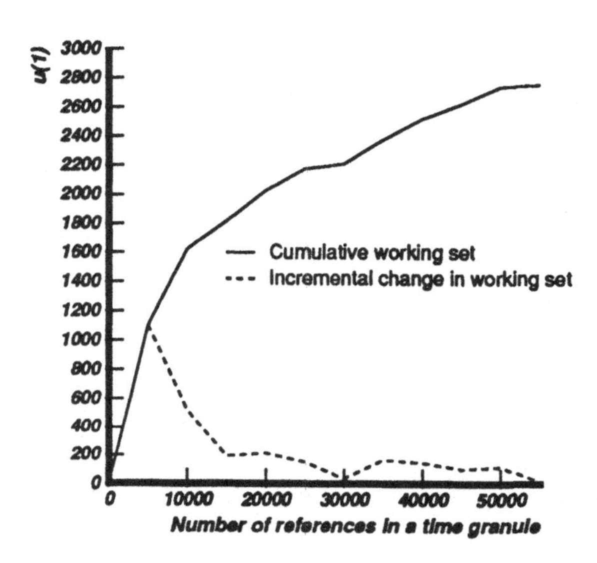

Figure A.1: Number of unique references per time granule, $u(1)$, versus granule size τ.

will be start-up induced anyhow.

Returning to our earlier discussion on the stability of the collision rate, once τ is greater than 10,000 references, increasing it further will cause little change in $u(1)$ and still less in the ratio of $u(B)$ to $u(1)$. Thus, we have showed that choosing τ greater than the start-up period will cause the intrinsic miss rate to be insensitive to changes in τ. For smaller values of τ, u varies enormously and potential for large errors exist. However, since changes proportional to $u(B)$ and $u(1)$ are expected in the numerator and denominator of the intrinsic miss rate equation, the differences should cancel out to first order and the miss rate should be reasonably stable.

Appendix B

Characterization of the Collision Rate c

The intrinsic interference model uses the collision rate c – the ratio of the total number of collisions to the number of colliding blocks – to quantize the dynamic interference component among program blocks. The product of the static number of colliding blocks and the average number of times a block collides, c, gives the average number of misses in the cache due to intrinsic interference in a time granule. The thesis is that c is reasonably stable for caches of different numbers of sets (rows) and block sizes. The collision rate, however, varies with set size (associativity or number of columns) and is not stable when the cache becomes much smaller than the size of the program working set. This section has the following parts to address these issues:

1. Provides an intuitive basis and some measured data for the assumption that c is stable for different cache sizes.

2. Extends c to all cache organizations.

B.1 On the Stability of the Collision Rate

We present the following argument as as intuitive substantiation of the claim that c is constant for most cache sizes and organizations. This is also verified by our measurement data, a sample of which is presented in Table B.1 for

Interconnect Verify. A direct-mapped cache with a block size of 4 bytes is assumed in the ensuing discussion unless otherwise stated.

Recalling, a *collision set* is a set with multiple blocks mapped to it, and a *colliding block* is a block that maps into a colliding set. The average number of collisions per block in a collision set will be an increasing function of the number of blocks present in that set. Clearly, the more the number of blocks in a collision set the greater the probability that a block will be purged by intervening references, and hence greater the collision rate. Therefore, c will show similar behavior to the parameter c' that we define to be the number of colliding blocks in an average collision set. Note that c' is not used to estimate c. In the cache shown in Figure 3.1, $c' = 2.5$.

Equation 3.3 gave the probability that a set has d blocks mapped to it. We repeat the equation here making the approximation that the binomial distribution tends to the Poisson for large u_i and small $(1/S)$:

$$P_i(d) = \frac{e^{-\frac{u_i}{S}} \left(\frac{u_i}{S}\right)^d}{d!} \tag{B.1}$$

As derived earlier, the number of colliding blocks is $u_i - SP(1)$ and the number of colliding sets is $S(1 - P(0) - P(1))$, yielding,

$$c' = \frac{u_i\left(1 - e^{-\frac{u_i}{S}}\right)}{S\left(1 - e^{-\frac{u_i}{S}} - \frac{u_i}{S}e^{-\frac{u_i}{S}}\right)}.$$

The following plot (Figure B.1) gives the variation of the above function. We also plot the collision rate, c, to check the correspondence. Clearly, c' (and hence a corresponding c) is stable for cache sizes as low as 512 sets because, above this value, both the number of collision sets and colliding blocks decrease in the same proportion with cache size. Below 512 sets, c' increases rapidly (c shows a similar anomalous upward trend) because the denominator starts to decrease in proportion to S and the numerator stays constant at u_i. Thus, c can be expected to remain stable if the cache size is greater that the working-set estimate, u_i. In addition, changing block size does not effect c for large caches as can be verified from Table B.1. The rationale is that the dynamic behavior of program blocks is statistically similar to that of their component words. For instance, if two words collide with each other in the cache, then the two blocks that contain the words will also collide at the same rate. The collision rate does depend on the set size and on cache size for small caches. This will be the subject of our discussion in the next section.

S	D	B	Coll-blks	Ms-lru	Ms-fifo	c-lru	c-fifo	c(est)
Vary Number of Sets								
32	1	4	1624	6859	6859	4.2	4.2	4.0
64	1	4	1624	5658	5658	3.5	3.5	3.6
128	1	4	1624	5049	5049	3.1	3.1	3.1
256	1	4	1622	3908	3908	2.4	2.4	2.7
512	1	4	1557	3106	3106	2.0	2.0	2.3
1024	1	4	1282	2391	2391	1.9	1.9	1.9
2048	1	4	914	1798	1798	2.0	2.0	1.9
4096	1	4	609	1305	1305	2.1	2.1	1.9
8192	1	4	254	413	413	1.6	1.6	1.9
16384	1	4	161	308	308	1.9	1.9	1.9
Vary Set size								
1024	1	4	1282	2391	2391	1.9	1.9	1.9
512	2	4	1355	1593	1680	1.2	1.2	1.3
256	4	4	1418	1404	1511	1.0	1.1	1.0
16384	1	4	161	308	308	1.9	1.9	1.9
8192	2	4	30	32	42	1.1	1.4	0.9
4096	4	4	8	10	19	1.2	2.3	0.5
Vary block size								
1024	1	4	1282	2391	2391	1.9	1.9	1.9
512	1	8	908	1784	1784	2.0	2.0	1.9
256	1	16	607	1268	1268	2.1	2.1	2.3
128	1	32	410	1017	1017	2.5	2.5	2.4
64	1	64	283	1037	1037	3.7	3.7	2.9
16384	1	4	161	308	308	1.9	1.9	1.9
8192	1	8	126	230	230	1.8	1.8	1.9
4096	1	16	93	163	163	1.7	1.7	1.9
2048	1	32	74	122	122	1.6	1.6	1.9
1024	1	64	65	102	102	1.6	1.6	1.9

Table B.1: Measured variation in the collision rate for IVEX. Coll-blks: number of colliding blks, Ms-lru and Ms-fifo: number of collision induced misses for LRU and random replacement, c-lru and c-fifo: measured values of c for LRU and FIFO replacement. B is in bytes.

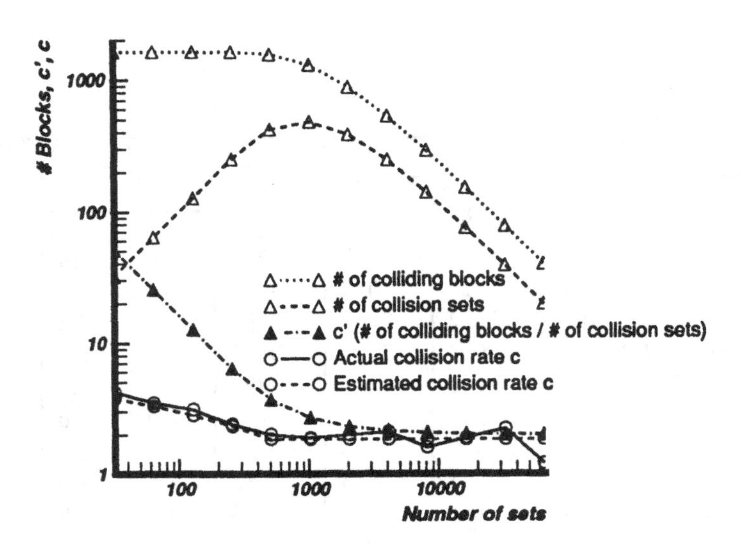

Figure B.1: Estimating the collision rate c in a direct-mapped cache.

B.2 Estimating Variations in the Collision Rate

We first derive c for non-unit set sizes. Let $c(D)$ denote the value of c for a cache with set size D. In a direct-mapped cache, a reference to a non most-recently-referenced address in the set will cause a miss. For a larger set size, however, reference to as many as $D-1$ blocks beside the most recently referenced one may not cause a miss. Assuming random behavior, the probability of a hit to any one of the d blocks mapped into the set is $(D-1)/(d-1)$. The most recently referenced block is excluded because its effect has already been included in c. The corresponding probability of a miss is one minus the above quantity. Therefore, $c(D,d)$, the collision rate for a set of size D with d overlapping blocks is $c(1)$ weighted by this fraction, where, as before, $c(1)$ is the collision rate for a direct-mapped cache with the same number of sets.

$$c(D,d) = c(1)\left(1 - \frac{D-1}{d-1}\right)$$

We can then obtain an average of $c(D,d)$ over all d's as

$$c(D) = \frac{\sum_{d=D+1}^{d=\infty} c(D,d)dP(d)}{\sum_{d=D+1}^{d=\infty} dP(d)}.$$

Table B.1 shows the variation in c for the benchmark IVEX. Estimated values of c and also measured values are provided. The number of colliding blocks and the actual number of collision induced misses are also shown. S, D, and B, represent the number of sets, set size and block size respectively. c seems relatively stable for direct-mapped caches when the cache size is greater than half $u_i(1)$. However, predictions of c for non-unit set sizes are often optimistic. Fortunately, even large errors in estimating c will not affect the miss rate if the number of colliding blocks is very small. For example, a 64K-byte cache with set size four, FIFO replacement, and block size four bytes, yields 8 colliding blocks, and only 19 collision induced misses for IVEX. The 78% error in the collision rate estimate clearly causes little error in the 2% miss rate.

We now provide a method of estimating the collision rate when the number of sets is much smaller than the number of program blocks. This region of the cache organization spectrum is only of marginal interest and hence this discussion is provided mainly for the sake of completeness. We had shown earlier that c is bounded as $0 \leq c \leq \tau/u$, the maximum being attained when the cache has only one set. Furthermore, Figure B.1 shows that c' is inversely proportional to S for very small caches. This leads to a rough approximation of c. We denote the stable value of c by c_0 measured for the representative cache with $S = S_0$. Let S_{u_i} be the power of 2 less than and closest to u_i. When the number of sets falls below S_{u_i}, all the sets will be occupied with a high probability. Then, empirical results show that c can be increased in inverse proportion to the log of the number of sets up to its maximum value for $S = 1$ as:

$$c = c_0 + \left[\left(\frac{\tau}{u_i}\right) - c_0\right]\left(1 - \frac{log(S)}{log(S_{u_i})}\right) \tag{B.2}$$

Figure B.1 shows the measured and calculated values of c. For number of sets less than 512 the log approximation appears to be quite good.

Appendix C

Inter-Run Intervals and Spatial Locality

We showed earlier that the distribution of run-lengths alone is not sufficient to characterize the spatial locality in programs especially for block sizes in excess of 8 words (32 bytes). We address this issue in this discussion by calculating the number of blocks needed to contain the reference stream in a slightly modified fashion to account for blocks that contain portions of more than a single run. The initial derivation assumes that the entire inter-run interval distribution is available, but later we will present a simplified formulation that requires just the average inter-run interval and gives comparable results.

As before, cover size for a run is the average number of blocks that have to be fetched to bring the entire run into the cache. Due to random alignment of the run, $B-1$ words in the cover are unused by the run on average; allocating all these extra words to the run inflates working set estimates as shown in Figure 3.9. The number of blocks in a cover actually allocated to contain the run (including both both forward and backward neighbors) is

$$\begin{aligned} &= \textit{Number of blocks needed to cover that run} \\ &\quad - \textit{number of blocks that include neighboring runs} \\ &= \textit{Cover size for the run} \\ &\quad - \frac{\textit{Number of words that include neighboring runs}}{\textit{Blocksize}} \end{aligned}$$

If the run length is l and the block size is B, the number of words in the cover (or set of blocks that contain the run) that do not contain any valid part of the run in question is $B-1$. Let $exc = B - 1$ denote the excess number of words and let $N(exc)$ denote the number of words out of exc that are utilized for neighboring runs. This means that the number of blocks actually used up by the given run is

$$\left\lceil 1 + \frac{l-1}{B} - \frac{N(exc)}{B} \right\rceil$$

and the total number of blocks as calculated before (see Equation 3.12) is

$$u(B) = \frac{u(1)}{l_{av}} \sum_{l=1}^{l=\infty} R(l) \left\lceil 1 + \frac{l-1}{B} - \frac{N(exc)}{B} \right\rceil \tag{C.1}$$

The total number of unique blocks in the entire trace, $U(B)$, is also calculated as above. We now need to derive the function $N(exc)$. Let $I(intvl)$ be the distribution of inter-run interval lengths. The expected number of words out of those left over in the cover (exc) used in covering *the first adjacent run* is given by,

$$\sum_{intvl=1}^{intvl=n} I(intvl) \sum_{l=1}^{l=\infty} R(l) MIN(l, exc - intvl)$$

where,

$I(intvl)$ = probability that an interval is of length $intvl$, and

$R(l)$ = probability that a run is of length l.

The maximum number of addresses of any run that can be covered is $exc - intvl$. $N(exc)$ can then be calculated in a recursive fashion, as follows:

$$N(exc) = \sum_{intvl=1}^{intvl=exc} I(intvl) \sum_{l=1}^{l=\infty} R(l) \left[MIN(l, exc - intvl) + N(exc - intvl - l) \right] \tag{C.2}$$

with $N(exc \leq 1) = 0$.

It is also reasonable to sacrifice some accuracy and lump the intervals into two values: I_{av} and ∞, where all intervals up to the maximum block size of interest are averaged to give I_{av}, and the remaining are categorized as ∞. Then,

$$N(exc) = f_{I_{av}} \sum_{l=1}^{l=\infty} R(l) \left[MIN(l, exc - I_{av}) + N(exc - I_{av} - l) \right], \tag{C.3}$$

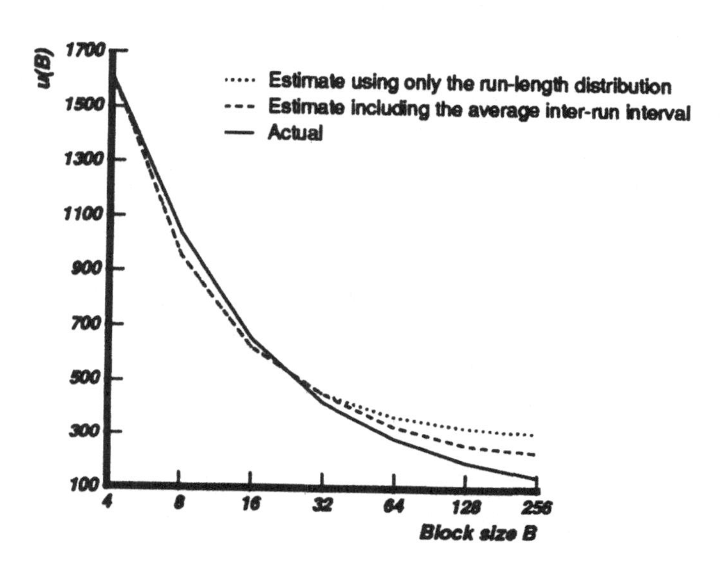

Figure C.1: The average number of unique blocks in a time granule, $u(B)$, versus block size B in bytes. The estimate using inter-run intervals is more accurate than with just the run-length distribution.

and $N(exc \leq 1) = 0$.

In the above equation, $f_{I_{av}}$ is the fraction of intervals that are averaged to give I_{av}. In the implementation, it is worthwhile to pre-calculate $R(l)$ and $N(exc)$ and store the values in arrays and use dynamic programming to eliminate recursion.

The total number of unique program blocks in a time granule, $u(B)$, and those in the entire trace, $U(B)$, can then be calculated as shown in Equation C.1 using the above formulation of $N(exc)$. Figure C.1 shows the variation in $u(B)$ as a function of block size to compare actual and predicted values. The predicted values are obtained using a measured average inter-run interval. These were not appreciably different from those calculated using the complete distribution of inter-run intervals. The variation in $u(B)$ using just run-length distributions is also shown. The difference between the dotted and the dashed curves can be attributed to the capture of multiple runs separated by inter-run intervals. The mean and maximum errors for the estimate using inter-run intervals are 19% and 64%, while those for the estimate excluding inter-run intervals are 33% and 115%.

Appendix D

Summary of Benchmark Characteristics

Tables D.1 through D.3 present the uniprocessor trace characteristics, and Table D.4 shows relevant multiprocessor trace statistics. The single-processor traces were obtained via ATUM and represent several applications running the VMS and Ultrix operating systems.

The multiprocessor traces were derived using ATUM-II. These traces correspond to versions of the MACH, VMS, and Ultrix multiprocessor operating systems running on one to four processor VAX 8350s.

Bench-mark	Total Refs.	Instr. Refs.	Data Refs.	System Refs.	User Refs.	Miss Rate (%)	
						C.S.	W.S.
ALLC	307	196	111	17	290	0.86	0.59
DIA0	336	197	139	186	150	5.20	5.84
IVEX0	307	180	127	228	79	5.80	4.87
IVEX3	397	171	225	35	361	2.34	2.28
IVEX	394	169	225	33	361	2.37	2.10
UMIL2	359	163	196	10	350	0.81	0.70
DEC0	335	170	164	18	317	1.75	1.42
DEC1	330	168	162	23	307	2.14	1.59
FORL0	314	156	158	122	192	4.37	3.51
FORL1	363	170	193	16	347	2.53	1.84
PASC0	559	175	383	22	536	0.28	0.22
PASC1	541	180	361	17	523	1.51	1.42
SPIC0	358	150	208	79	279	2.16	1.67
SPIC1	423	173	250	11	412	1.27	0.92
LISP0	263	147	116	14	249	2.56	2.29
LISP1	261	146	115	14	247	3.37	3.40
MUL3	1086	544	542	82	1004	2.94	3.19
MUL6	1187	523	663	194	992	3.10	3.60
MUL10	1094	540	554	196	899	3.55	2.94
NMLST	373	195	179	190	183	4.09	4.88
SAVEC0	388	190	199	129	260	3.07	3.19
SAVEC1	386	196	190	154	232	4.51	3.49
SAVEC2	388	190	198	170	218	3.13	2.81
SAVEC3	219	134	84	212	6	1.50	1.98
SAVEC	1380	710	671	665	715	2.99	2.38

Table D.1: Summary of benchmark statistics. The cold start (C.S.) and warm start (W.S.) miss rates are for a 64K-byte direct-mapped cache with a block size of 16 bytes using PIDs. The number of references are in thousands.

Bench-	Working-set size for T=									
mark	128	256	512	1K	2K	4K	8K	16K	32K	64K
UMIL2	74	115	184	279	319	393	522	659	752	933
ALLC	48	73	101	151	241	357	521	818	1323	1902
DEC0	72	116	175	253	382	565	828	1213	1582	2329
DEC1	71	114	174	263	415	618	960	1438	1924	2573
DIA0	58	97	152	242	397	665	1057	1564	2245	2789
FORL0	79	138	224	353	559	927	1334	1903	2645	3869
FORL1	85	145	232	357	532	800	1164	1740	2646	3976
IVEX0	54	95	170	303	549	1002	1748	3205	4432	6264
IVEX3	78	134	235	354	511	729	1131	1332	1508	1901
LISP0	89	150	217	290	383	510	706	1029	1471	2123
LISP1	89	151	219	294	386	500	668	933	1464	2284
PASC0	45	72	120	195	228	265	336	391	460	557
PASC1	73	87	114	165	267	472	879	1541	2363	4008
SPIC0	79	112	164	251	386	615	992	1562	2032	2440
SPIC1	82	98	128	187	302	517	901	1608	2676	3689
AVE	71	113	173	262	390	595	916	1395	1968	2775

Table D.2: Individual benchmark (VMS) working-set sizes for user references only. T represents the time window.

Bench-	Working-set size for T=									
mark	128	256	512	1K	2K	4K	8K	16K	32K	64K
UMIL2	76	119	191	297	360	470	659	833	1001	1229
ALLC	53	84	124	196	321	484	710	1111	1737	2443
DEC0	74	122	188	283	432	640	968	1413	1971	2634
DEC1	74	120	190	297	472	725	1143	1711	2343	3021
DIA0	87	154	267	401	582	881	1379	2212	3274	4563
FORL0	92	164	271	414	655	1076	1666	2339	3408	5139
FORL1	87	149	244	382	580	860	1256	1855	2816	4420
IVEX0	71	122	200	337	567	971	1686	3011	5036	9150
IVEX3	81	141	250	394	598	922	1454	1832	2270	2813
LISP0	91	156	233	330	444	604	857	1209	1688	2134
LISP1	91	155	235	335	450	604	857	1254	1884	2773
PASC0	48	78	133	223	279	337	442	587	788	1121
PASC1	74	93	126	189	312	524	947	1654	2454	3926
SPIC0	82	123	192	319	535	880	1507	2472	3325	3912
SPIC1	83	103	138	207	338	555	959	1687	2854	3891
AVE	77	125	198	306	461	702	1099	1678	2456	3544

Table D.3: Individual benchmark (VMS) working-set sizes for user plus system references. T represents the time window.

Trace Name	OS	# Instr	# CPU	# Proc.	R/ Instr	Instr/ C.S.
ABAQUS	VMS 4.4	520	2	6	1.9	2
CAYENNE	VMS 4.4	1,606	2	8	1.8	2
JUN9	VMS 4.4	552	2	6	1.7	2
SITES1	VMS 4.x	99	1	3	1.9	5
DHRY	Ultrix 2.0	104	2	2	1.9	35
MAKEX	Ultrix 2.0	414	2	7	1.9	28
THOR	MACH	1,629	4	5	2.1	78
PERO	MACH	1,834	4	5	1.9	262
POPS	MACH	1,769	4	10	1.8	47
POPS5	MACH	1,719	4	3	1.9	246

Table D.4: Multiprocessor trace characteristics. Instruction counts are in thousands. "Instr" stands for instructions, R for memory references, Proc. for processes, and C.S. for context swap.

Appendix E

Features of ATUM-2

Multiprocessor address tracing encounters several issues that do not arise in tracing single processors. This section touches on some of these. We also briefly discuss the problem of trace and patch microcode storage. While the latter issues are not unique to tracing multiprocessors, handling several CPUs certainly exacerbates the problem.

E.1 Distributing Trace Control to All Processors

The user controls tracing by interfacing to a high-level process that has the ability to change tracing state on the processor it is running on. Because the multiprocessor can schedule this process on any processor, it is not possible to determine a priori which processor will change its tracing state. Therefore a way to communicate this change to all the processors is needed. To maintain ATUM-2's transparency to the operating system, a requirement was that the OS should not be involved in this operation.

We built a microcoded inter-CPU communication facility to distribute trace state. The processor on which the trace state changes first writes a new state value into one of its registers visible to the other CPUs. Each CPU periodically checks all the other CPUs to see if they have posted a state change. If so, each CPU changes its own state to match that change. These checks and updates are patched into the hardware timer interrupt routine so that the checking happens at least every 10 msec. This period is sufficient for our purposes.

E.2 Provision of Atomic Accesses to Trace Memory

The problem of retaining the relative sequencing of memory references of the various processors is solved by providing the tracing routines on all the processors access to a common trace memory region. Address recording in this trace memory is sequentialized by the common system bus. To distinguish between the references of the various processors, every address stored here has a tag that includes the processor number in addition to information regarding the type of the reference. Thus, the traces contain an interleaved stream of references made by the various processors in the order they were generated by the processors.

Providing all processors access to a common trace memory, as opposed to several private regions, means that the accesses to this common memory must be atomic. That is, the entire operation of reading the pointer to the next location in trace memory, incrementing it and writing it back, must be atomic. Because accesses to trace memory must use physical addresses, and because the micromachine does not provide atomic physical memory operations, we achieve the same effect by disabling virtual to physical memory translation and using a virtual memory interlocked microinstruction. Translation is reenabled after the operation. (It is ironic that this atomic access causes huge amounts of inter-CPU cache interference while tracing. Clearly, these memory references are not recorded and hence do not distort the traces.)

E.3 Instruction Stream Compaction Using a Cache Simulated in Microcode

Due to limited microcode patch RAM space, it is not possible to patch all microinstructions that access memory. To obtain the memory references corresponding to complex VAX instructions, we record instead certain other relevant information such as the stack pointer and the register mask corresponding to that instruction. In addition we record the instructions themselves or the instruction-stream data. Besides helping in regenerating the references, the opcodes in the instruction stream are valuable information in themselves. This information is all the more useful in a multiprocessor environment, for example, to identify special instructions such as the interlocked ones. Because VAX instructions are of variable length, one has to record the worst-case length of every instruction to retain complete information. Unfortunately, recording these instruction stream values for every instruction considerably increases the trace memory space required to capture trace data for a given amount of time.

Since the instruction stream values do not change with time, we can filter out repeat instruction stream values to roughly double the amount of useful information in a trace of given length. The trace microcode implements a small filter cache indexed by instruction address and PID. Essentially, each instruction address is looked up in this filter cache, and if found, nothing is added to the trace; if not found, that instruction is added to the trace and its address put in the cache. By this means, the entire instruction stream is recorded with only a 10% increase in the size of the trace.

E.4 Microcode Patch Space Conservation

On the VAX 8350 processor the patching is done by loading new microcode into a patch RAM. The size of the RAM determines the maximum number of microcode patch instructions that can exist. It was clear that the multiprocessor ATUM-2 would be severely constrained by this limit given that single processor ATUM itself was. The solution adopted was to use ***microcode overlays***. The method of overlays also helped achieve an additional goal that normal machine execution be at full speed when tracing is off.

Our current implementation has a base set of patches that are loaded at boot-up time. These set aside memory for tracing and the instruction stream cache, and also contain the microcode necessary for loading and unloading patches. The XFC instruction patch for tracing control is also included in the base patches. Then there is one overlay that supports all our tracing operations. This overlay scheme also makes it easy to write microcode trace packages with different functionalities without worrying about the RAM space.

Bibliography

[1] Anant Agarwal. *Trace Compaction using Cache Filtering with Blocking.* Computer Systems Laboratory TR 88-347, Stanford University, January 1988.

[2] Anant Agarwal, Paul Chow, Mark Horowitz, John Acken, Arturo Salz, and John Hennessy. On-Chip Instruction Caches for High Performance Processors. In *Proceedings of the Conference on Advanced Research in VLSI, Stanford,* pages 1–24, March 1987.

[3] Anant Agarwal, Richard Simoni, John Hennessy, and Mark Horowitz. An Evaluation of Directory Schemes for Cache Coherence. In *Proceedings of the 15th International Symposium on Computer Architecture,* IEEE, New York, June 1988.

[4] Anant Agarwal, Richard L. Sites, and Mark Horowitz. ATUM: A New Technique for Capturing Address Traces Using Microcode. In *Proceedings of the 13th Annual Symposium on Computer Architecture,* pages 119–127, IEEE, New York, June 1986.

[5] A. V. Aho, P. J. Denning, and J. D. Ullman. Principles of Optimal Page Replacement. *JACM,* 18(1):80–93, January 1971.

[6] D. Alpert, D. Carberry, M. Yamamura, Y. Chow, and P. Mak. 32-bit Processor Chip Integrates Major System Functions. *Electronics,* 56(14):113–119, July 1983.

[7] Donald Alpert. *Performance Tradeoffs for Microprocessor Cache Memories.* Computer Systems Laboratory 83-239, Stanford University, December 1983.

[8] James Archibald and Jean-Loup Baer. An Economical Solution to the Cache Coherence Problem. In *Proceedings of the 12th International Symposium on Computer Architecture,* pages 355–362, IEEE, New York, June 1985.

[9] James Archibald and Jean-Loup Baer. Cache Coherence Protocols: Evaluation Using a Multiprocessor Simulation Model. *ACM Transactions on Computer Systems*, 4(4):273–298, November 1986.

[10] Robert Baron, Richard Rashid, Ellen Siegel, Avadis Tevanian, and Michael Young. MACH-1: An Operating System Environment for Large-Scale Multiprocessor Applications. *IEEE Software*, July 1985.

[11] James Bell, David Casasent, and C. Gordon Bell. An Investigation of Alternative Cache Organizations. *IEEE Transactions on Computers*, c-23(4), April 1974.

[12] John F. Brown and Richard L. Sites. A Chip Set Microarchitecture for a High-Performance VAX Implementation. *Micro-17 Proceedings*, September 1984.

[13] Richard E. Calcagni. A Patchable Control Store for a Reduced Microcode Risk in a VLSI VAX Microcomputer. *Micro-17 Proceedings*, September 1984.

[14] Lucien M. Censier and Paul Feautrier. A New Solution to Coherence Problems in Multicache Systems. *IEEE Transactions on Computers*, c-27(12):1112–1118, December 1978.

[15] H. Cheong and A. V. Veidenbaum. A Cache Coherence Scheme with Fast Selective Invalidation. In *Proceedings of the 15th International Symposium on Computer Architecture*, IEEE, New York, June 1988.

[16] David R. Cheriton, Gert A. Slavenberg, and Patrick D. Boyle. Software-Controlled Caches in the VMP Multiprocessor. In *Proceedings of the 13th Annual Symposium on Computer Architecture*, pages 367–374, IEEE, New York, June 1986.

[17] James Cho, Alan Jay Smith, and Howard Sachs. *The Memory Architecture and the Cache and Memory Management Unit for the Fairchild CLIPPER Processor*. Computer Science Division (EECS) UCB/CSD 86/289, University of California at Berkeley, April 1986.

[18] C. K. Chow. Determining the Optimum Capacity of a Cache Memory. *IBM Technical Disclosure Bulletin*, 17(10):3163–3166, March 1975.

[19] C. Y. Chu. MILS: MIPS Instruction Level Simulator. September 1985. Unpublished Report, Computer Systems Laboratory, Stanford University.

[20] D. W. Clark and J. S. Emer. Performance of the VAX-11/780 Translational Buffer: Simulation and Measurement. *ACM Transactions on Computer Systems*, 3(1):31–62, February 1985.

[21] Douglas W. Clark. Cache Performance in the VAX-11/780. *ACM Transactions on Computer Systems*, 1(1):24–37, February 1983.

[22] Ron Cytron, Steve Karlovsky, and Kevin P. McAuliffe. Automatic Management of Programmable Caches. In *Proceedings ICPP*, August 1988.

[23] P. J. Denning. The Working Set Model for Program Behavior. *Communications of the ACM*, 11(5):323–333, May 1968.

[24] Michel Dubois and Faye A. Briggs. Effects of Cache Coherence in Multiprocessors. In *Proceedings of the 9th International Symposium on Computer Architecture*, pages 299–308, IEEE, New York, May 1982.

[25] M. C. Easton and R. Fagin. Cold-start vs. Warm-start Miss Ratios. *Communications of the ACM*, 21(10):866–872, October 1978.

[26] Malcolm C. Easton. Computation of Cold-Start Miss Ratios. *IEEE Transactions on Computers*, c-27(5), May 1978.

[27] M. D. Hill et al. Design Decisions in SPUR. *Computer*, 19(10):8–22, November 1986.

[28] S. J. Frank. Tightly Coupled Multiprocessor System Speeds Up Memory Access Times. Electronics, 57, 1, January 1984.

[29] John Fu, James B. Keller, and Kenneth J. Haduch. Aspects of the VAX 8800 C Box Design. *Digital Technical Journal*, 41–51, February 1987.

[30] James R. Goodman. *Cache Memory Optimization to Reduce Processor/Memory Traffic*. Department of Computer Sciences, University of Wisconsin-Madison, 1985.

[31] James R. Goodman. Using Cache Memory to Reduce Processor-Memory Traffic. In *Proceedings of the 10th Annual Symposium on Computer Architecture*, pages 124–131, IEEE, New York, June 1983.

[32] Anoop Gupta, Charles Forgy, and Robert Wedig. Parallel Architectures and Algorithms for Rule-Based Systems. In *Proceedings of the 13th Annual Symposium on Computer Architecture*, IEEE, New York, June 1986.

[33] Ilkka J. Haikala. Cache Hit Ratios with Geometric Task Switch Intervals. In *Proceedings of the 11th Annual Symposium on Computer Architecture*, pages 364–371, IEEE, New York, June 1984.

[34] Ilkka J. Haikala and Petri H. Kutvonen. Split Cache Organizations. In *Performance '84*, pages 459–472, 1984.

[35] W. J. Harding, M. H. MacDougall, and W. J. Raymond. *Empirical Estimation of Cache Miss Ratio as a Function of Cache Size.* Technical Report PN 820420-700A, Amdahl, September 1980.

[36] J. L. Hennessy. VLSI Processor Architecture. *IEEE Transactions on Computers*, C-33(12), December 1984.

[37] Robert R. Henry. Tracer - Address and Instruction Tracing for the VAX Architecture. University of California, Berkeley, November, 1984.

[38] Mark Hill and Alan Jay Smith. Experimental Evaluation of On-Chip Microprocessor Cache Memories. In *Proceedings of the 11th Annual Symposium on Computer Architecture*, pages 158–166, IEEE, New York, June 1984.

[39] P. G. Hoel, S. C. Port, and C. J. Stone. *Introduction to Stochastic Processes.* Houghton Mifflin Company, Boston, 1972.

[40] M. Horowitz and P. Chow. The MIPS-X Microprocessor. In *Proc. IEEE WESCON 85*, San Francisco, CA, 1985.

[41] Mark Horowitz, John Hennessy, Paul Chow, Glenn Gulak, John Acken, Anant Agarwal, Chorng-Yeung Chu, Scott McFarling, Steven Przybylski, Steve Richardson, Artuto Salz, Richard Simoni, Don Stark, Peter Steenkiste, Steve Tjiang, and Malcolm Wing. A 32-Bit Microprocessor with 2K-Byte On-Chip Cache. In *IEEE International Solid-State Circuits Conference*, 1987.

[42] William N. Johnson. A VLSI Superminicomputer CPU. In *IEEE International Solid-State Circuits Conference*, pages 174–175 and 334–335, February 1984.

[43] J. L. Hodges Jr. and E. L. Lehmann. *Basic Concepts of Probability and Statistics.* Holden-day, Inc., San Francisco, 1964.

[44] Rupert G. Miller Jr. *Beyond Anova - Basics of Applied Statistics.* John Wiley and Sons, Inc. New York, 1986.

[45] K. R. Kaplan and R. O. Winder. Cache-Based Computer Systems. *Computer*, 6(3):30–36, March 1973.

[46] R. H. Katz, S. J. Eggers, D. A. Wood, C. L. Perkins, and R. G. Sheldon. Implementing a Cache Consistency Protocol. In *Proceedings of the 12th International Symposium on Computer Architecture*, pages 276–283, IEEE, New York, June 1985.

[47] B. Kumar. A Model of Spatial Locality and its Application to cache Design. 1979. Unpublished Report, Computer Systems Laboratory, Stanford University.

[48] Subhasis Laha, Janak H. Patel, and Ravishankar K. Iyer. Accurate Low-Cost Methods for Performance Evaluation of Cache Memory Systems. Coordinated Science Laboratory, University of Illinois, 1986.

[49] Edward D. Lazowska, John Zahorjan, G. Scott Graham, and Kenneth C. Sevcik. *Quantitative System Performance.* Prentice Hall, 1984.

[50] J. S. Liptay. Structural Aspects of the System/360 Model 85, Part II: The Cache. *IBM Systems Journal,* 7(1):15–21, 1968.

[51] Doug MacGregor, Dave Mothersole, and Bill Moyer. The Motorola MC68020. *IEEE Micro,* 101–118, August 1984.

[52] R. L. Mattson, J. Gecsei, D. R. Slutz, and I. L. Traiger. Evaluation Techniques for Storage Hierarchies. *IBM Systems Journal,* 9(2):78–117, 1970.

[53] E. McCreight. *The Dragon Computer System: An Early Overview.* Technical Report, Xerox Corp., September 1984.

[54] Steve McGrogan, Robert Olson, and Neil Toda. Parallelizing large existing programs - methodology and experiences. In *Proceedings of Spring COMPCON,* pages 458–466, March 1986.

[55] G. Milandre and R. Mikkor. VS2-R2 Experience at the University of Toronto Computer Centre. In *Share 44 Proceedings, Los Angeles, CA.,* pages 1887–1895, March 1975.

[56] J. Moussouris, L. Crudele, D. Freitas, C. Hansen, E. Hudson, R. March, S. Przybylski, T. Riordan, C. Rowen, and D. Van't Hof. A CMOS RISC Processor with Integrated Systen Functions. In *COMPCON,* pages 126–131, IEEE, March 1986.

[57] Charles J. Neuhauser. *Instruction Stream Monitoring of the PDP-11.* Computer Systems Laboratory 156, Stanford University, May 1979.

[58] Robert Olson. Parallel Processing in a Message-Based Operating System. *IEEE Software,* July 1985.

[59] Mark S. Papamarcos and Janak H. patel. A Low-Overhead Coherence Solution for Multiprocessors with Private Cache Memories. In *Proceedings of the 12th International Symposium on Computer Architecture,* pages 348–354, IEEE, New York, June 1985.

[60] D. A. Patterson and C. H. Sequin. Design Considerations for Single-Chip Computers of the Future. *IEEE Transactions on Computers*, C-29(2):108–116, February 1980.

[61] David A. Patterson, Phil Garrison, Mark Hill, Dimitris Lioupes, Chris Nyberg, Tim Sippel, and Korbin Van Dyke. Architecture of a VLSI Instruction Cache for a RISC. In *Proceedings of the 10th Annual Symposium on Computer Architecture*, pages 108–116, IEEE, New York, =May 1983.

[62] Bernard L. Peuto and Leonard J. Shustek. An Instruction Timing Model of CPU Performance. In *Proceedings of the 4th Annual Symposium on Computer Architecture*, pages 165–178, IEEE, New York, March 1977.

[63] Andrew R. Pleszkun and Matthew K. Farrens. An Instruction Cache Design for Use with a Delayed Branch. In *Proceedings, M.I.T. VLSI Conference*, pages 73–88, 1986.

[64] Thomas R. Puzak. *Analysis of Cache Replacement Algorithms*. PhD thesis, University of Massachusetts, Department of Electrical and Computer Engineering, February 1985.

[65] G. Radin. The 801 Minicomputer. In *Proceedings of the ACM Symposium on Architectural Support for Programming Languages and Operating Systems*, pages 39–47, Palo Alto, CA, March 1982.

[66] G. S. Rao. Performance Analysis of Cache Memories. *JACM*, 25(3):378–395, July 1978.

[67] B. R. Rau. *Sequential prefetch strategies for instructions and data*. Technical Report 131, Digital Systems Laboratory, Stanford University, January 1977.

[68] George Rossman. November 1986. Private communication. Palyn Associates, San Jose, CA.

[69] L. Rudolph and Z. Segall. Dynamic Decentralized Cache Consistency Schemes for MIMD Parallel Processors. In *Proceedings of the 12th International Symposium on Computer Architecture*, pages 340–347, IEEE, New York, June 1985.

[70] Jerome H. Saltzer. A Simple Linear Model of Demand Paging Performance. *Communications of the ACM*, 17(4):181–186, April 1974.

[71] Arturo Salz, Anant Agarwal, and Paul Chow. *MIPS-X: The External Interface*. Computer Systems Laboratory, TR 87-339, Stanford University, April 1987.

[72] Richard L. Sites and Anant Agarwal. Multiprocessor Cache Analysis using ATUM. In *Proceedings of the 15th International Symposium on Computer Architecture*, pages 186–195, IEEE, New York, June 1988.

[73] Alan Jay Smith. A Comparative Study of Set Associative Memory Mapping Algorithms And Their Use for Cache and Main Memory. *IEEE Transactions on Software Engineering*, SE-4(2):121–130, March 1978.

[74] Alan Jay Smith. Bibliography and Readings on CPU Cache Memories and Related Topics. *Computer Architecture News*, 14(1):22–42, January 1986.

[75] Alan Jay Smith. Cache Evaluation and the Impact of Workload Choice. In *Proceedings of the 12th Annual Symposium on Computer Architecture*, pages 64–73, IEEE, New York, June 1985.

[76] Alan Jay Smith. Cache Memories. *ACM Computing Surveys*, 14(3):473–530, September 1982.

[77] Alan Jay Smith. CPU Cache Consistency with Software Support and Using One Time Identifiers. In *Proceedings of the Pacific Computer Communications Symposium*, IEEE, New York, October 1985.

[78] Alan Jay Smith. *Line (Block) Size Choice for CPU Cache Memories.* Computer Science Division 85-239, University of California, Berkeley, June 1985.

[79] Alan Jay Smith. Two Methods for the Efficient Analysis of Memory Address Trace Data. *IEEE Transactions on Software Engineering*, SE-3(1), January 1977.

[80] James E. Smith and James R. Goodman. A Study of Instruction Cache Organizations and Replacement Policies. In *Proceedings of the 10th Annual Symposium on Computer Architecture*, pages 132–137, IEEE, New York, June 1983.

[81] James E. Smith and James R. Goodman. Instruction Cache Replacement Policies and Organizations. *Proceedings of the 10th Annual Symposium on Computer Architecture*, C-34(3):234–281, May 1983.

[82] J. R. Spirn. *Program Behavior: Models and Measurements. Operating and Programming Systems Series*, Elsevier, New York, 1977.

[83] Harold S. Stone and Dominique Thiebaut. Footprints in the Cache. In *Proceedings of the ACM Sigmetrics Conference on Measurement and Modeling of Computer Systems*, pages 4–8, May 1986.

[84] W. D. Strecker. Cache Memories for PDP-11 Family of Computers. In *Proceedings of the 3rd Annual Symposium on Computer Architecture*, pages 155–158, IEEE, New York, January 1976.

[85] William D. Strecker. Transient Behavior of Cache Memories. *ACM Transactions on Computer Systems*, 1(4):281–293, November 1983.

[86] C. K. Tang. Cache Design in the Tightly Coupled Multiprocessor System. In *AFIPS Conference Proceedings, National Computer Conference, NY, NY*, pages 749–753, June 1976.

[87] George S. Taylor, Paul N. Hilfinger, James R. Larus, David A. Patterson, and Benjamin G. Zorn. Evaluation of the SPUR Lisp Architecture. In *Proceedings of the 13th Annual Symposium on Computer Architecture*, pages 444–452, IEEE, New York, June 1986.

[88] Charles P. Thacker and Lawrence C. Stewart. Firefly: a Multiprocessor Workstation. In *Proceedings of ASPLOS II*, pages 164–172, October 1987.

[89] Shreekant S. Thakkar and Alan E. Knowles. A High-Performance Memory Management Scheme. *Computer*, 19(5):8–22, May 1986.

[90] Kishore. S. Trivedi. *Probability and Statistics with Reliability, Queuing, and Computer Science Applications.* Prentice Hall, 1982.

[91] *VAX-11 Architecture Reference Manual.* Digital Equipment Corporation, Bedford, MA, 1982. Form EK-VARAR-RM-001.

[92] M. K. Vernon and M. A. Holliday. Performance Analysis of Multiprocessor Cache Consistency Protocols Using Generalized Timed Petri Nets. In *Proceedings of SIGMETRICS 1986*, May 1986.

[93] J. Voldman and Lee W. Hoevel. The Software-Cache Connection. *IBM Journal of Research and Development*, 25(6):877–893, November 1981.

[94] J. Voldman, B. Mandelbrot, L. W. Hoevel, J. Knight, and P. Rosenfeld. Fractal Nature of Software-Cache Interaction. *IBM Journal of Research and Development*, 27(2):164–170, March 1983.

Index